Paul Green's
The House of Connelly

Paul Green's
The House of Connelly

A Critical Edition

Paul Green

Edited by Margaret D. Bauer

Introduction by Laurence G. Avery
Afterword by Jim Grimsley

McFarland & Company, Inc., Publishers
Jefferson, North Carolina

Frontispiece: **Paul Green (courtesy Paul Green Foundation).**

LIBRARY OF CONGRESS CATALOGUING-IN-PUBLICATION DATA

Green, Paul, 1894–1981.
[House of Connelly]
Paul Green's The house of Connelly : a critical edition /
Paul Green ; edited by Margaret D. Bauer ; introduction by
Lawrence G. Avery ; afterword by Jim Grimsley.
p.   cm.
Includes bibliographical references and index.

ISBN 978-0-7864-9444-6 (softcover : acid free paper) ∞
ISBN 978-1-4766-1791-6 (ebook)

1. Green, Paul, 1894–1981 House of Connelly.
2. Green, Paul, 1894–1981—Criticism and interpretation.
3. Carolina (Motion picture)
I. Bauer, Margaret Donovan, 1963–   II. Title.
PS3513.R452H7 2014   812'.52—dc23   2014028507

BRITISH LIBRARY CATALOGUING DATA ARE AVAILABLE

© 2014 by the Paul Green Foundation and
Margaret D. Bauer. All rights reserved

*No part of this book may be reproduced or transmitted in any form
or by any means, electronic or mechanical, including photocopying
or recording, or by any information storage and retrieval system,
without permission in writing from the publisher.*

On the cover: *The House of Connelly* Act II, Scene 3,
performed by the ReGroup Theatre (2014) featuring
Selena C. Dukes as Big Sue and Sheila Simmons as Big Sis;
© Mikiodo Media (ReGroup Theatre Company, Inc.)

Printed in the United States of America

*McFarland & Company, Inc., Publishers
Box 611, Jefferson, North Carolina 28640
www.mcfarlandpub.com*

For Mary Jane Bauer,
with love, admiration, and gratitude

Table of Contents

Preface and Acknowledgments	1
Introduction: *The House of Connelly*, Paul Green, and the Way He Worked, by Laurence G. Avery	3

The House of Connelly, A Drama of the Old South and the New, in Two Acts, by Paul Green — 9

Act I, Scene 1	10
Act I, Scene 2	21
Act I, Scene 3	39
Act II, Scene 1	51
Act II, Scene 2	67
Act II, Green's original Scene 3	82
Act II, Scene 3, revised ending for the Group Theatre	96

Paul Green's *The House of Connelly*, a Play (and Playwright) "worth bothering about": A Scene-by-Scene Analysis, by Margaret D. Bauer — 107

The House of Connelly from Script to Stage	109
Act I, Scene 1	112
Act I, Scene 2	115
Act I, Scene 3	118
Act II, Scene 1	120
Act II, Scene 2	123
Act II, Scene 3	126
Act II, Scene 3, the original ending	128
Act II, Scene 3, the revised ending	130

Two Endings, One Theme: The Need for Change	131
From Stage to Screen: *Carolina*	135
Paul Green Revisited	146
Afterword, by Jim Grimsley	149
Appendix: Reviews of the 1931 Broadway Performance	151
Notes	152
References	155
About the Contributors	157
Index	158

Preface and Acknowledgments

The House of Connelly is reprinted here with the permission of the Paul Green Foundation. Several print editions of the play were consulted as the transcription of the play was prepared, beginning with the edition published electronically by *Twentieth-Century Drama*, which includes both versions of the play: as Green ended it originally and as it was performed by the Group Theatre on Broadway. Preparing the manuscript of the play for republication, my research assistants and I consulted the original publication of the play, with the Broadway-performed ending, in *The House of Connelly and Other Plays* (1931); the version, still with this revised ending, in Green's collection *Out of the South: The Life of a People in Dramatic Form* (1939); and, with the original ending that Paul Green wrote, in his collection *Five Plays of the South* (1963). For my own writing about the play, I consulted *Best American Plays, Supplementary Volume, 1918–1958*, edited by John Gassner (1961), which is the first publication of the play with both endings included. With very few minor exceptions (mainly formatting), this edition's transcription remains true to Green's. Where there were discrepancies between editions, which mainly occurred with dialect, I took a lesson from Laurence G. Avery's essay in this volume, and opted for the version in which Green used standardized spelling.

I thank the Paul Green Foundation for its support of my work on Green over the past several years. In particular, I appreciate the funding from the Foundation to have the George Eastman House, International Museum of Photography and Film, create a DVD of the film *Carolina* so that I could finally watch it. I also thank East Carolina University's Harriot College of Arts and Sciences for providing additional funding for a master of the film, which came with permission to share the movie with audiences and thus allowed me to show it to my classes. Thanks also go to ECU for three Undergraduate Research grants awarded to Maggie Rogers, Michael Avery, and Rachel Ward, who each helped with different stages of this research and with preparing the manuscript of the play for publication.

The people of the Paul Green Foundation, particularly Laurence Avery, Jim Clark, and Marsha Warren, have helped me to promote this play through numerous events at which they arranged for me to present my work on the play. I also appreciate Laurence and Jim, both of whom are supposedly retired, for taking their time to read my analysis of the play and for their valuable revision suggestions. I also thank Laurence, who is the preeminent Green scholar, for writing an introduction to Green for this volume, and North Carolina writer Jim Grimsley, whose oeuvre includes drama as well as fiction, for writing an afterword. I appreciate Jim's willingness to read the play, in the middle of his own current book project, and his enthusiasm about it, which confirmed my view of it as a treasure worthy of bringing back into the public eye. I also appreciate my colleagues Bob Siegel, a playwright, who read and offered feedback on the play, and Randall Martoccia, who taught the play and film with me in 2012. And I thank Lorraine Hale Robinson for providing most of the translations of the Latin and Greek phrases used by Uncle Bob in the play. Thanks also to Richard Krawiec, who organized a reading of the play in Carrboro, North Carolina, and to the ReGroup Theatre Company, Inc., of New York for providing me with the opportunity, finally, to see an actual stage production of *The House of Connelly* and for inviting me to participate in a talk back with the actors and audience.

    Lastly, I express my appreciation to the people at McFarland for their immediate enthusiasm about this book project. It has been a pleasure working with them to bring years of my work into print with a new edition of this extraordinary Paul Green play.

Introduction: *The House of Connelly*, Paul Green, and the Way He Worked

by LAURENCE G. AVERY

Paul Green's *The House of Connelly* has been produced and published with two strikingly different endings, and that feature of its textual history will be fully explored by this volume's editor, Margaret Bauer, elsewhere in this edition. Meanwhile, she has asked me to place the play in the context of Green's career, and there is no better way to do that in a brief piece than to point out that Green's radical revision of *Connelly* is far from unusual and, in fact, is typical of him as a writer.

William Butler Yeats, Irish poet and playwright, himself an inveterate reviser, had a neat phrase for why writers revise when their work is republished or reproduced: to keep the work contemporary with themselves. In addition to keeping a work in tune with his current outlook, Green revised in order to accommodate what he learned from audience responses to his work. Sometimes that involved reducing the level of dialect in dialogue that listeners or readers found hard to follow. Sometimes it meant adding or deleting or moving episodes to encourage intended audience responses. It could also mean a change, in structural terms, from a comic to a tragic ending, or vice versa.

Green got his start as a writer in the early 1920s at the University in Chapel Hill as a member of Frederick Koch's Carolina Playmakers program, where the whole emphasis was on folk plays. By definition "the folk" are not city dwellers or highly educated people, but the rural peasantry. And Green took seriously Koch's injunction that characters in folk plays should sound like themselves. He saw himself in those days as, almost, an anthropologist recording the actual speech (words, phrases, pronunciations) of the people he wrote about. As a result, practically everything he wrote during the 1920s was heavy with dialect.

In Abraham's Bosom, Green's Pulitzer Prize play from the 1926–27 season, is an example. In the first scene of the play Abe, a mulatto who has attacked his white half-brother, is beaten by his white father. Even though the beating is to save Abe from a possible lynching, it is still hard punishment, and while Abe recovers, Goldie, his wife-to-be, tries to comfort him. In the produced and first published script, she says:

GOLDIE—[*Her face alight, a sort of reckless and unreal abandonment upon her.*] I knows where dere's a cool place under a big tree. And dey's cool green moss dere and soft leaves. Le's go dere, boy. I gwine tend to you and feed you....
ABE—[*Moved out of himself.*] Yeh, yeh, I come wid you. I don't keer foh nothing, not nothing no mo'. You, des' you'n me [*Field God* and *In Abraham's Bosom* 43].

Late in the next decade, Green published a large anthology of his plays, *Out of the South: The Life of a People in Dramatic Form*, and for that book he revised several of the plays, including *In Abraham's Bosom*. In this 1939 text the previous exchange is as follows:

> GOLDIE. (*Her face alight, a sort of reckless and unreal abandonment upon her.*) I knows where there's a cool place under a big tree. And there's cool green moss there and soft leaves. Let's go there, boy. I gwine tend to you and feed you....
> ABE. (*Moved out of himself.*) Yeh, yeh, I come with you. I don't care for nothing, not nothing no more. You, just you'n me [*Out of the South* 221–22].

It's clear what Green did here. "Gwine," a legitimate if substandard word like "ain't," is still there, and the grammar of the speakers is still shaky, but gone are the "dey's," "dere's." "fohs," and "keers." These attempts to evoke the sound of folk speech with phonetic spellings are replaced with standard spellings.

A more complex example of the same sort of revision occurs in *The No 'Count Boy*, a one-act play that was the first work to carry Green to national attention. Published in *Theatre Arts Monthly,* in November 1924, it was produced the next month by a Little Theater in Chicago, then in 1925 was taken to New York by another Little Theater from Dallas, where it won the prestigious Belasco Cup as the best one-act play of the year. Also in 1925, Green included "The No 'Count Boy" in his first book, *The Lord's Will and Other Carolina Plays*.

In those productions and that publication, the play is set in "the small yard immediately before a Negro cabin." It involves Pheelie, "a neat Negro girl of seventeen," and her beau, Enos, "a short stocky Negro of twenty." They get into an argument because Pheelie prefers looking at a book to talking with him.

> ENOS. Whut sorter book is it, Pheelie?
> PHEELIE. Whut difference do it make to you? You ain't int'rested in no book.
> ENOS. 'Speck dat's right. But you sho' seems mo' tuk wid it dan anything I ever seed you have befo'.
> PHEELIE. It's a fine pitchture book [*Lord's Will* 145].

When Green prepared the play for his 1939 anthology *Out of the South*, he revised the text just as he did with *In Abraham's Bosom*, moving away from phonetic spellings of folk speech toward standard spellings. But when he published *The No 'Count Boy* still later, in 1953, he went further. In the 1953 publication, the play is set in "a yard immediately before a small farm house." Pheelie is "a neat young country girl of seventeen," and Enos "is a short stocky farm lad of twenty or more" (*No 'Count* 5). The argument given above now goes like this:

> ENOS. What sort of book is it, Pheelie?
> PHEELIE. What difference does it make to you? You're not interested in any book.
> ENOS. I expect that's right. But you sure seem more taken with it than anything I've seen before. What's in a book anyhow?
> PHEELIE. It's a fine picture-book [*No 'Count* 6].

Here the language is standardized even more fully than in *Out of the South*, but the striking thing is the change in the race of the characters. Unlike *In Abraham's Bosom*, in "The No 'Count Boy" there is no thematic point to their race, so Green changed them from black to white. In my own library is the script he used to make the revisions, a script he went through from beginning to end, crossing out, in pencil, words and phrases to be cut and adding in margins and between lines the new language of stage directions and dialogue. The 1953 text of the play is the last one published in Green's lifetime.

The Lost Colony shows another kind of revision Green sometimes made, the recasting of scenes in an effort to insure certain audience responses. *The Lost Colony* opened on Roanoke Island in the summer of 1937 on the site of the first English colony in North America, established in 1587, and was staged to celebrate the 350th anniversary of that event. The play was so popular that it has been repeated every summer since 1937, except for four years during World War II, and has inspired a whole movement in outdoor historical drama throughout the country. Green himself wrote sixteen additional history plays and saw them performed under the stars from Florida to California.

There is a small irony about *The Lost Colony*. The play, conceived to celebrate English colonization, actually celebrates the breakdown of stratified English society in the frontier conditions of Roanoke Island and, in its place, the emergence of the ideal of an egalitarian democratic society for America. Ananias Dare, an important character in the play, epitomizes the huffy, aristocratic Englishman who can't function well in the unstructured environment of Roanoke Island. He is a military captain, and back in England, Eleanor White's father, for reasons of social status, insisted that she marry Dare despite her love for a young tenant farmer, John Borden. On Roanoke Island, Dare is killed in a battle with Indians, and subsequent events push Eleanor Dare and John Borden together. For audiences, a gratifying development at the end of the play is that finally, in the egalitarian society of Roanoke Island, the love of Eleanor and John is free to flourish.

In the years before World War II, however, Dare's death was not shown on stage. He was last seen leading a party of soldiers off stage in pursuit of attacking Indians. Then the Historian, a narrator in the play, reads out the names of the colonists killed in battle, Dare's name among them. In those years, Green occasionally got scolding letters from people disturbed that he would show a married woman carrying on with another man when her husband must be somewhere about. Such behavior flew in the face of morality, these correspondents felt, and made the play an encouragement of infidelity—which means, of course, that the letter writers had missed Dare's name in the list of those killed in battle.

With German U-boats patrolling our east coast, *The Lost Colony* did not play in the summers of 1942, 1943, 1944, and 1945, and during that time Green made several changes in the play, a notable one in the staging of Dare's death. Beginning with the reopening in 1946, Dare still led his troops off in pursuit of the Indians, but then audiences saw him stagger back on stage, an arrow clearly visible in his back as he spun and fell and expired, his head in the lap of his wife, who in a few new lines announced to the colonists—and the audience—that her husband was dead. Green's pointed revisions to the scene—almost humorous when you know the background—made it impossible for anyone to miss Dare's death, and smoothed the way to full appreciation of the new classless society unfolding in America.

The last revision I will mention is similar to the changes Green made in the conclusion of *The House of Connelly*. *The Field God* was Green's second Broadway production, opening in April 1927, while *In Abraham's Bosom*, which opened the previous December, was still running. The Provincetown Players had moved to New York City by then, and Green's New York agent had shown them the two plays, both of which they accepted for production.

The Field God is set in the first decade of the twentieth century in a farming community much like the Harnett County in which Green grew up. In fact, the central character of the play, Hardy Gilchrist, is as close to an autobiographical character as any Green created. Hardy glories in his physical strength and stamina, is a hard working and successful farmer, has real compassion for others and goes out of his way to help them, is widely liked and respected,

Paul Green (courtesy Paul Green Foundation).

yet is fiercely independent in his humanistic views in the face of the fundamentalist and puritanical outlook of his wife and neighbors. That last trait, of course, is the root of the conflict in the play.

As the play opens, Hardy's wife, Etta, in poor health for years, has sent for her niece to come down from Durham to care for her and the Gilchrist household. The niece, Rhoda, is twenty-three, beautiful, gracious, and vivacious. The men of the community are smitten, and soon Etta is sure her husband has lusted after the young woman and accuses them both of sin. In fact, an understandable bond is developing between Hardy and Rhoda, two perfectly compatible individuals, but they have committed no infidelities as they care for Etta, and Rhoda, especially, is hurt by the accusation. As Hardy, putting an arm on her shoulder, tries to comfort Rhoda, Etta enters the room, sees them in what she takes to be an embrace, and in shock dies, cursing them to everlasting damnation.

The rest of the play shows the world collapsing around Hardy and Rhoda. Several months after Etta's death, they marry. Then a drought descends on the area, and their crops wilt. Hardy's prize hog takes sick and dies. A former friend, who coveted Rhoda for himself and is now sick with jealousy, commits suicide in their front yard. And their baby son dies in his cradle. Hardest of all to bear is the constant harangue of the local preacher and church members, who, convinced that Hardy must repent and be saved before these plagues will go away, not only hold prayer vigils for him at church, but also show up constantly at his house demanding an attentive ear to their message.

Hardy is shaken by the calamities and accusations and contemplates suicide: "The God of these fields, the God of the whole universe says I got to make sacrifice unto Him" (294). In the 1927 version, Rhoda is strong and reminds Hardy continually of her love for him, and his for her. When the Preacher urges Hardy to live in "the blessed light of God's love," Hardy corrects him:

The light of our love.... The light of life. Not the light up there, not the light from heaven.... The light here in my breast and in [her] breast. The light of human beings that lighteth every man into this world.... And it will give us strength to go forth again in the morning.... [*The Preacher stares at him in perplexity.*] Now again we'll go into the fields and sow and reap and bring forth the fruits of life.... We are God—Man is God. That's the light, that's the truth. It will set [us] free. And love shall abide among us to the end [300–301].

The 1927 version of *The Field God* is slow-moving, with talky dialogue and too many plot points, and over the years Green revised the play. In 1929, for instance, he sent a revised script to his agent, saying, "The play has cost me two or three weeks hard work. It's a better play now, but I fear a far from perfect one. I succeeded in clearing out many things and continued to save Gilchrist's life, though it would have been so aesthetically easy to let him kill himself and repeat the Job story with a different ending only" (Avery 157). Green continued to work on the play, and by 1939, when he included it in *Out of the South*, *The Field God* was reduced from three acts to two and was more streamlined in its action (several plot points were cut, such as the baby who dies in the 1927 version). But the most striking difference is the outcome.

The 1939 version of *The Field God* ends with Hardy killing himself, thus "repeat[ing] the Job story with a different ending." Green brought about that conclusion by altering Rhoda's trajectory in the play. Unlike her strong role in the 1927 version, where she is steadfast in her love for Hardy, in the 1939 version she is crushed by the accusations of the religious fanatics around them and ends as a weak, pathetic figure. "I can't stay here any more," she tells Hardy. "It's a sin—something tells me it's so. And I'm afraid" (*Out of the South* 165). For his part, Gilchrist refuses to cave in to the pressure. Looking at the story of Job in the Bible, where Job repents in dust and ashes, Gilchrist wonders, "For what? For what? He was a righteous man. He did no evil." And he hurls the Bible across the room (*Out of the South* 169). Deprived of his wife and her supportive love, however, Gilchrist realizes, "It's me now alone against you all, against you and your God. So let it be, and I'll face it... me, Hardy Gilchrist... by myself... a man... man against you and your God. And you'll not beat me down. I'll save myself from you" (*Out of the South* 172; ellipses in original). He goes to another part of the house with the large knife he uses to butcher hogs, and soon there are hysterical wails from several church members. The Preacher rushes to look, then comes back to end the play, telling Rhoda, "It was the Lord's work.... He's killed himself" (*Out of the South* 173; ellipses in original).

Later on, when Green talked about the changed ending of *The Field God*, he said that both the pessimistic and the optimistic endings reflected his experience in the South, were "cued out of life" (Avery 504). But he continued by pointing out that plays are works of art, not mere transcripts of life. While a play must resonate with human experience, it has a form that springs from the author's sensibility, "his ethical intuition" (Avery 507). And Green's own temperament inclined him toward tragic outcomes—toward instances of suffering, injustice, defeat. That is why, even before he changed the ending of *The Field God*, he could tell his agent, "it would have been so aesthetically easy [was so aesthetically *tempting*?] to let [Hardy] kill himself." Beyond his plays and fiction, this inclination toward the tragic can be seen most clearly in Green's social commitments. In the world around him he gravitated toward mistreated cotton mill workers, exploited and unjustly treated African Americans, downtrodden Native Americans, people caught up in the state penal system—in chain gangs or facing the death penalty—victims of abuses of power by state and national governments. During adulthood he spent almost as much time on behalf of those suffering life's misfortunes as he did on his writing—and thus became known in his own day as a crusader for social justice. So the tragic ending of *The Field God*, which shows a man who has lost the core relationship of his life "saving" himself from his tormentors by means of suicide, came to feel more "right" to Green, more in tune with life as he perceived it, than the earlier optimistic ending.

Making changes in a play, as he did with *The House of Connelly*, the focal play of the current volume, was, therefore, not the exception in Green's career as a writer, but rather the rule.

The House of Connelly, a Drama of the Old South and the New, in Two Acts

By Paul Green

To Elizabeth Lay Green

First presented by the Group Theatre at the Martin Beck Theatre, New York City, September 28, 1931.

CHARACTERS

BIG SIS and BIG SUE, *Negro field women*

PATSY TATE, *daughter of a tenant farmer on the Connelly plantation*

WILLIAM BYRD (WILL) CONNELLY, *son of the mistress of Connelly Hall*

MRS. (ELLEN) CONNELLY, *of Connelly Hall*

ROBERT (UNCLE BOB) CONNELLY, *the uncle,* MRS. CONNELLY'S *brother-in-law*

GERALDINE and EVELYN CONNELLY, *daughters of the mistress of Connelly Hall*

VIRGINIA BUCHANAN, *from South Carolina*

JESSE TATE, *a tenant farmer living on the Connelly plantation*

DUFFY, *a Negro tenant*

ESSIE, *a Negro servant girl*

Tenant farmers on the Connelly plantation:

    MACK LUCAS, *a fiddler*

    UNCLE REUBEN

    UNCLE ISAAC

    ALEC

    JODIE

    HENRY

    TYLER

    RANSOM

    CHARLIE

    ALF

    OTHERS

AN IDIOT BOY

YOUNG MEN *and* YOUNG WOMEN, *serenaders, children of tenant farmers on the Connelly plantation*

Time   *The early years of the twentieth century.*

Place   *An old aristocratic plantation somewhere in the southern part of the United States.*

ACT I
Scene 1   A field on the Connelly plantation, Christmas afternoon.
Scene 2   The dining room in Connelly Hall, evening a few hours later.
Scene 3   The ruined garden of Connelly Hall, a night in spring several months later.

ACT II
Scene 1   The dining room, mid-morning a few days later.
Scene 2   The dining room, summer a few months later.
Scene 3   The dining room, Christmas evening, one year after Scene 2 in Act I

ACT I, SCENE 1

A late winter afternoon is over the fields, and across the land to the west a murky cloud creeps up the sky, lighted along its edge by a bluish tinge from the hidden sun. The air is raw and has the feel of snow in it. A rail fence grown up with an unkempt hedgerow of dead fennel weeds, poke stalks, and sassafras bushes crosses the foreground, rotten and spraddled, with a disused stile near the center. Close beyond it in the field, three stackpoles, now empty and gaunt, stand up like black gallows trees, with ragged wisps of hay clinging to the crosspieces above. The decaying stalks and weeded hedge exude the rot of death into the air, and the mood of a heavy loneliness is over the earth.

Two old sibyl-like Negro women come in from the right, one carrying a hoe and the other a tow sack, and both chewing tobacco in their toothless jaws. They are huge creatures, sexual and fertile, with round moist roving eyes and jowled faces smooth and hairless as a baby's. The mark of ancient strength and procreation still remains in their protuberant breasts and bulging hips. Under old coats their broad shoulders and arms are muscled like men's.

Big Sis [*as if talking into the air*]. Dere. *She gestures toward an uprooted stump behind the hedge where a clump of sassafras grows.*

Big Sue [*answering likewise*]. Yeh.

They lumber through the hedgerow, the rotten rails breaking under them. Big Sis *turns and strikes the fence with her hoe.* Big Sue *lets out a teasing cackle.*

Big Sis [*snarling in simulated anger as she goes behind the stump and begins digging*]. Hee-hee! Laugh, laugh! [*A twisting smile creeps around the corners of her mouth.*]

Big Sue [*softly, her gaze stopping on the haypoles*]. Look at them haypoles—like the gallows where they hung nigger Purvis on.

Big Sis [*now looking up with a wakeful eye*]. G'won. Yah, do—gallows where the old General Connelly hung nigger Purvis on.

BIG SUE. Like bunches of hair hanging on 'em too—Jesus!

BIG SIS. Old General stood up in his long robes and said silence in the court—Purvis to be hung by the neck till dead—and Lord have mercy on your poor soul! Uhm—

BIG SUE [*gazing restlessly about her*]. Uhm—yah, and the sky look black same like when they killed the Son o' God.

BIG SIS. Poor Purvis!

BIG SUE. Poor General!

BIG SIS. Own flesh and blood make no difference. The law say hang.

BIG SUE. The General say hang.

BIG SIS. Purvis can't say "Pappy."

BIG SUE. General can't say "Son." No, Lord, no!

BIG SIS [*half musing as she digs*]. Uhm—poor Purvis—that nigger twist about like a worm on a fishhook the day they hang him.

BIG SUE. Uhm—didn't he? And people everywhere—setting on tops of houses like buzzards—uhm—and some of 'em fainted and fell off when he 'gan wiggle on that rope.

BIG SIS. Old General riding by in his great carriage with his head bent down.

A gun is fired off far down in the field. They listen a moment without saying anything. Then in unison and without looking at each other they point their forefingers in the direction of the sound and make a falling hammer motion with their thumbs, after which they break into a peal of laughter.

BIG SUE. Poor nigger. Some of 'em say they hear him whisper, "Give me some air under this black cap, sweet Lord Jesus."

BIG SIS. But like the deadfall of the grave they had him though—Old General Connelly and the law, yeh, had him. [*Digging furiously.*] Come out of that 'ere ground, old root. I gwine boil you and drink your sap. [BIG SIS *wrenches a root out and hands it up to her sister. The gun goes off again down in the field.*]

BIG SIS. Shoot them doves, Mr. Will Connelly! You can't hit 'em and they feets red with blood. Oughter know it.

BIG SIS. Where they tromped in the blood of the Saviour—nunh—unh.

BIG SUE. Mr. Will couldn't hit 'em if they feets were black like Satan. [BIG SIS *bursts into a peal of laughter.*] Whyfore?

BIG SIS [*straightening up and looking at her sister with a merry glistening eye*]. He can't shoot. Can't like his pappy.

BIG SUE [*laughing till her broad bosom heaves*]. Popgun.

BIG SIS [*spitting*]. Pop goes the weasel. [*With sudden anger she lifts a huge fist and makes a sweeping gesture over the earth.*] He can't do nothing. Creep about. Let the world rot down. Can't do nothing.

BIG SUE. Yah. [*Softly.*] But Lord, his daddy.

BIG SIS. Old General Connelly was a shooting man. [*She slaps her thigh at some far-off remembrance.*]

BIG SUE. Shoot to kill. [*After a moment—slyly.*] Tu-chu, a hossman too and heavy riding man.

They double over in great gales of laughter.

BIG SIS. Yah, and knowed the law. [*Now with sudden mournfulness again.*] But he done gone—gone to his long home.

BIG SUE [*forlornly*]. Yah—yah—and the Old Man is there where Purvis is.

BIG SIS [*prying among the roots and singing in the deep voice of a man, to which her sister adds a low melodious alto*].
> In the cold earth the sinful clay
> Wrapped in a sheet is laid away—hah!
> Rock to the hill to the trees do mourn—
> Pity poor man ever were born—hah!

BIG SUE [*with moody overcast countenance*]. He were good though—in the heart. The Old Man were good. When us wanted meat he give it to us. [*Touching* BIG SIS *on the shoulder and gesturing to the right with her head.*] Look who there.

BIG SIS. Hunh, 'fore God!

BIG SUE. That new tenant gal picking old poke berries. Unh-unh, sees us.

BIG SIS. Sees everything.

BIG SUE. Do that. Been moved on this plantation three weeks and see everything.

BIG SIS. Us sees too—unh-unh. Hee-hee.

BIG SUE. Do—yeh, us do. Hoo—hoo.

BIG SIS [*digging and grunting*].
>   They grabble his eye, they work in his head,
>   Man don't feel 'em, three days dead—hah!
>   And all up above him the wind do mourn—
>   Pity poor man ever were born—hah!

BIG SUE [*wrenching a broken rail out of the fence and standing it up*]. Ho-ho, now she watch us snatch firewood.

BIG SIS. You done said.

BIG SUE. Poor white trash.

BIG SIS. Like all of 'em—scrounging and a-gouging. Poor white trash!

BIG SUE. Pushing up in the world—reaching and a-grabbing at the high place of the quality and the roof over our heads!

BIG SIS. Uhm—

PATSY [*coming in at the right with a bucket*]. Tearing down the fence Big Sue?

BIG SUE [*singing*]. The sparrow sot with her head in her wing—

> PATSY *is a lithe full-figured girl of twenty or more, with cheeks pink in the cold, and dark gipsy-like eyes—eyes which at times have a bright hard look. She wears a cloak buttoned close up under her throat and a stocking cap pulled down over her ears.*

BIG SUE [*snickering*]. Heigho, Miss Patsy.

PATSY. The hogs'll get through that hole.

BIG SUE. Yeb'm, that's so.

PATSY. Better put it back.

BIG SUE [*mumbling*]. Yeb'm. [*She replaces the rail with infinite and sassy slowness.*]

PATSY. What's the matter, got no firewood?

BIG SIS [*snickering also*]. Nob'm.

PATSY [*impatiently*]. There's plenty of it in the woods. [*She begins picking the scattered berries from among the dead stalks and leaves along the hedge.*]

BIG SIS [*facetiously*]. Thought the birds had them berries all by this time.

BIG SUE [*softly*]. Her make no answer.

> *They snicker in disrespect as* PATSY *moves off toward the right.*

PATSY [*calling back*]. You seem to be feeling good.

BIG SUE. Yeb'm.

BIG SIS. Yeb'm.

BIG SUE [*after a moment, as* PATSY *starts away again*]. Gwine find the hunter?

PATSY. What hunter?

BIG SIS. Hunter down in the cornfield there—shooting.

BIG SUE. But can't hit nothing.

> *Again as before they hee-haw with laughter.*

PATSY [*returning along the hedge toward them*]. Why you laugh so?

BIG SIS [*jumping about with her hoe*]. Us feeling good.

PATSY. Do you?

BIG SIS [*with mock forlornness*]. Us feel bad, feel lonesome then with nobody to love us.

BIG SUE [*picking up a handful of damp holly leaves*]. Us tell your fortune about loving.

PATSY [*coming nearer—with slight airiness*]. Can you?

BIG SIS. Us both can.

BIG SUE. Us don't miss um neither. [*Prancing before her and holding a leaf up.*] Name one them points your sweetheart's name.

PATSY [*glancing at her sharply*]. Hm—m—

BIG SUE [*sweetly, mammylike*]. Gwine tell your fortune, honey.

BIG SIS. Yah, name your man, honey.

BIG SUE [*shambling away*]. All right, then—now listen, folkses, and catch the truth.

BIG SIS. That's right, speak it, sister.

BIG SUE. Done made many a match with a holly leaf. Toodle-de-doo. And broke up many one.

PATSY. Oh, yes.

BIG SIS. Yeb'm.
>All of us turn and face the west,
>See who the man that she love best.

They turn and face toward the left and presently PATSY, *smiling, does likewise.* BIG SUE *brings her arm over in a circle and touches each point of the leaf.*

BIG SUE. Heenery-hinery-hikum-ho,
>Answer my answer there below.
>Speak with my finger, say with my voice—
>Shall this woman have her choice?

[*Softly.*] None them points show any urgement yet. [*Chanting.*]
>Slimmery-slissum-slickum-slo,
>Answer my answer there below.
>Who is the man this woman'll wed—

[*She poises her hand in the air, listening.*]

BIG SIS [*grunting*]. Who she gonna keep warm with in bed?

BIG SUE. Don't hear no answer, sump'n wrong.
>Mischief-meevery-miny-mo,
>Answer my answer there below.
>Gimme some motion, gimme some sound—

WILL CONNELLY *comes in at the right and stands watching them, partly concealed by the hedge. He is a gentleman farmer of thirty or thirty-five, with slightly stooping shoulders and thin clean-shaven face. A gun hangs loosely from the crook of his arm.* BIG SUE *has again poised her hand in the air and waits as if for an answer.*

BIG SIS [*starting and crying out*]. Death gwine take her church-wedding bound.

BIG SUE [*tearing the leaf in two and throwing it down*]. There. [*With humorous malice.*] You name one man and us tell you another—hee-hee.

PATSY [*narrowly*]. That's funny.

BIG SIS [*loudly again*]. Mought's well take your mind off'n him.

BIG SUE. Off'n the hunter. Sure God had.

PATSY [*snapping her fingers above her head*]. Hah.

BIG SUE. Her say hah—hee-hee.

BIG SIS. Walk about and look greedy. [*Now snapping her fingers likewise.*] Done got her cap sot, by golly.

WILL, *who has been wiggling himself uneasily, comes forward.*

WILL. Sis!

BIG SIS. Lord Jesus, Mr. Will! [*She begins digging quickly among the bushes.*]

BIG SUE [*dropping on her knees and scratching among the leaves*]. Us just getting sassafras roots, Mr. Will.

In a lightning flash the cunning of their nature has disappeared, and to the casual observer they are no other than two obsequious and ignorant old Negro women.

WILL [*his voice full of indulgent and fatherly patronage*]. Ah-ha.

BIG SIS [*softly, to her sister*]. Let's be going. This'll make tea for a long spell.

BIG SUE [*coming out of the hedge, now shiningly bland and subservient*]. Couldn't give us a quarter for this Christmas Eve, could you, Mr. Will?

WILL [*after a moment, leaning languidly on his gun*]. Reckon I could. [*He pulls out a coin and tosses it toward them. It rolls under the leaves and they fall down on their knees searching for it.*]

BIG SIS. Where is you, new money? Ehp, here she is.

They clamber to their feet.

BIG SUE. Ain't got no little drinkum stuff for us at the big house, has you?

WILL. Come around, I'll see.

BIG SIS *and* BIG SUE. Thanky, suh, thanky, suh. Us'll be there. [*Bowing and scraping they go out at the left. Presently in the distance they are heard roaring with laughter. Then, silence.*]

WILL [*partly to himself*]. A little thing makes 'em happy as larks. Poor creatures. [*He gazes at the ground a moment as if absorbed in thought, and then stares after them with a gentle whimsical smiling.*]

PATSY [*watching him and trying to hide her confusion*]. Yes, poor things.

WILL. Pathetic! Helpless like children. [*Musingly.*] All the Negroes on this plantation are.

PATSY [*neutrally*]. Yes. [*As if pondering.*] Who are they?

WILL. Big Sis and Big Sue?

PATSY. Yes.

WILL. Connelly Negroes. They were slaves of my father's. Everybody knows Big Sis and Big Sue.

PATSY. Are they crazy?

WILL. Gracious, no! Why you ask that?

PATSY. They look at you funny, don't they? [*Hesitating.*] I mean at me funny.

WILL [*presently*]. Pshaw, they tell fortunes and that sort of stuff, but they don't mean any harm.

PATSY. No?

WILL [*glancing at her*]. Of course not.

PATSY [*wiping her stained fingers with her handkerchief and smiling at him with sudden brightness*]. Kill anything?

WILL [*still as if his mind were away*]. Shot at some doves far off. Just to scare 'em. [*Presently.*] I wouldn't like to kill a dove, you know.

PATSY. Yes. They're hard to hit too, ain—aren't they?

WILL. They fly like the wind. [*Setting his gun down and leaning on it—musingly.*] I killed one once.

PATSY [*watching his bowed head*]. You did?

WILL. Never wanted to since.

PATSY. They are pretty things.

WILL. It stared out of its eyes—so— [*Starting.*] Aren't you cold?

PATSY. Look. [*She touches him on the arm.*] There's a line of doves coming this way. [*In a kind of quick excitement.*] Shoot 'em.

> WILL *raises his gun and follows the flight of birds across the sky, then lowers it without firing.*

WILL [*sheepishly*]. I won't shoot 'em now. They're going to their roost down in the pasture. [*Uncomfortably, as he searches for something to say.*] How do you find the house?

PATSY. Fine.

WILL. You're not too crowded?

PATSY. We can get along.

WILL. How do your father and your brothers like it?

PATSY. All right, I guess.

WILL. It ought to've been repaired before you came.

PATSY. Father and I have fixed it up a lot.

WILL. Yes, I know. The yard looks nicer. The house too. I saw it yesterday—and—things all look nicer. [*Staring before him, he awkwardly tips his cap and starts away.*]

PATSY. Look, there's another line of them! [*She suddenly pulls the gun out of his arm, aims at the flying doves, and fires twice in quick succession.*]

WILL. Gracious!

PATSY [*looking up at him with flushed face*]. What do you think of that?

WILL. There, they're falling down. There—in the edge of the field—two of them—gracious!

PATSY [*unbreaching the smoking gun and taking out the shells*]. They fly fast and are hard to kill. Their feathers are so thick.

WILL [*staring at her in a kind of blinking intentness*]. You're a good shot.

PATSY. Used to I'd win turkeys at the shooting matches—eighty yards. I'll run and get them. [*She hands him the gun.*]

WILL [*sharply*]. No, let them be. [*Turning around.*] I'll be going now. [*Stopping.*] What are you doing with those berries?

PATSY [*with a flashing bright smile*]. Your young tenant people are going on a Christmas serenade tonight.

WILL. Are? Why, they haven't serenaded in years. Ah, no, they haven't. [*Stopping again.*] And will you be wearing—dough-faces we used to call them?[1]

PATSY. Yes. Some of us will paint up with this berry juice and look terribly funny. Come and go with us tonight.

WILL. Granny's children play at that! I did long ago.

> JESSE TATE, *a heavy-set farmer of fifty with swarthy face and iron-gray hair, comes in at the left. He carries a knob-gnarled cudgel in his hand, and walks and talks with heavy and lightless deliberance.*

TATE [*slightly touching the rim of his hat with his forefinger*]. Howdy, Mr. Connelly.

WILL [*looking around*]. Evening, Mr. Tate.

TATE [*slowly, after a moment*]. Any luck hunting, sir?

WILL. Your daughter here has just shot two doves. No, I haven't killed anything.

TATE [*pecking at the ground with his stick*]. She's about as good as Daniel Boone when it comes to guns. She is that. [*He stares at the ground as if absorbed with something he sees there.*]

PATSY. Pshaw. Father raised me up same as a boy to ride and hunt, Mr. Will.

WILL. Yes. Good training, I reckon. [*Pulling his coat tight.*] Cold weather, like snow. [*His gaze travels around the field and he fingers his gun.*]

TATE [*with his heavy observation*]. Don't know. The sky's got a sort of glassy glaze to it, don't look like a muggy thickish snow cold.

WILL. No. [*After waiting for someone to speak.*] Hope you're not too disappointed in the farm.

TATE. Well, no. I been down looking over that tract you spoke of my tending.

WILL. Hope you can handle it.

TATE. I'll have to, won't I? It's washed about and bogged up with briars and bushes, but I'll clean that out by March.

WILL [*hurriedly*]. Well, don't freeze in this cold, Miss Patsy. Good evening. [*Again he tips his cap in half embarrassment as he starts off.*]

PATSY *and* TATE. Good evening.

> WILL *walks away at the right.*

TATE [*presently*]. Seems like a nice sort of landlord.

PATSY [*turning to her berrypicking*]. Yes.

TATE [*pushing his stick down into the ground*]. But he ain't no farmer. I knew the Connelly farm when I lived in this neighborhood as a boy. I wish you could have seen it then.

PATSY. I do.

TATE. He's no more like his father than black is white. The old General Connelly was a rip-snorter. Things moved around him. [*Sighing.*] Still he was right much of an ungodly person, and I reckon the world evens up somehow, I don't know. Yes, I reckon so.

PATSY. They say Mr. Will is one of the best men in the neighborhood.

TATE. But a man old as him ought to have a family and be making things go along.

PATSY. I don't know. Oh, well, that's not our business, is it?

TATE. No, there's nobody good enough for him, and never will be according to his mother—and his sisters. Never was anybody good enough for a Connelly. [*Looking off to the left.*] There they all set in that great house. [*Turning back, his eyes sweeping the wide stretch of half-fallow land.*] If I had this farm— [*Muttering to himself.*] Well, no matter, I say.

PATSY. What?

TATE [*thinking to himself*]. Walking over these fields today I'd a-give anything, anything in good honesty, to have owned them. [*Half murmuring.*] It's purty land, purty land, and level as a table, two thousand acres of it.

PATSY. You'll have your own farm yet—some of these days you will.

TATE [*with a touch of moroseness*]. No, I won't. I'll die the other fellow's man—a tenant. [*After a moment.*] You will too.

PATSY [*sharply*]. I won't.

TATE. Oh, but you'll come to it.

PATSY. No.

TATE. Let's go home. [*He climbs over the stile and goes diagonally away at the left, bumping his stick on the ground before him.*]

> PATSY *stands looking after him a moment, and then, turning, stares across the fields to the left, gradually growing absorbed in thought about something. Presently she tosses her head and, whistling, turns once more to picking berries.* BIG SIS *and* BIG SUE *creep back along the hedge at the left and begin digging sassafras roots again, acting all the while as if in ignorance of her presence.*

PATSY. What you want now?

BIG SIS [*swinging her hoe*]. Raise her up—hah—bring her down—hah.

PATSY [*eying them*]. Hope you work like that when chopping cotton time comes.

BIG SUE [*tearing her piece of rail out of the fence*]. I stick this up for a headboard at the grave. Already I sticks it up, and watch her rouse mad. [*She jabs it into the earth and watches it swaying as if reading some mystic meaning there.*]

PATSY [*bursting into a laugh*]. That's right, tear the old fence down. We'll put up a wire one where it was.

BIG SUE. And the wind and the rain can write the name.

> PATSY *watches them wryly and half perplexed a moment and then walks away to the left. Just as she goes out of the scene she begins jiggling her bucket and whistling, apparently in high spirits.*

BIG SIS [*winking and singing*].
> The sparrow sot with her head in her wing,
> The snake crope up and begun to sing—

As if with simultaneous understanding they turn and thumb their noses after PATSY, *then at the sky, wagging their heads and breaking into loud blasphemous laughter. Between their staccato guffaws,* PATSY *is heard whistling in the distance.*

Fade-out.

ACT I, SCENE 2

A few hours later supper is being laid in the old Connelly mansion. The tall candles and the firelight in the dining room illumine an interior once pretentious but now falling to decay. The walls, paneled and decorated in proud Georgian style, are yellowed and cracked, and the portraits of the Connelly ancestors hang moldering in their frames. The furniture is early eighteenth century, with mahogany table, sideboard, chairs, and tapestries here and there. A wide fireplace is at the left, set between fluted pilasters and under an ornate mantel. At the rear a heavy door opens to a latticed side portico, with airy windows on either side. The room is decked with stray bits of Christmas holly and mistletoe. If once the frilled and pompous gentlemen spent many a joyous evening here in the days gone by—when the guests sat to the board and slaves handed on goblets of liquor and wine, as they said—it is so no longer. For now the grace of hospitality is gone, the jovial host is gone, gone is the slave. The furniture is falling to pieces, the brass candlesticks on the walls and the useless chandelier hanging over the table are cankered and green. The ivory wood trimmings are peeling off in brickish patches, and great gaping cracks run leeringly across the plastered ceiling. The dead Connellys, erect in their frames, wait for the end.

The two surviving daughters of Connelly Hall, now late middle-aged spinsters, are laying supper in this dining room, fetching dishes of food from the kitchen at the left. GERALDINE *is tall and somewhat prim, with pallid aristocratic features;* EVELYN *is a few years younger and less austere.*

GERALDINE. I heard a gun shoot twice. And I looked out and saw her and Will standing together there in the fields.

EVELYN. Pshaw, Deenie, there's no harm in that, is there?

GERALDINE [*tapping the knuckles of one hand against the palm of the other, a habit she has when she is worried or undecided about something*]. I thought I'd speak of it to you, that's all.

EVELYN. Oh, he was talking to her about the farm. Uncle Bob says there never was such a person for farming.

GERALDINE. We don't know what sort of woman she is—I mean—you know, Evelyn.

EVELYN [*bending over and smelling the ham*]. Oh, isn't that heavenly? Well, anyway, she's about as pretty a poor-white girl as I ever saw.

GERALDINE [*with a faintly peculiar intonation*]. She's handsome if that's what you mean. [*She busies herself at the table.*]

EVELYN [*examining the ham*]. It browned splendidly, didn't it? [*With a low halfhearted laugh.*] Now Uncle Bob will be sick at his stomach again. [*Picking up the leather-headed gong stick.*] Shall I ring now?

GERALDINE [*standing back and appraising the table*]. Our Christmas supper is ready at last. Yes, ring.

> EVELYN *turns to the sideboard and strikes the gong with slow measured strokes. The two women grow still in their tracks listening as the soft musical tones go echoing through the house.*

EVELYN. I never get tired of listening to it.

GERALDINE [*softly*]. Yes, it's beautiful.

EVELYN. Something so lonely beautiful in it. [*Half musing.*] For a hundred years it has called our people into this dining room. [*Softly also.*] A hundred years.

GERALDINE [*turning with quick nervousness toward the door at the left*]. I was forgetting the coffee.

> *She goes into the kitchen and* EVELYN *moves over to the hearth and leans her head against the mantel. After a moment* GERALDINE *returns with the coffeepot, which she places on the table.*

EVELYN [*staring at the fire*]. Through all the rooms it goes calling. [*Echoing the gong with sentimental and heartaching mournfulness.*] Nobody. Nobody.

GERALDINE. Of course there's somebody.

EVELYN [*with sudden and tearful melancholy*]. How warm this fire is. It burned just like this Christmas years ago. I was standing here and Father came in from town. He'd brought me a new fur coat—You remember that coat, Deenie?

GERALDINE. Let's think of tonight, not some other night. Now that's it.

EVELYN. Oh, there was so much fun then. We had so many friends.

GERALDINE [*with a touch of sharpness*]. We have friends now, Evelyn.

EVELYN. Yes. Mother, and Will, and Uncle Bob, and you and me. There were so many more then. Father—Grandfather—Aunt Charlotte and Uncle Henry. Soon there'll be Uncle Bob and Will and you and me; then you and me and Will; then—

GERALDINE [*gazing about the room as if willing herself into the attitude of an interior decorator*]. These ivy leaves look better in the center of the table. [*She moves them from the sideboard.*]

EVELYN [*gazing about the room also*]. It looks beautiful, Deenie—beautiful and sad.

GERALDINE [*aloofly and as if conscious that the portraits heard*]. This room is always beautiful—and happy—to me.

EVELYN [*lighting the candles*]. Sad like a funeral. [*Childishly.*] Why don't you ever say so? You know it is.

GERALDINE. Set out the wine please, Evelyn. Mother says we must have some tonight.

EVELYN [*going to the window at the rear and looking out*]. It's getting dark and you can't see anything down in the garden there. [*With her face against the pane.*] Remember the Christmas we had that orchestra from Richmond? You danced with a Naval officer that night—hours.

GERALDINE [*with a little laugh*]. You remember a lot.

EVELYN. Sometimes I do.

GERALDINE. Come away from the window, silly, you'll catch cold.

EVELYN [*turning impulsively toward her*]. Deenie!

GERALDINE. Go see if Uncle Bob is ready.

EVELYN. Yes, I will. [*Dabbing her eyes with her handkerchief, she goes out at the right.*]

GERALDINE *stands lost in thought a moment and then brings glasses from the corner cupboard and fills them with water.* WILL *comes in from the door at the rear. He is dressed in the same dark suit as before, except that he has dispensed with his hunter's leggings. He comes up to the fire without a word and stands warming himself, his head bent over in its usual sag.*

GERALDINE. Any mail?

WILL. A letter or two and some circulars—papers, a few Christmas cards too. Cousin Vera sends her regular "Merry Christmas" and nothing more. Where's Evelyn?

GERALDINE. Gone to hurry Uncle Bob. Shall I take the mail to Mother?

WILL. Do. I'll be along to fetch her in a minute if she's to eat with us.

GERALDINE. She is. [*She takes the letters and goes out at the right.*]

WILL *looks into the kitchen, then turns and starts out at the right as* EVELYN *returns.*

EVELYN [*coming in*]. Supper's ready, Will.

WILL. I was looking for you. [*Stepping outside the rear door and bringing in a package.*] Here you are.

EVELYN. For me?

WILL. Yes.

EVELYN [*with almost a cry*]. Thank you, Will!

WILL. It's not from me. Your loving neighbor sent it.

EVELYN. Will.

WILL. Sid Shepherd, of course. Oh, I don't mean to tease you. [*She starts to lay the package in the sideboard drawer.*] Open it. He came by on the road and asked me to give you this Christmas present with his compliments. [*He looks at her with a touch of fond amusement.*]

EVELYN. Thank you and him both. [*She opens it and takes out a flashy toilet set.*] In spite of the—taste, it's nice.

WILL. Taste nothing. [*Hurriedly.*] Sid Shepherd's all right—if he did grow up from poor-white folks.

He goes out. EVELYN *handles the package a moment, her face a mixture of feeling. Then she puts it away and stands by the fire. Presently she picks up the stick and strikes the gong as before, the blows seeming to wait and listen in themselves.* GERALDINE *returns.*

GERALDINE [*sharply*]. There's no need to ring again, Evelyn.

EVELYN. Oh, excuse me, Deenie.

GERALDINE [*brightly*]. Here's Uncle Bob and I'm surprised.

UNCLE BOB *creaks in from the right and stands surveying the supper. He is a run-down old southern gentleman of sixty-five or seventy—dressed in moth-eaten evening clothes of the style of the seventies—with a ragged mustache, pointed scraggly beard, and the pale mottled face of a consistent drinker. His eyes are soft and womanish.*

UNCLE BOB [*in a high thin voice as he pulls out his watch and surveys the table*]. Hah, eight o'clock. Is supper ready? [*Putting a spray of ivy in his coat and singing as no one answers him.*]
        Hop light, ladies, on the ballroom floor,
        Never mind the weather if the wind don't blow.

EVELYN. Merry Christmas to you.

UNCLE BOB. Merry Christmas. You're looking fine, cheeks pink. Purty as that new Tate gal. Merry Christmas, Geraldine. What, don't hear me?

GERALDINE [*starting*]. Merry Christmas, Uncle Bob. Could you lay that large log on, please?

UNCLE BOB. Where's your mother? Shall I bring her?

GERALDINE. No, she's coming with Will.

UNCLE BOB. Is she feeling better?

GERALDINE. I think she'll be able to sit to the table. She says so.

UNCLE BOB *gets the log on but rips his coat.*

UNCLE BOB [*resting on his knees and peering around at* GERALDINE]. It hath been proved of old times—one coat will not last a man his three score and more. [*Spying the wine.*] Heigho, the old Madeira shows up again, ho?

GERALDINE. Come in, Mother.

WILL *helps* MRS. CONNELLY *in from the right and seats her at the head of the table. She is near* UNCLE BOB'S *age but appears much older, a shell of a woman, but with something of the dignity and strength of the matriarch yet remaining to her. Her head dodders with palsy, but her mouth is firm, even stern at times, and her eyes are alert. She is crippled and walks with the aid of a crutch. Her dress of heavy black silk, surmounted by a lace cap, comes down voluminously around her.*

MRS. CONNELLY [*when she is settled in her chair*]. Merry Christmas, Robert.

UNCLE BOB [*getting up from his knees and kissing her hand gallantly*]. Same to you, Ellen. How're you feeling?

MRS. CONNELLY. Better, thank you.

UNCLE BOB. Good, good. You'll throw away that crutch when spring comes.

MRS. CONNELLY. You're always so nice. Thank you. You are indeed.

    EVELYN *comes in and they all arrange themselves quietly and with conscious dignity at the table.*

WILL [*with an embarrassed laugh*]. Well, this is nice, Mother, to have you with us.

MRS. CONNELLY. Thank you. [*To* GERALDINE *and then* EVELYN.] How splendidly you girls have arranged things! [*After a moment bowing her head and reciting in a quavering singsong.*] On this hallowed evening we bow our heads before thee. Bless us, bless this food to our use and to thy name's honor and glory. Bless this house. Teach us to hold sacred its memory and the memory of our fathers. We humbly beg in the name of the blessed Redeemer. Amen.

    For a moment they sit in silence.

UNCLE BOB [*rubbing his hands*]. Well, here we are—the napkins folded and the crystal goblets and all.

EVELYN. And I've never tasted better ham, if we did cook it.

UNCLE BOB. A festive board. *Dum Roma deliberat Saguntum*[2] starves to death.

    WILL *begins carving the ham.* EVELYN *and* GERALDINE *preside over the other dishes.*

WILL. That's for you, Mother.

UNCLE BOB [*genially*]. If this keeps up you'll have to go in for big farming again, William Byrd. But *carpe diem*, I say with Horatius.

WILL. Hardly a second time, Uncle Bob. Geraldine. [*He hands on a plate.*]

UNCLE BOB [*shivering*]. It's cold in here. The fire hardly warms us.

EVELYN [*elated*]. Yes, let's have some wine, Deenie. And we have some lovely wine whey for you, Mother.

A still from Act I, Scene 2, performed by the Group Theatre on Broadway, 1931 (courtesy Paul Green Foundation).

MRS. CONNELLY [*laughing*]. Am I as ill as that? Open a bottle.

> GERALDINE *pours the wine.*

UNCLE BOB. Once more we gather 'mid scenes of delight.

EVELYN. Yes, once more. [*Holding a glass between her and the fire, her face flushed with happiness.*] What wonderful flames dance in it.

UNCLE BOB [*admiringly*]. The color of your face, ah—Better as it nears the end. Hence, melancholy. Rustle up another pirate uncle in the vineyards of the Barbados.

GERALDINE. None of the Connellys ever were pirates, Uncle Bob. [*She smiles at him with her fine weary eyes.*]

UNCLE BOB. They should have been. [*Smiling also.*] Well, whoever furnished it, here's to him. [*He drains down his glass, gesturing slightly with his free hand toward* GERALDINE.]

I can remember back in '87 when Ed Waddell and me—the honorable Ed he came to be in Congress—put away a whole cask of this same stuff and went out to 'dress the Democrats. I laid Zeb Vance in the shade that day.

MRS. CONNELLY [*presently*]. Help Uncle Bob again, Geraldine.

GERALDINE pours him a second glass, now prim again as if faintly offended at his boorishness.

UNCLE BOB. Thanks. [*He raises his glass to his lips and then stops.*] A toast. [*There is no answer, and he rises.*] On this Christmas Eve, marking the one hundred and fiftieth year [*He draws out the words in deep oratorical sonority.*] this house has stood, we lift our cup to the present keeper of its ancient hearth—one who bears the sacred name of Mother, one who shared her husband's [*With a gesture toward the portrait above the mantel.*] accomplishments and his glory, one who is the proud possessor of all the virtues known to womanhood and not one blemish— [*His voice full of real and genuine feeling.*] one whose life has been an inspiration to us all; to you, Ellen, we drink.

They rise, clink their glasses, and drink.

MRS. CONNELLY [*in a low voice*]. Thank you, thank you.

They reseat themselves and go on eating. Someone softly heighoes beyond the door at the rear.

WILL [*calling out*]. Come in!

A middle-aged Negro opens the door and stands with his cap in his hand and a tow sack on his shoulder.

DUFFY. Evening, missus, evening, ma'am.

MRS. CONNELLY. Howdy, Duffy.

DUFFY [*embarrassed, but artfully obsequious*]. I want to see Mr. Will a minute, ma'am.

WILL [*glancing at* MRS. CONNELLY]. Warm yourself by the fire. I'll be through directly.

He comes in, a ragged nondescript fellow, and sits down meekly on the edge of a chair near the fire. They go on with their supper.

MRS. CONNELLY [*graciously and yet the perfunctory mistress*]. How's your baby, Duffy?

DUFFY. Right peart, ma'am.

EVELYN. What's Santa going to bring them all?

DUFFY [*snickering*]. Got so many he can't do much visiting this year.

UNCLE BOB. Why you niggers have so many young'uns anyhow?

DUFFY [*hiding a grin behind the bag*]. The Good Book say 'splenish the earth, Mr. Bob.

WILL [*pushing himself back from the table*]. I'll finish later. Excuse me. How much meat you want, Duffy?

DUFFY. Much as you kin spare, suh.

WILL. Is that all right, Mother?

MRS. CONNELLY. Let him have fat back if you have it.

WILL. That's all gone.

MRS. CONNELLY. Well, whatever's there.

DUFFY. Thanky, ma'am.

    WILL *and the Negro go out.*

GERALDINE [*motionless*]. We must do something about that, Mother.

MRS. CONNELLY. He has to eat.

EVELYN. And we too.

UNCLE BOB. Pray for a miracle. [*Raising his pudgy fist aloft, his voice full of sudden anger.*] Oh, I'd step in and give Duffy's old woman the worst beating she'd ever had. I'd say, get out of that bed, you old whelp, and get to work, you and your puppies. And then I'd fall in on Duffy, and then I'd stretch three or four of his young'uns out cold.

EVELYN. It's not slave days any more, Uncle Bob.

UNCLE BOB [*excitedly, his voice high and thin*]. That's it! A Yankee or a Jew, I don't know which is slickest. The Yankees first sold us nigger property, then took it away from us in the name of Christianity and paid us nothing for the loss. But they kept the money they'd got for the trade, b'God! [GERALDINE *suddenly pours her mother a glass of wine.*] The Yankees, the damned Yankees. All that shall go in my book. The truth has never been told. [*He falls to eating again, and no one says anything.*]

WILL [*coming in at the rear and going quietly to the table*]. Oh, yes—the book. Still working on it?

UNCLE BOB. My Lord, feeding a nigger on ham!

WILL. I'm the Good Samaritan. [*He smiles wanly at* UNCLE BOB.]

UNCLE BOB. Why don't you get fatback for him at the store?

WILL. Lend me ten dollars and I will.

UNCLE BOB. As soon as they straighten my pension.

    MRS. CONNELLY *makes a slight gesture of impatience.*

GERALDINE. Sugar, Evelyn?

EVELYN. No, thanks. The butter, please, Uncle Bob.

    WILL *drops his knife and fork on his plate and leans his head on his hand.*

MRS. CONNELLY. Pass Will the jam.

WILL. I'm not very hungry, Mother.

UNCLE BOB [*in mock sympathy as he regains his spirits*]. Not hungry for Christmas dinner? Must be in love. Any bad news in the mail, Will?

WILL. The bank would like to see me. [*Hurriedly.*] Oh, well, let's talk of that later. [*He takes up his knife and fork again.*] By the way, the paper says we may have snow tonight or tomorrow.

EVELYN. And let's get out that old sled, Will. [*To* GERALDINE.] You remember that big snow when Will and Duffy killed so many rabbits—we were riding on the sled and you stuck that awful splinter in your hand. [*Putting an arm around her affectionately.*] But you didn't cry one bit. No, you didn't, Deenie.

GERALDINE. I remember.

UNCLE BOB. Look out, honey, that wine's mighty strong. Any mail come for me, Will?

WILL. Nothing, Uncle Bob.

UNCLE BOB [*feeling his drinks*]. Used to I got it by the carload, office piled full of it, running over in the courthouse—to the Honorable Robert Randolph Connelly, Solicitor, Third District, Legislator. [*Eying them.*] Oh, yes!

    MRS. CONNELLY *bows her head a trifle in shame for him.*

GERALDINE [*to* EVELYN]. Virginia Buchanan writes she is coming in the spring.

EVELYN. Isn't that lovely? We—

UNCLE BOB [*with dogged and conscious perversity*]. I fought the battle of the Wilderness— at Gettysburg I fought. I yielded up my arms at Appomattox. But I never was whipped. I'm not whipped now. [*Foolish and ashamed.*] Ah, Ellen.

MRS. CONNELLY [*smiling*]. Of course not.

EVELYN. We must begin to plan for Virginia's visit.

GERALDINE. We could have the Grahams up from Wilmington.

UNCLE BOB [*emboldened again*]. Our day is not over. Chance, luck that makes the great, makes success. A heavy rain is what beat the Confederacy. Our guns were stuck below the hill. It happened to rain. But our day will come. [*Drawing up his shoulders.*] And when it does, a Jeff Davis won't have to hide in a woman's clothes then. Nor will a Robert E. Lee have to pray to God so much. It'll be minnie balls and not prayer.

MRS. CONNELLY. Perhaps so, Robert. [*Turning to* EVELYN.] Virginia say she's looking forward to being here.

UNCLE BOB. Pass me the wine, Geraldine. Virginia Buchanan, you say? *Te morituri salutamus.*[3] She's worth two million sweated out of the niggers of South Ca'liny.

MRS. CONNELLY [*with a touch of impatience in her voice*]. Now, Robert.

UNCLE BOB [*drawing his coat about him*]. Selah.[4]

WILL [*dropping his knife with a clatter*]. Talk, talk.

GERALDINE [*after a moment*]. Will!

WILL. Yes, I said talk, talk. God help me. God help all of us!

They eye him in astonishment and MRS. CONNELLY *now sits up straight, offended.*

UNCLE BOB. God? Thou hast not read the Stoics, son. Pass the pickles, Evelyn.

WILL [*angrily*]. Stoics, Epicureans, Atomists! Cicero, Horace! They don't tell you how to feed hungry niggers, how to meet overdrafts and pay mortgages. Do they?

MRS. CONNELLY. Lift me up, Robert. [*Agitated.*] I—I must lie down.

UNCLE BOB. No, no, forgive us, Ellen. Will, what in the name of goodness!

MRS. CONNELLY. Never mind, I'm tired—that's all.

WILL. Mother—I'm—sorry—

MRS. CONNELLY [*in a low disturbed voice*]. Tomorrow I have some little gifts for you. I'm sorry I can't finish. [*They all rise except* WILL.] No, don't bother. [*With sudden sharpness.*] The Connellys have stood more than poverty without losing their pride. Good night.

WILL [*contritely—jumping up*]. I'll help you, Mother. Here, this way—gently. [*He takes her by the arm and quietly goes out with her,* GERALDINE *leading the way with a candle.*]

UNCLE BOB [*his face haggard and drawn*]. Sleep well, Ellen! Good night. [*To himself.*] Sleep—ah. *De mortuis*—ah—[5]

EVELYN [*bursting into tears*]. Now—now— [*Furiously.*] Why couldn't you talk of something pleasant? Mother's sick.

UNCLE BOB. What's got into Will? He's laughed at my joking before. Now—Oh, don't cry, honey. [*With sharp self-hate.*] Fool! [*Rising.*] I'll go to her—No, I'll sit right down again.

EVELYN *sits down by the fire, her face buried in her hands. Presently she springs up again.*

EVELYN. I can't stand to live like this.

UNCLE BOB. Well, Sid Shepherd's a rich farmer. He'd marry you in a minute.

EVELYN. And that beautiful Dauphine pudding wasted!

UNCLE BOB. That's what's wrong. The damned Connellys are too proud to live in this world. Pudding? We'll eat it. [*Sighing and going to the fire.*] *Desicco, desiccare*[6]—huhm, principal parts—dry, by God—dry and proud!

EVELYN. And I'm glad we are proud.

WILL [*coming in—smiling*]. Is that Livy talking again, Uncle Bob?

UNCLE BOB. And what's swelled up your spleen this Christmas Eve?

WILL. I'm sorry you missed your toast to the General— [*Glancing up surreptitiously like a boy.*] who in the front of war hath held— [*He turns and pokes the fire hurriedly and aimlessly.*]

UNCLE BOB [*gazing up at the portrait draped in the Confederate flag above the mantel*]. He can spare it and I can too.

WILL [*pouring himself a large glass of wine*]. Good. [*He stirs the fire faster, holding the wine untasted in one hand.*]

UNCLE BOB [*softly*]. Let's all take poison and die. Burn up the house. Leave the crickets and the field mice to their inheritance. You hear me?

EVELYN *goes into the kitchen.* WILL *throws out his hands in a gesture and sits down by the fire, looking through the newspaper and sipping his wine.*

WILL [*wearily*]. Yes, Uncle Bob.

UNCLE BOB. And I can tell you how to change it, if you would.

WILL. Yes.

UNCLE BOB. Turn the farm over to old man Tate and his gal, Patsy. Or turn it over to her.

WILL. They've only been on the plantation three weeks.

UNCLE BOB. I knew Jesse Tate years ago. He was a good farmer then.

WILL. He doesn't seem to have prospered—coming back here as a tenant.

UNCLE BOB. And of course you've prospered, sonny. It would pay you to quit, if you want my advice. You can—oh—ho—ride around and look at the purty girls in the evening time.

WILL. Don't let the wine make you mean, Uncle Bob.

UNCLE BOB. And another thing. Get married.

WILL. Here, now. Really?

UNCLE BOB. When Virginia Buchanan comes up here—

WILL [*throwing down his paper in vexation*]. Virginia Buchanan—and I beg her pardon—never had a thought but for her blue blood and the Confederate flag and something she thinks her folks did on the battlefields of Virginia.

UNCLE BOB. Ho-ho-ho! [*Narrowly.*] Did you and Miss Patsy kill any game this evening? I saw you banging away together there by the hedgerow. Sweet, ain't she?

WILL [*going to the kitchen door*]. Can I help you with the dishes?

EVELYN [*within*]. No, thank you.

   After a moment EVELYN *comes in and stands with her head leaned on the mantel.*

WILL. Have a headache?

EVELYN. No.

UNCLE BOB [*twiddling his thumbs and talking half to himself*]. Pray with this penknife prick thou this vein. And let there be no tears, tears. The ivy creeps in at the doors, the beams yield under the roof, the beetles bore with their sharp little augers, and the flood pours in. Hold fast the laces, preserve the frills, though the heavens fall. [*Singing in squeaky dolefulness.*] *In-teg-er vi-tae, sce-le-ris-que pu-rus— / Non e-get Mau-ris ja-cu-lis nec ar-cu.*[7] [*He picks up the newspaper which* WILL *has dropped and begins reading.*]

EVELYN [*clearing the table,* WILL *aiding her*]. Want any more supper?

WILL. No, much obliged.

UNCLE BOB. And a little Greek becomes it—*Menin aeide thea—Peleia—dos Achilleus oulomen—en—*[8]

> GERALDINE *returns and helps* EVELYN, *going back and forth into the kitchen with dishes.*

WILL. You're very witty tonight, Uncle Bob. [*Smiling.*] Not that I mind it.

UNCLE BOB. Selah. [*Outside and far away come the sounds of bells and horns intermingled with the faint music of guitars and fiddles.*] Listen. Serenaders, bless my life! [*Excitedly.*] First time I've heard them in years, Will. [*The music is heard more distinctly a moment and then is silent. Disappointed.*] Gone on by, I reckon. [*He returns to his paper.*]

> BIG SIS *and* BIG SUE *open the door at the rear and creep in.*

WILL. What is it?

BIG SIS. We came for our little drinkum stuff, Mr. Will.

WILL. Go into the kitchen. Evelyn, give Big Sis and Big Sue a little wine.

BIG SIS *and* BIG SUE. Thanky, suh, thanky, Mr. Will.

UNCLE BOB. What's all that racket out there, Big Sis?

BIG SIS. Serenaders coming up the gyarden with bull fiddle and bells. Yes, suh.

> GERALDINE *takes a bottle of wine and two glasses and follows the Negro women into the kitchen.*

EVELYN. Won't that be fine!

> *Outside there is a sudden burst of horns, ringing of bells, and yells let loose.*

GERALDINE [*coming in*]. That will disturb Mother. Stop them, Will. [*She too listens a moment and then goes out at the right.*]

UNCLE BOB. There's the spirit—hah—hah!

> *Presently the clamor dies down, the rude country string band strikes up a ballad, and the serenaders join in singing, led by a young woman's clear voice.*

EVELYN [*listening, her face full of naive delight, then half singing with the girl's voice outside, forgetful for the moment of her surroundings*].

> The Brown Girl she has house and lands.
> Fair Elinor she has none.
> It's my advice to you, my son,
> Go bring the Brown Girl home.

UNCLE BOB *goes to the rear door, opens it, and waves unsteadily to the serenaders outside.*

UNCLE BOB. Heigh, heigh, boys!

The music suddenly stops and a group of singers come up under the portico, snarling and snapping in joyous abandon at UNCLE BOB *like a gang of dogs. He steps back into the room and they stand in the door, loath to come in, yelling, ringing their bells and tooting their guano bugles. They are dressed in all sorts of outlandish garbs—some wearing their clothes backwards, some with masks or dough-faces on, and others painted like Indians on the warpath.*

A BOY [*ringing his bell above his head*]. Wake up, it's Christmas!

VOICES [*yelling and tooting*]. Christmas, merry Christmas, everybody!

UNCLE BOB [*catching sight of someone through the door*]. Heigh you, Mack Lucas, bring in that fiddle! [MACK LUCAS, *a shy stoop-shouldered man, wearing a stage-villain's mustache, slips just inside the door. He carries a fiddle in his hand.*] Give us a piece. [*Waving his hand unsteadily over them.*] A piece, musicianers! [*His head doddering.*] Christmas comes but once a year. [*Singing.*]
> Hop light, ladies, on the ballroom floor,
> Never mind the weather if the wind don't blow.

The serenaders titter and giggle, and the country musicians strike up a country favorite, "Noah's Ark." UNCLE BOB *listens a while and then pulls* EVELYN *out into the room and pushes her through a step or two.*

VOICES. Hooray!

EVELYN [*confused and embarrassed*]. Let me go. [*She shakes herself from him and flees to the fireplace.*]

UNCLE BOB [*surveying the crowd as he begins cutting steps*]. Come on, partner, where are you hiding?

The serenaders gradually move into the room, but showing all the while that they are somewhat timid about it, no matter how much noise they make outside.

A VOICE. The old bird's right.

VOICES. Patsy, come in here!

Now with shouts and laughter they push PATSY *through the group and into the room. She is dressed in the garb of a gypsy with a scarlet band around her head, a flouncy flowing dress, and with stained lips and cheeks, and painted eyebrows and lashes.* WILL *turns around in his chair and looks up at her in mild astonishment.*

UNCLE BOB [*clapping his hands gleefully as he moves toward her*]. Ho—ho—and what's the matter? Don't run back.

VOICES. Dance with him, Patsy.

PATSY [*with a glance that passes by* WILL]. We'd better go, maybe. We all didn't mean to come in and disturb you so. [*She apparently tries to push her way through the door, but now emboldened they hold her back.*]

VOICES. Dance off that piece for him.

UNCLE BOB [*still clapping his hands to the music*]. Dance all around. [*He snatches a girl, with a pigtail hanging down over her forehead, from the crowd and begins dancing up and down the room. Those not dancing begin to clap their hands rhythmically.* WILL *sits bowed over in his chair, staring at the floor.* PATSY *becomes a partner to a youth wearing his clothes reversed, a floursack over his face and a mask surmounted by a cap tied on the back of his head. Another fantastic gnarl-visaged fellow makes his way over to* EVELYN *and drags her unwillingly into the dance. After a moment she partially enters into the spirit of the occasion.* WILL *stands up, eying* EVELYN *and the roisterers in embarrassment.* UNCLE BOB, *aroused with wine and excitement, wheezes and shouts as he thumps about.*] Let her roll. Swing your partner. Sashay to the right, sashay to the left. Promenade all! Hands all around. Rah-rah for our side! [*He lets go his partner and pulls* PATSY *into his arms as she passes.*]

VOICES. That's a dancing man.

PATSY *and* UNCLE BOB *pass close to* WILL.

PATSY [*half teasing*]. Come on, play, Mr. Will.

WILL *makes no answer.*

UNCLE BOB [*blowing*]. A regular fox chase.

  PATSY *falls to doing a sort of crude gypsy dance in the middle of the room.*

VOICES. Hooray, hooray! [*A firecracker is shot off outside. The serenaders turn for an instant toward the door and yell.*] Merry Christmas!

A BOY [*with a high cry*]. God the Saviour is born!

  The music changes from "Noah's Ark" to the ballad of "Gypsy Davie." The others stop dancing and stand watching PATSY. EVELYN, *as if suddenly upset by her part in the shindig, turns abruptly and leaves the room.*

PATSY [*weaving her hands around her and singing*].

> It was all upon a cold river bank,
> The water was deep and a-muddy, O.
> The tears ran down his face like rain,
> When first he saw his a-lady, O.

[*The* OTHERS *join in.*]

> Last night I lay on a warm featherbed,
> My arms were around my a-baby, O.
> Tonight I'll lie on some cold river bank,
> In the arms of my Gypsy a-Davie, O.

UNCLE BOB [*singing*]. For she's gone with the Gypsy a-Davie, O. [*Squealing.*] Purty bird in my cup—Jenny Wren! [*Full of devilment he catches* PATSY *by the hand and leads the singing dancers in a circle around* WILL.] Mack Lucas, saw on your strings! Great God!

VOICES [*singing*].

> Pull off, pull off them fine kid gloves,
> All made of Spanish leather, O,
> And give to me your lily-white hand,
> And we'll shake hands together, O.

They shake hands and the boys kiss the tips of the girls' fingers and bow. A country boy, dwarfish and idiotic, springs out into the floor with a squeal. He begins dancing round and round by WILL, *giggling and leering at him. The serenaders roar with laughter.*

WILL [*suddenly grabbing the boy by the collar*]. Stop that laughing!

The serenaders stop and look around sheepishly, giggling, murmuring, and begin to move toward the door at the rear.

UNCLE BOB [*pouring himself a glass of wine*]. A toast, ladies and gentlemen. [WILL, *ashamed, releases the boy, who slinks back to his companions, gurgling foolishly.*] To all of ye a Merry Christmas and a happy New Year! [*He climbs up on a chair and raises his glass.*]

VOICES [*tittering and nodding at him*]. He's gonna speak.

MRS. CONNELLY, *supported by* GERALDINE *and* EVELYN, *appears in the doorway at the right.*

MRS. CONNELLY. What is this! What are you doing here?

The serenaders back away before her.

UNCLE BOB [*waving his hand to her and gesturing with his glass at the portrait above the mantel*]. Saul hath slain his thousands, David his tens of thousands, and on this blessed Christmas Eve, ladies and gentlemen, I lift this cup to the blessed—

Again the serenaders snicker and murmur among themselves and some laugh aloud.

WILL [*whirling upon them wrathfully*]. Be quiet!

UNCLE BOB [*staring intently at* MRS. CONNELLY]. To the blessed memory of a gallant soldier and a great gentleman—the dead husband of our dear lady and erstwhile master of this house. [*As he goes on* MRS. CONNELLY *moves farther into the room, and she and her two daughters stand holding hands and looking up at the portrait.* WILL *has again dropped his head on his chest and is staring at the floor. The serenaders, as if awed by some uncomprehended ritual, begin to steal out of the room one by one.* UNCLE BOB, *oblivious to all around him, slowly continues, his voice deepening with emotion.*] To him we drink who in the face of death mounted The Stars and Bars above the rampart of the enemy; the first at Manassas, last at Appomattox, farthest at Gettysburg—to thee we lift this cup— [*As if addressing a living person.*] to thee, suh, jurist, patriot, soldier, citizen, we drink—General William Hampton Connelly of Connelly Hall!

VOICES [*outside*]. Ha-ha-ha! Hooray!

> UNCLE BOB *drinks and after a moment steps heavily down from the chair, looking round the room, from which all the serenaders save* PATSY *have gradually gone.*

MRS. CONNELLY. Thank you, Robert.

EVELYN [*clapping her hands*]. Uncle Bob. [*She runs up to him and kisses him on the cheek.*]

GERALDINE [*catching* EVELYN'S *arm and continuing to gaze at the portrait*]. Don't.

UNCLE BOB. *Arma virumque cano.*[9] How great a thing to have an honored name. Ah, we shall not look upon his like again. [*He moves to the fireplace and stands looking closely at the portrait. Lifting his arm, disclosing a wide rip in his coat, he goes on in the voice of one at prayer.*] In our poor way we honor thee. [*Stretching his other hand back toward* WILL *who looks up somewhat sheepishly.*] And may this, thy son, wear the mantle of his father, with profit and renown. May he become conscious of the name he bears, and from this day forth determine by the help of God— [*He stops and sits down in an armchair near the fire, his head bent over.*]

VOICES [*outside*]. Come on, Patsy, le's go!

MRS. CONNELLY. We will excuse you.

PATSY. I—all right. Thank you, ma'am. [*Now ignoring* MRS. CONNELLY.] Come on, Mr. Will, and go with us a-serenading.

WILL [*starting up*]. Me? [*Foolishly.*] Ha-ha-hah.

GERALDINE. You can go out this way.

PATSY. We're going to stop at the millpond and have an egg-fry. All of you come.

UNCLE BOB. I'll go.

PATSY [*controlling the tremor in her voice*]. The young folks told me to ask you. [*As no one says anything.*] I'm sorry we disturbed you, sorry we disturbed you. [*Impetuously.*] Why're you all so—so solemn? [*She turns and walks with dignity from the room. As she passes* GERALDINE *at the door she looks up and nods with a smile.*]

MRS. CONNELLY [*after a long silence*]. Please see to the fire before you go to bed tonight, Will.

WILL. All right, Mother.

MRS. CONNELLY. Help me to my room, will you, Geraldine? GERALDINE *helps her out.*

UNCLE BOB. Old and solemn, mournful as whippoorwills. [EVELYN *goes into the kitchen and leaves them. He pours himself another glass of wine and gestures heavily toward the portraits.*] Ladies— [WILL *suddenly picks up his hat and starts out at the rear.*] Where to, Galahad?

WILL. I'll look about the barn a minute.

UNCLE BOB [*staring after him and spanking his thigh*]. Ho-ho! [*Calling*] Don't fall in the millpond. By Jesus! [*Gesturing around again at the portraits.*] Gentlemen—

Fade-out.

ACT I, SCENE 3

A night in early spring several months later. The ruined garden of Connelly Hall with the moonlit fields showing off to the right. Rose brambles, briers, and honeysuckles grow in unkempt profusion among the ragged trees. In the foreground is an old scraggly crepe myrtle tree with a garden seat under it, to the right of which is a stone pool grown up into a mush of lilies and flags. Farther back in the distance the tombstones of the family burying ground glitter in the moonlight, the sarcophagus of General William Hampton Connelly standing lordly above the rest. Between the pool and the garden seat is an old wooden pump, and beyond the pump in the background the gaunt form of a lightning-blasted cypress lifts itself out of the underbrush like a gnarled disfigured hand. A path leads in from the right foreground through the grass and briers, passes by the pump, and goes crookedly off toward the side portico, the steps and columns of which can be dimly seen at the left rear. The garden is partially illuminated through the lighted windows of the mansion. Contrasting with the mournfulness of the decaying garden and the pallid light of the moon are the gay strains of a waltz coming from an orchestra in the house. Once again a ball is being given in Connelly Hall and the rooms are alive with youthful laughter and music. Twinkling feet go up and down the broad staircase, hands are squeezed and hearts are fluttered as was told of in the old days.

BIG SIS and BIG SUE come up the path from the right and stop by the pump. They are dressed in long loose wrappers.

BIG SIS. Bet there's muskrats in that pool big as the old black sow.

BIG SUE. Mought be other varmints in this old Connelly garden—ghostes. Look at them tombstones.

BIG SIS. And that poor moon hanging sick with grief.

BIG SUE. Tchee-tchee—but listen at that music. Ain't no grief there.

BIG SIS. Plenty loving. [*Standing by the myrtle tree.*] Lord, they's cutting up there. Sure giving that Miss Virginia a blowout—uhm!

BIG SUE [*coming over and standing with her*]. That Miss Virginia sure God is a queen. Look how she sashay!

BIG SIS. Sashay her tail off, do her no good with Mr. Will.

BIG SUE [*hugging her sister and prancing about*]. Lord, look like old days done come back to Connelly Hall.

BIG SIS [*grabbing* BIG SUE *by the arm*]. There that huzzy bitch Patsy!

BIG SUE. Jesus, hugging up with the quality.

BIG SIS. Gwine get hugged up—eigh Lord.

BIG SUE. Uh-huh, now!

She catches her sister's hand and they cut a step or two, their wrappers flapping about their bare shanks, and BIG SIS *moaning softly.*

BIG SIS.
                Rank-tuh-ma-tank, I'm gwine to the fair,
                To see them ladies comb their hair.

BIG SUE [*mocking the fiddles in the house*]. Tweedle-duh-dee.

BIG SIS. S'lute yo' pardner. [*The music in the house stops, followed by applause and the chattering of many voices.*] There come somebody.

They hurry along the path to the rear as WILL *emerges from the thicket at the left, hatless and dressed in ill-fitting evening clothes.*

WILL. Who's that?

He waits a moment, and hearing no reply rolls a cigarette and lights it. He paces up and down muttering to himself. Presently he goes over and stands looking down into the pool. A light form glides through the trees and VIRGINIA BUCHANAN *comes out into the clearing.*

VIRGINIA [*in a cool drawling voice*]. Heigho, Will?

WILL. Yes, Virginia.

VIRGINIA [*coming over to the garden seat*]. Isn't this the quietest place? I've been out in this garden hours since I came. Yesterday I sat here and read *Lorna Doone* half through and nothing came to disturb me.[10] That's the sweetest story.

WILL. Yes, it's quiet here.

VIRGINIA. Quiet and lovely.

WILL. Yes.

> VIRGINIA *is a tall gracious woman of twenty-five, somewhat irregularly featured, with a girlish giddy voice that goes prattling along like a bubbling brook. But underneath her giddiness there now and then show through a weariness and subtlety that she strives constantly to keep concealed. She is wearing a filmy white evening dress with a light scarf thrown over her shoulders and a bouquet of carnations at her waist. Sitting down, she makes way for* WILL.

VIRGINIA. Oh, of course some things came to disturb me.

WILL. Yes, they usually do.

VIRGINIA. A girl can't get away from her thoughts, you know.

WILL. What was worrying you?

VIRGINIA [*leaning over and tapping the toe of her shoe with her fan*]. Lor, you'll think I'm foolish.

WILL. I reckon not.

VIRGINIA. I was thinking about you. [*Archly.*] Now don't say I'm too forward.

WILL [*with hidden wryness*]. I won't.

VIRGINIA. Look, there's the moon again. A new moon.

WILL [*rolling another cigarette*]. Yes, there it is again.

VIRGINIA. "Late, late yestre'en I saw the old moon / With the new moon in its arms. / I fear, I fear, my master dear—" Do you know that poem? It's beautiful. Oh, me, I believe it's the new moon that has the old moon in its arms, isn't it? Please sit down and cool your fevered thoughts.

WILL [*sits down awkwardly beside her*]. I'm not very well up on poetry and the moon.

VIRGINIA. I declare you haven't said three words to me the whole evening. What's the matter?

WILL. Haven't I? I'm sorry.

VIRGINIA. You haven't said much to me the whole week. I didn't know you smoked.

WILL. I've taken it up lately. Oh, may I?

VIRGINIA. That's all right. But Father used to say a true southern gentleman chewed tobacco or smoked nothing weaker than cigars.

WILL. I'm not a true southern gentleman, maybe.

VIRGINIA. Oh, Will!

WILL. Am I?

VIRGINIA. Of course you are. What's the matter? What is it worries you so? I'll declare. You seem worried all the time.

WILL [*turning and looking at her intently*]. All right, then, I won't be.

VIRGINIA. That's nice now. Who is that country girl in there, Will?

WILL. Who?

VIRGINIA. Patsy Tate, or some such name?

WILL. She's a girl lives on the plantation.

VIRGINIA. A tenant girl?

WILL. Yes.

VIRGINIA. What's she doing at the dance?

WILL. Everybody's not as proud as you and Geraldine.

VIRGINIA. Oh, Lor, I don't care. I just wondered who she was. [*Whistling softly to herself.*] You're not glad to have me up here, are you? I looked forward to it for months.

WILL. Of course I'm glad.

VIRGINIA. La, oh, I declare. [*Looking off to the left also.*] Don't those white dresses look perfect against those old columns?

WILL. Aren't you cold? Shall I bring your wrap?

VIRGINIA. Oh, no! I think Connelly Hall is the loveliest place. I've fallen in love with its sad ancient grandeur.

WILL. Sad.

VIRGINIA [*touching his arm timidly*]. You're not happy, Will. You're tired. There's something worrying you. [*Laughing again.*] You ought to come to Charleston and take a vacation. The old homes and lovely gardens there would cheer you up. Lor, I guess for sheer beauty they're not to be equaled anywhere. Still there's something about this place—Did you ever see such boxwood! [*Laughing.*] I never did in my life. I wonder how high those at the front are?

WILL. Some over thirty feet.

VIRGINIA. It's the loveliest place. I declare it is.

WILL [*looking at her*]. A northern man offered me five hundred dollars apiece for them.

VIRGINIA. How foolish! Money couldn't buy them, of course. [*Half singing.*] Late, late yestre'en, I saw the old! moon—You don't like poetry, do you? Do you know Longfellow's "Excelsior?"[11]

WILL. I learned it the year Uncle Bob ran for the legislature.

VIRGINIA. Isn't he the funniest man? He's having the time of his life. [*As the music starts up again.*] Listen at the waltz. Have you ever been to Vienna?

WILL. I should say not.

VIRGINIA [*laying her hand gently on his arm*]. Don't be mournful.

WILL [*standing up quickly*]. Mournful little boy—hah?

VIRGINIA [*starting back*]. Of course not.

WILL. Well, then, that's nice of you, really.

VIRGINIA. There Patsy is by the window with her black eyes, Will—and outlandish dress. [*Laughing.*] I declare. But she doesn't seem to mind though.

WILL. I don't reckon she minds.

VIRGINIA. She's forward, don't you think?

WILL. How do you mean?

VIRGINIA. A bit—you know—coming.

WILL. Well, that would not be so bad—maybe.

VIRGINIA. Oh, my, I've dropped my fan. [*He picks it up and hands it to her.*] Thank you.

WILL. Don't mention it. [VIRGINIA *breaks into a peal of laughter.*] I lack style, Virginia. I wasn't born for a courtier.

VIRGINIA. I'll declare you're funny. [*She touches him lightly on the cheek with her fan.*]

WILL. I know it.

VIRGINIA [*looking out before her*]. Cousin Geraldine said that hollow down there was where you used to have the race track.

WILL. It's nothing but a canebrake now.

VIRGINIA. Do you ever think of getting it in shape again? It would be wonderful to do it. I'll declare. Think of the people from Richmond and Washington, Charleston and Savannah, all coming here and betting their money! It would be perfectly lovely. And the jockeys all dressed in their funny clothes and caps! And the marvelous crowds!

WILL. Great goodness!

VIRGINIA. It could be done. And it would be more fun than a little. Please sit down.

WILL. Does this place look like there's any money to spend on race tracks, Miss Virginia?

VIRGINIA. "Miss Virginia." Will—I declare, I call you Will like I'd known you all my life.

WILL. Everybody calls me Will—you can. [*He sits down again.*]

VIRGINIA. Shows people like you.

WILL. Really? [*Bitterly.*] Ha!

VIRGINIA. Of course I've known the Connellys through Father for a long time. [*Laughing.*] Didn't you know he used to kind of love Cousin Geraldine?

WILL. Well, I know something about it. He used to come here when I was a little boy.

VIRGINIA. I wonder why it never went any further. I've heard Mother tease him about the aristocratic Miss Geraldine.

WILL [*sharply*]. Aristocratic over the dead! That explains a lot.

UNCLE BOB [*calling from off the left*]. Virginia, come in! We want you to sing for us!

VIRGINIA. I don't understand you, Will.

WILL. And your little moon shines on the tombstones. That's the poetry of it. [*As if quoting into the night.*] And all the great past that comes to dust.

VIRGINIA [*with sudden vehemence*]. No!

UNCLE BOB [*calling again*]. Come on and sing, Virginia!

> *Other voices call her.*

WILL. No, you can't tell me anything about it. I've already thought it out. You'd better go in now.

VIRGINIA. Come in and I'll sing for you then.

WILL [*standing up*]. The great Connellys are all dead. The fools and the weak are left alive. Good night.

VIRGINIA [*half angrily*]. Now you are being silly. I go in alone?

WILL. Virginia, stop this mockery!

VIRGINIA. Silly boy, you're not the only one that's had bitter thoughts. We have something in common, Will. [*Laughing but with a touch of anger left.*] Au revoir.

WILL [*resentfully*]. Oh, yes. Good night.

> VIRGINIA *turns and goes quickly out by the crepe myrtle tree to the left.* WILL *sits hunched over with his head in his hands. After a while* UNCLE BOB *comes waddling along the path from the portico. He is pulling* PATSY *by the hand.*

UNCLE BOB [*peering forward*]. They're gone now. Just ask her to sing and she'll come a-running. A voice like a goose in March.

PATSY. What do you want?

UNCLE BOB [*pulling her on*]. Wait a minute, sweet Arabia.

PATSY. This is far enough.

UNCLE BOB. There's a seat over there. [WILL *rises and wanders off into the shrubbery back of the pool.* UNCLE BOB *and* PATSY *come in. He is dressed in the same old moth-eaten evening clothes as before.* PATSY *wears a dark dress cut low across her bosom. A single bedraggled flower is in her hair. Still holding her hand, he sits down.*] Phew, I've cut up like a boy tonight. [*Singing.*] A wounded snake I was, and now a fleet greyhound. [*Tugging at her hand.*] Sit down. [*She does so and he tries to put his arm around her.*] You've put new life in this old hulk. Real life this time, it ain't whisky.

PATSY [*pushing him away*]. Why did you say I was invited to the party when I wasn't?

UNCLE BOB. Will wanted you to come. He's too timid—you know. So I asked you. It's right, honey, he's glad you're here. Ah, Patsy, you'd put new life into any man, even mournful Will.

PATSY. You had something to tell me?

UNCLE BOB [*teasing and laughing at her*]. Maybe it was and maybe not.

PATSY. Then I'm going home. [*She tries to move along the path toward the right, but he pulls her back.*]

UNCLE BOB. Yes, I have, real important. Now sit down and listen to your Uncle Robert.

PATSY [*sitting down apart from him*]. Go ahead then.

UNCLE BOB. Ho, who could a-thought it? Forty-odd years ago I sot here on a bench and made love to another gal—not nigh as purty as you. Still going strong—unh?

PATSY [*laughing*]. You ain't making love to me, I can tell you.

UNCLE BOB. Ain't I? [*He pushes himself close against her.*]

PATSY. What was it? Go on, tell me.

UNCLE BOB. Still interested—unh?

PATSY. I wouldn't a-come out here if you hadn't said it was so important.

UNCLE BOB [*grinning at her amorously*]. *Ego amo te.*

PATSY [*laughing again*]. What's that, the Lord's Prayer?

UNCLE BOB. Man's prayer. [*He suddenly grabs her hand and kisses it.*]

PATSY. Let me a-loose.

UNCLE BOB. *Ego amo te*, I love you.

PATSY [*giggling*]. Lord-a-mercy!

UNCLE BOB [*with a threatening growl*]. You laugh at me—hanh? [*She claws at his face and he holds her tight.*]

PATSY [*panting*]. Let me a-loose—oh!

UNCLE BOB. So you come a-walking in the dark—anh? Humhn-unhn—you're soft as a kitten. [*She frees one hand and strikes him in the face.*] This is one of the old boys, honey! The bull of the woods!

WILL *bounds through the shrubbery at the left and snatches* PATSY *from* UNCLE BOB.

WILL [*sputtering with helpless anger*]. Get away—get away from here quick!

UNCLE BOB [*clattering to his feet*]. Can't you see we're at private—

PATSY [*to* WILL—*laughing*]. That's all right, I'm not afraid of him.

UNCLE BOB. God A'mighty, you won't do nothing! Well, for Christ's sake, he's got a puny arm around her!

WILL [*moving toward him*]. Say another word and I'll kill you.

UNCLE BOB [*staring at him in astonishment*]. You will, hanh?

WILL [*flying at him*]. You old hog, get away from here! [*He springs upon* UNCLE BOB *and knocks him down.*]

PATSY [*rushing between them*]. Please, Mr. Will, please.

UNCLE BOB [*crawling up on his haunches*]. Now you see—now— [*spluttering*]. I'll get my gun—I ought to shoot you like a dog for that—I ought to—Will Connelly, are you gone crazy?

WILL [*his voice breaking between a sob and a whine*]. Get away from here—right quick—

UNCLE BOB [*backing away from him*]. All right—all right. I'm going. [*Tauntingly.*] Let the moon shine, let it be dark around, you'd do nothing with her.

WILL. Don't say another word to me—Uncle Bob!

UNCLE BOB [*sneering*]. Ha, you happen to knock an old man down and it turns your stomach. Now take her, see'f there's any blood in you, sissy! [*He throws up his hands in an indecent gesture and goes off at the left.*]

PATSY [*bursting into a laugh*]. You sure laid him out flat.

WILL. I don't think it's funny at all. I don't see a thing to laugh at.

PATSY [*soberly*]. It's not funny. [*After a moment.*] Why do you want to hurt my feelings, Mr. Will? [*She sinks down close to him on the seat.*]

WILL. What have I done now?

PATSY. I wouldn't have come to the party if I'd a-known you didn't want me.

WILL. Well, maybe I wanted you to come.

PATSY. Mr. Bob said you did, or I wouldn't.

WILL [*furiously*]. That's just it. He wanted you to come so he could do what— [*Grieving like a boy.*] I hit him right in the face with my fist. Lower and lower. Now we fight like dogs.

PATSY. What a strong man you are, Mr. Will!

WILL. My hands are trembling. It scared me—I'm ashamed of myself.

PATSY [*taking one of his hands in hers*]. Your hand is big and strong too. You didn't hurt my feelings by what you said.

WILL. Oh, I don't know what I said. My head's all to pieces now. [*Looking at her.*] Why do you do that?

PATSY [*softly*]. Please don't mind.

WILL [*brokenly*]. Your hand is nice—it's cool.

PATSY. I'm glad it's so. I feel sorry because you're sad—you weren't sad the night you went serenading with us. You had a lot of fun.

WILL [*stammering, as he draws his hand away*]. I stood in the shrubs and heard it all and I was scared. I didn't know what to do. And then something seemed to go all over me—it made me blind of a sudden and the next thing I knew I was out here and had hit him. [VIRGINIA *is heard singing in the house* —"After the ball is over, after the break of day"—] Oh, God, what a mess! Let me tell you something. I'm done.

PATSY [*sharply*]. What do you mean?

WILL. I'm going to work in town somewhere. The farm may go to hell and all with it.

PATSY. No.

WILL. Listen there! Fools, fools we are. Borrowing our last cent to give Virginia a big party, having an orchestra and—My God! I'm done—done!

PATSY [*catching his hand in hers*]. Let me help you, Will.

WILL. I wish you could, I do.

PATSY [*in a low voice*]. I can.

WILL [*raising his head*]. No, you're like the rest. You pity me. I am nothing. Even the niggers laugh at me.

> *She bends down suddenly and kisses him on the lips. Incredulous, he stands awkwardly up and then sits down again, nervously fingering his coat.*

PATSY. I could help you. [*Hesitating.*] And you could help me. You'd be running away like a coward if you left. You'll do it. I'll help you—we'll do it—work—work—together. [*Throwing out her hands.*] I know how to work with the earth. [*Gazing at him with intensity.*] I know her ways. I could teach you. [*Bending vehemently over him as he looks at her with a forlorn smile.*] See, I talk to you—I pour out my heart for you.

WILL. Patsy. [*Murmuring.*] You make it almost real. With you—yes—I might do something. But I'm numbed, cold, empty. I've stayed in this old house too long—

PATSY. No, you must live—live! Wipe away all these gullies and broom-straw patches—and waste—waste.

> *In the background the two Negro women are seen creeping softly forward through the trees and watching them.*

WILL [*staring at her in a sort of stupefaction*]. It seems strange—like a dream. Yes, I could—maybe we could. [*Suddenly starting.*] No, I don't know you. No—

PATSY [*catching him by the shoulders*]. Yes, yes, you do. [*Putting her arms suddenly around his neck.*] I love you, I do, Will. [*Tugging at his arm and whispering.*] Come with me. [*The Negro women have crept up the path nearer, listening.*] We'll walk in the fields.

WILL [*almost with a pleading shout as he sweeps her suddenly into his arms*]. Yes! Out of this death and darkness—into the light! [*He starts out with her, impelled by his burst of feeling, and then stops.*]

> PATSY *puts her arm around him and with her head upon his shoulder leads him on. The Negro women wobble in by the crepe myrtle trees.*

BIG SIS. This darkness, bless God!

BIG SUE. That light, hallelujah!

BIG SIS. Ehp, her don't know that Connelly blood her messing with mebbe.

> *They hug each other over the pump.*

BIG SUE. Her think that sassafras water.

BIG SIS [*tossing her head*]. Water can turn to blood.

UNCLE BOB [*blundering through the underbrush at the left*]. O little moon, what have I seen? Cock-a-doodle-do! [*He crows like a rooster and flaps his arms up and down.*]

A still from Act I, Scene 3, performed by the ReGroup Theatre, 2014, featuring Selena C. Dukes as Big Sis, Anthony Laciura as Uncle Bob Connelly, and Sheila Simmons as Big Sis (photography by Mikiodo Media, courtesy of ReGroup Theatre Company, Inc.).

BIG SIS *and* BIG SUE. Uhp! [*He cuts a goatish step before them.*] Us done see and foresee.

UNCLE BOB [*like a crier*]. William Byrd Connelly is now out farming. Oh yus! Oh yus! [*Calling after* WILL *and* PATSY.] Ain't no fences round your crops—ehp! Let the hogs root.

BIG SIS *and* BIG SUE [*guffawing*]. Uhp—Lord!

UNCLE BOB [*beginning to pat his hands*]. Go to it, old squealers. [*The sisters begin hopping up and down, their wrappers flopping about.*] Great doings ahead. Amen.

BIG SIS *and* BIG SUE [*as they dance*].
                    Mischief-meevery-miney-mo,
                  Answer my answer there below.
[*They begin doing a hootchee-kootchee dance facing each other.* UNCLE BOB *rolls around on the ground clapping his hands and peering at their huge flashing legs and joggling bodies.*]

UNCLE BOB. Hurrah! [*He rises to his knees, beating time and reaching out his hands to the night in a drunken blasphemous call.*] Our Father who art in heaven, hallowed be the sin which now doth flourish forth to salvation. Ecch, set to it, old cows, we'll all go home at milking time. [*He goes on foolishly clapping his hands. Presently, emitting a long sigh, he stretches himself out flat on the ground.*]

Curtain

ACT II, SCENE 1

A few days later, in the Connelly dining room. It is midmorning and still cold enough to have a fire going. WILL, *dressed in rough outdoor clothes, is seated at the table finishing his breakfast.* ESSIE, *a mulatto girl about eighteen years old, comes in with a plate of biscuits.*

ESSIE. The vittles warm enough?

WILL. All right.

ESSIE. Everything 'bout to get cold waiting.

WILL [*taking a biscuit*]. I've had a lot to do.

ESSIE [*laughing*]. You sho' got an appetite, Mr. Will.

WILL. Yes. Have the others eaten?

ESSIE. The ladies done et early to get to the station.

WILL. Duffy drive Miss Virginia over?

ESSIE. Miss Deenie and Miss Evelyn went too. They waited to say good-by, but you didn't come.

WILL. Yes.

ESSIE. Yes, suh, I told 'em you'd gone round to the tenants on business.

WILL *goes on eating, saying nothing, and* ESSIE *watches him with merry half-closed eyes.*

WILL [*after a moment*]. Clear everything away. I'll need the dining room. [*He pulls out a notebook and figures in it as she goes about stacking up the dishes.*]

ESSIE. Gonna bring them menfolks in here?

WILL [*handing her a key*]. And go down in the cellar and fetch up a jug of wine.

ESSIE. Yes, suh.

UNCLE BOB *comes in at the right.*

UNCLE BOB. Essie, Mrs. Connelly wants her breakfast in her room.

ESSIE. Yes, suh. [*She gathers up the dishes on a tray and goes into the kitchen.*]

UNCLE BOB. She'd like to see you too, Will.

WILL. All right, later. How's she feeling?

UNCLE BOB. Not so spry after the stir this morning. Oh, saw ye fair Inez as she gaed into the South.[12] You've just played hell, ain't you?

WILL [*smiling*]. Not that I know of.

UNCLE BOB.
     The Brown Girl she has house and lands,
     Fair Elinor she has none—
 Danged if you ain't becoming a moon-eyed ladies' man.

WILL [*laughing*]. Poetic, by God!

UNCLE BOB [*angrily*]. And it ain't funny.

WILL. Isn't it?

UNCLE BOB. Must be an interesting little book there.

WILL. Getting ready to address my constituency.

UNCLE BOB. Running for constable? [*Looking out at the rear.*] Your tenant gang. What's up?

WILL. Having a meeting about the crops.

UNCLE BOB. Hustling landlord, like Sid Shepherd, ain't ye?

WILL [*with a glance at him*]. Going to put everybody to work.

UNCLE BOB. And what holy transubstantiation has happened to you?

WILL. Your words are too long for business.

UNCLE BOB. Ho-ho! Going to labor under the sign of Venus—eh?

WILL. Go to hell.

UNCLE BOB [*gleefully*]. Jesus my Saviour, he's getting fiery!

A Voice [*outside*]. Heigh, Mr. Will!

WILL [*going to the door and opening it*]. You all come in here.

>   UNCLE BOB *goes over and stands by the fireplace. Fifteen or twenty tenant farmers troop in, the Negroes behind the whites, and* TATE *in the lead. They all take off their hats as they enter and arrange themselves around the room. With the exception of* TATE *they are a scurvy nondescript crew. Three or four ancient ebony darkies with faces wizened as aged monkeys beneath their flaring white hair stand respectfully near the table.* WILL *pushes chairs toward them.*

WILL. Uncle Reuben, you and Uncle Isaac sit down.

>   *They sit down and stare about them with dull blinking eyes. There are a few middle-aged white men with ragged mustaches and beards, thin gaunt fellows, hollow-eyed and hopeless, their faces burnt like leather by the wind and sun. Some of the Negroes are middle-aged, tattered and mournful like* DUFFY. *And the others are younger, more greasy and merry, with bold gleaming eyes that roll in their sockets as they take in the splendor of the room. One of the Negroes is taller and more dignified than the rest. He is dressed in the garb of a preacher with a high celluloid collar coming up under his chin and a bluish coat that reaches below his knees. Most of the Negroes are mulattoes. They speak to* WILL *as they enter, some shyly and with embarrassment, others more boldly and with little or no respect in their voices.*

TATE. Good morning, Mr. Will.

WILL. How're you, Mr. Tate?

TATE. Well, I thanky.

OTHERS. Good morning, Mr. Will—good morning. Howdy. Right here on the dot.

WILL. Good. Make yourselves comfortable.

OTHERS. Howdy, Mr. Bob.

UNCLE BOB. Howdy, all. [WILL *looks around in some embarrassment at the pinched and weary faces, and nervously fingers his notebook. Then he sits down at the table, turning through the notebook making notations, very businesslike. The tenants are themselves ill at ease until* UNCLE BOB *goes around among them, shaking hands, asking after their health and the health of their families.*] Well, help my life, Reuben. Isaac, how are you?

>   *They rise and shake his hand with a dignity that hides all their knowledge of his sins and meannesses.*

UNCLE REUBEN *and* UNCLE ISAAC. Still here, suh, still hanging on.

UNCLE BOB [*making his way among them like a lord*]. How're you, Alf? Good morning, Duffy. And here's the preacher—the orator of Shady Grove. [*He shakes hands with the Negro preacher.*] Who'll ask after my soul when you are gone? Ah, Alec, how's your windpipe?

ALEC [*overwhelmed with delight*]. Getting her down now so she'll roar, suh.

UNCLE BOB. More like your mammy every day. [*There is a giggling and snickering among the group.*] Well, he is, folkses. Coming to hear you preach in August, Alec. The last time I heard you you had the sinners on the floor licking sweat. It's good to see you all. [*He shakes hands with a thin sad-faced white man.*] How you, Jodie?

JODIE. Purty well, Mr. Bob.

UNCLE BOB. How's your wife?

JODIE. Ain't mended none lately.

UNCLE BOB. Get her some Pluto water to drink, that'll fix up her stomach. Swamp root's good too. Morning, Henry. Howdy, Tyler.

HENRY *and* TYLER [*two fellows with long plow-handle arms*]. Howdy, sir, howdy, sir.

WILL [*standing up*]. I won't keep you long, not long.

UNCLE BOB. See you got business to attend to. This young landlord'll be running for the legislature next. Glad all my friends looking so well. *Vale et vatque.*[13] Vote for him. [*He goes through the rear door, and regretfully they watch him leave.*]

ALF [*a sad fellow, to his neighbor*]. All right!

NEIGHBOR [*tapping his head*]. Something in there besides shucks.

WILL [*his embarrassment disappearing as he goes on*]. I asked you to come over here so we can talk about the plantation together. Some of you see me now with my work clothes on perhaps for the first time. [*Smiling intimately.*] Ain't it so?

A YOUNG WHITE FELLOW [*wearing galluses and with a mop of mangy hair protruding over his forehead like a cap*]. That's about so, Mr. Will.

WILL [*as several of the men nod to one another and some of the Negroes snicker*]. Go ahead and laugh. Well, I'm going to work. I want to talk to you and I want you to talk to me. This is the first time we've ever got together and that's what it's for. What's been the matter with this farm? Somebody tell me. [*Nobody says anything.*] What would you say, Ransom?

RANSOM [*a middle-aged white man with long drooping mustaches and stooped shoulders*]. I don't know. I don't just know, Mr. Will.

WILL. There's something been wrong, ain't there?

RANSOM. Seems like it.

CHARLIE [*in the rear—softly*]. Sho' God is.

WILL. Who was that?

VOICES. Charlie over here.

WILL. All right, Charlie, what's been wrong?

CHARLIE [*a little dried-up Negro of thirty or forty*]. Nothing, Mr. Will. Sho' ain't nothing! Everything fine!

WILL. Don't be afraid to talk out. [*He waits and no one says anything.*] Well, I'll tell you. We ain't been working. Year after year we've lived from hand to mouth. We've let the soil wash away, bushes grow up in the fields, half-plowed the land. [*With nervous impetuosity.*] I've been a damn poor manager.

VOICES. You been all right, Mr. Will.

A WHITE MAN. You sure have.

OTHER VOICES. Good Lawd, sho' he has!

A NEGRO. Sho' the truth, Mr. Will.

WILL. Maybe I been too good to you, good and no backbone. But that's not all the trouble. We sleep too much on this place.

A NEGRO [*as if in alarm*]. Uh-uh!

WILL [*tapping the table*]. From this day we're going to change. Ransom, you got children—grown boys and girls somewhere in a factory. They couldn't stand this dead place. They oughta be here with us. We oughta made it so they'd stay. And Jodie's got boys, gone from home, he don't know where they are. The young folks run away from this place like partridges from a hen. Why? We got no life here, that's why. I been figuring on all these things and we're going to take a new start. We're going to be real farmers. We got a lot of land broke but we're going to break a lot more and break it deep. Next week I'll have new plows and more stock. The first thing we'll do is to clean up the hedgerows, patch the fences, and shrub the bushes out of the fields. Everybody's got to work. I'm going to work—we're all going to work. Work won't hurt any of us, will it? And everybody works will get rations. I'm going to start a commissary to furnish you. And I'll see who deserves to eat and who don't.

UNCLE BOB [*applauding in the hall*]. Hooray!

He is heard clapping his hands. The farmers chuckle and murmur among themselves. WILL *controls his impatience and turns to* TATE.

WILL. Is that right?

TATE [*solemnly*]. Sounds right.

WILL. Yes. Well, there's no reason why we can't make this land pay. How does it compare with the land farther south, Mr. Tate?

TATE [*more solemnly still*]. The land's all right. Just needs work. [*Monotonously.*] It just needs work and peas and clover now and then.

WILL. I'll get the money to swing this, and if I don't get the money I'll get the credit somehow. [*He stops suddenly and looks at them.*]

A NEGRO [*softly*]. Sounds mighty good.

ANOTHER NEGRO. Sound right.

A THIRD NEGRO. I don't mind work.

A FOURTH NEGRO. Me neither. Work, work, I don't mind work. Just so I gets my rations. [*He makes a sound of spitting on his hands preparatory to swinging an ax.*]

FIRST NEGRO [*softly*]. Rations.

WILL. Anybody want to say anything?

VOICES [*after a moment*]. No, suh, Mr. Will.

WILL. Go ahead and talk out. [*But they look at him dumbly.*] All agree to that?

VOICES. That's right. That's all right. We're satisfied.

WILL [*now at ease—laughing boyishly*]. Does it suit you, Alec? You're a preacher, but you don't have to preach till August.

ALEC. Yes, suh, yes suhrree. [*He stands bowing up and down in confusion as a roar of laughter bursts around him.*]

WILL. You'll have to get off that long coat and collar, Alec. Can't plow in them. *A fleeting glimpse of wrath crosses* ALEC's *face, but he goes on bowing and grinning.*

ALEC. Yes, suh, yes suhree.

WILL. I'll come around and see each one of you separately. I've already figured out the number of acres you ought to tend and what you ought to make on them. And remember—everybody that works gets his rations. I'll put an oath on it. Every damn one of you that don't, don't eat, and he don't stay on this land either.

ALEC [*with a touch of grim piety*]. Now, now.

VOICES. Uh-uh!

WILL. Any questions? All right, meeting's adjourned to the back porch where we'll have a taste of wine. [*He goes to the kitchen door and calls.*] Essie, get out some glasses in there. [*With the exception of* TATE, *all the men go out and are heard laughing and talking outside.* WILL *turns back.*] Have some wine, Mr. Tate?

TATE. Thanky, I don't drink. [*Looking around the room.*] Sure is a fine place here, Mr. Will.

WILL. Thank you.

TATE. Don't blame you to wanter keep it going.

WILL. We've started, haven't we?

TATE. They know you mean business now. You've got 'em going. They'll work.

WILL. I meant what I said, too.

TATE. It was all right. Well, I got to get back to my plow. Good day. [*He puts on his hat.*]

WILL. Good day.

TATE [*goes out and* WILL *walks out onto the porch after him*]. Count on me to help when I can.

WILL [*outside*]. Thank you. [*To the men.*] I'll be around to see you all later in the day.

VOICES. All right, Mr. Will. Yes, suh.

They are heard guffawing and uttering joking cries. MRS. CONNELLY *comes in at the right, helped along by* UNCLE BOB. *He settles her in an armchair by the fire and puts a hassock under her feet.*

UNCLE BOB. I wouldn't talk to him now, Ellen.

MRS. CONNELLY. I'm all right. Tell him to come in, please.

UNCLE BOB. He's all set up over his plans.

MRS. CONNELLY. I'll speak to him now.

UNCLE BOB [*at the rear door*]. Will, come here a moment, please.

WILL [*comes in with a glass of wine in his hand*]. I was coming to your room, Mother. You feeling better?

MRS. CONNELLY. I'm very well, thank you. [*She waits a moment.* UNCLE BOB *goes out at the rear and closes the door behind him.*] Sit down.

WILL [*going to the fire*]. Let me stand up if you don't mind.

MRS. CONNELLY. I've got to be plain with you.

WILL. What's the matter, Mother?

MRS. CONNELLY. You've hurt us all terribly. I want you to know that.

WILL. I'm sorry.

MRS. CONNELLY. Virginia's gone home. You weren't even here to tell her good-by.

WILL. I told her good-by last night. I had to be away this morning.

MRS. CONNELLY. Why, why do you act this way? Please tell me.

WILL. Well. We just didn't get along together and that's all. It's past now.

MRS. CONNELLY. She's asked you to come down hunting in the fall. I want you to go.

WILL. The harvest will be on then. [*Fumbling his notebook.*] I have a lot to do now, Mother. [*He drinks down his wine and comes over and pats her on the shoulder, as if to leave the room.*]

MRS. CONNELLY. Please don't go. It's not that I've offended you in some way, is it?

WILL. Why, no.

MRS. CONNELLY [*agitated*]. Don't you have any love for this plantation and the carrying on of your father's name? It means that to us, Will. [WILL *turns and looks in the fire, saying nothing.*] It's hard for me to talk like this to you.

WILL. I know it is.

MRS. CONNELLY. Listen to me then. [*Catching his hand.*] Write to Virginia, make it up with her. It's not too late.

WILL. No. There's nothing to make up.

MRS. CONNELLY. I wish you would. [*She waits and he says nothing.*] The rest would take care of itself.

WILL. I'll tell you why. Because I'd go on being the same kind of weakling I've always been. It would be her money that did everything, not me. I want to do something.

MRS. CONNELLY. You've not been weak. I've always known you'd make me proud of you.

WILL. I know what I've been.

MRS. CONNELLY. You could do things then, all the great things we dream about. [*Softly.*] And our name will go on.

WILL [*turning and looking at her*]. We've thought too much about our name anyway.

MRS. CONNELLY. Will!

WILL. It's true, Mother.

MRS. CONNELLY [*dropping his hand*]. Then, excuse me, Will. The plantation and everything will keep on going to pieces. What will the end be? You know—poverty—poverty—to the end.

WILL. Not if I can help it.

MRS. CONNELLY. You can't help it and you know it.

WILL. I can too and I shall.

MRS. CONNELLY. How?

WILL. By starting right here and making things over. It was once the great Connelly plantation and I'll make it so again. [*In excitement.*] I will, Mother.

MRS. CONNELLY. And that's but half of it, even if you could.

WILL. What do you mean?

MRS. CONNELLY. You know very well whom I mean.

WILL [*turning again to the fire*]. I don't. [*He picks up the empty glass and tries to drink from it.*]

MRS. CONNELLY. Somebody else will do everything, not you.

WILL. I'll do it myself.

MRS. CONNELLY [*in a soft cold voice as she watches him*]. Can't you see that girl's designs upon you, upon us all?

WILL [*hotly*]. You know nothing about it, Mother.

MRS. CONNELLY. Geraldine and Evelyn see it too. She's making use of you to get what she wants.

WILL [*grimly*]. I reckon she's not.

MRS. CONNELLY. She's set out in cold blood to become mistress of Connelly Hall and you're helping her to it.

WILL. She's not.

MRS. CONNELLY. You've been spending more time over at her house—your own tenant's house—the last week than you have here. Haven't you any pride?

WILL. We've been working out plans for the farm— [*He stops in embarrassment.*]

MRS. CONNELLY. Of course she— [*She waits a while and then—suddenly changing her tone of voice.*] Well, she loves you?

WILL [*after a moment*]. Yes.

MRS. CONNELLY [*smiling*]. You don't know a thing about such women as she.

WILL [*defensively, like a boy*]. I know she does.

MRS. CONNELLY [*smoothing out her dress*]. And how do you know?

WILL [*in a low voice*]. I know.

MRS. CONNELLY [*after a moment*]. Do you mean what I think—

WILL [*looking at her in shamed triumph*]. Well, whatever you think, I know she—loves me.

MRS. CONNELLY [*quietly*]. It proves everything I've said if she's gone as far as that.

WILL. It does not.

MRS. CONNELLY. Any honest woman would tell you she's done that to trap you.

WILL. I don't believe it.

MRS. CONNELLY. I'm a woman and I know. [*After a moment, smiling.*] Well, the Connellys are famous for that. You're one of them after all, aren't you? If she wants to play with fire, then let her get burnt. It won't be you, for you're not the woman. [*She looks at him, telling her meaning in her eyes and finally he turns away and looks again in the fire.*]

WILL [*helplessly*]. I don't know what to say to you, Mother.

MRS. CONNELLY. Then let's don't talk about it any more. [*In a changed voice.*] After all, I do trust you, Will, you see?

WILL [*abstractedly*]. Thank you.

MRS. CONNELLY. Now let's talk over your plans for the farm—

WILL [*dragging forward an answer*]. They're not all worked out yet.

MRS. CONNELLY. What was the meeting about?

WILL [*mechanically*]. I'm going to put 'em all to work.

MRS. CONNELLY. What did you say to them?

WILL. That.

MRS. CONNELLY [*She waits, but he says nothing more in reply*]. We'll go over it all later, then. [*Watching his face.*] Help me out in the sun now, please.

WILL [*throwing down the poker and turning to her*]. Don't you see, Mother—

MRS. CONNELLY [*quietly as he stops*]. Yes?

WILL. How you're destroying my confidence in—

MRS. CONNELLY. In what?

WILL. In—well—in myself then.

UNCLE BOB's *teasing voice is heard in the kitchen.*

UNCLE BOB. Good morning, sweet arbutus.[14]

MRS. CONNELLY. I haven't said anything about you, Will.

WILL [*hastily*]. All right, all right then. [*Vehemently.*] But it's me—me she cares for, Mother.

MRS. CONNELLY. It's the Connelly land and the Connelly name she wants. [*Turning to him.*] Only selfishness and greed would make a woman violate herself.

WILL. My God!

MRS. CONNELLY [*almost gently*]. And Geraldine says Big Sis and Big Sue have heard her scheming in the fields with her father.

WILL. No! No! They're lying.

UNCLE BOB [*comes in from the kitchen*]. Another farmer in here wants to see you, Will.

   WILL *makes no answer.*

MRS. CONNELLY. Help me into the garden, Robert.

UNCLE BOB. Excuse me for interrupting you.

MRS. CONNELLY. We've just finished. [*Sticking her crutch under her arm and climbing up to her feet.*] Go ahead with your plans. We'll talk them over after supper. Robert. [*She goes out at the rear leaning on* UNCLE BOB'S *arm.*]

   WILL *sits looking at the fire a moment, then picks up his notebook from the table, glances at it, and sticks it sharply into his pocket. From the same pocket he pulls out a small bag of tobacco and starts rolling a cigarette. There is a knock at the kitchen door to which he pays no attention.* UNCLE BOB *re-enters at the rear. The knock is repeated.*

UNCLE BOB. Wake up.

WILL. Come in.

   PATSY *enters dressed in rough clothes and with a shawl over her shoulders.* WILL *looks up at her saying nothing and throws his unfinished cigarette into the fire.*

UNCLE BOB [*bringing forward a chair for her*]. Sit down.

PATSY [*pulling some rolls of paper from under her shawl*]. I just brought these plots for you. They're all finished—name, acres, and all.

WILL [*taking them*]. Thank you. Sit down.

UNCLE BOB. Let me take off your shoes. Your feet are wet as water.

PATSY [*laughing*]. No thanky. [*Sitting down and stretching her feet out to the fire.*] A terrible heavy dew this morning. Same as August. [WILL *turns through the papers.*] Are they all right?

WILL. They look all right.

PATSY. Look at Duffy's plot. I've marked off sixty acres for him.

WILL. He's never farmed more than twenty-five.

PATSY. Him and his crowd ought to tend sixty.

WILL. Yes, that's so. [*He goes on turning through the papers nervously.*]

UNCLE BOB. You oughta been here and heard the speech.

PATSY. Father said it was all right—everything was fine.

UNCLE BOB. Oh yes, lots of applause. Such a change—rejuvenation. Two weeks ago he couldn't have stood up and faced 'em. Now he speaks like an orator. [UNCLE BOB *stands watching them with squinting eyes, his lips stuck out in a whistling pucker.*]

   WILL *says nothing and* PATSY *stares at him questioningly once or twice.*

PATSY. Want me to go over them with you?

WILL. Everything's all right, I reckon.

PATSY. Well, I'll get on back.

UNCLE BOB. What's the hurry? *Abusum non tollit usum.*[15]

WILL [*angrily*]. Go to the devil!

UNCLE BOB [*staring at him and then waddling across the room*]. *Persona non grata.* [*He grins at them and goes out into the kitchen.*]

PATSY [*as* WILL *says nothing*]. I used to think he was so funny.

WILL. And you don't think so now?

PATSY [*childishly*]. There's something deep behind his fun, ain't there?

WILL. Yes he's deep, like his lust, and that's deep as hell bottom. All the Connellys were like him—ha-ha—deep.

PATSY. What's the matter?

WILL. Not a thing in God's world. What's the matter with you?

PATSY. Nothing.

WILL. We're all well then.

PATSY [*eying him*]. Won't your mother agree about selling the boxwood bushes?

WILL. We didn't get to that.

PATSY. I don't understand why you're so—like that.

WILL. Don't say I'm too clever for you.

PATSY [*half angrily*]. I won't.

WILL. Sure you wouldn't. [*With sudden overbuoyancy as he springs up from his chair and comes over to her.*] Won't that be a big harvest—cotton, tobacco, corn, peas, potatoes—mountains of crops? [*Patting her on the head.*] Give me a kiss. [*He tries to fondle her.*]

PATSY [*pushing him away*]. What did you say to your mother? [*Her face full of pain.*] Please, please don't do like that with me.

WILL. Oh, I told her we'd be out of debt by Christmas.

PATSY [*rising from her chair, a half smile shutting around her lips.*] I can guess what she said. Please don't joke with me, Will.

WILL [*looking at her intently*]. You're so clever. The poor Connellys are the simple ones.

PATSY [*stammering but never losing her poise as she searches out her reply*]. What I've done is not clever. Any woman would tell you that. [*She smiles up at him, now suddenly wistful.*]

WILL [*catching her tightly by the shoulders*]. You do love me, don't you?

PATSY [*with turned head*]. You already know that.

WILL [*eagerly*]. Yes, yes, I do. [*He hugs her to him and kisses her.*]

PATSY [*her head still bowed*]. Now don't worry any more. She'll see different later when everything is going fine.

WILL [*in a low voice*]. Oh, I'm not worrying.

PATSY [*quickly*]. There's nothing to be so sad over. [*Brightly.*] Now you must see after your men and I've got to get to work. You come by later.

BIG SIS *and* BIG SUE *open the door at the rear and stand unobserved, looking in.*

WILL [*taking up his wineglass again*]. Yes, later. [*Like a servant.*] Other orders?

PATSY [*ignoring his manner*]. I'll see you this evening then. [*Gazing at the floor.*] There's something I want to talk with you about.

WILL. Well, talk to me now.

PATSY. No, later. [*She rises to go and then seeing the two Negro women starts back.*]

WILL, *noticing her manner, looks up and sees* BIG SIS *and* BIG SUE.

WILL. What you want?

BIG SUE. Us wanted to borrow a little flour.

WILL. Go around to the kitchen and wait for Miss Geraldine.

They close the door and go away.

PATSY. I don't like the way they follow me.

WILL [*staring at her intently*]. Good gracious.

PATSY. Their eyes shining at me—like—like— [*She shivers.*] like maybe they're planning something.

WILL. I've told you they're harmless—like children.

For a while neither says anything.

PATSY. I must go now. [*She starts out at the rear.*]

WILL. Mother's out that way.

PATSY [*softly*]. I don't mind.

WILL. I do—Patsy. [*Loudly.*] This way!

PATSY [*whirls around, her eyes shining suddenly*]. Who're you talking to!

WILL [*starting back from her*]. You, by God. [*He snatches her arm half fondly and half angrily.*]

PATSY. Well, stop it. [WILL *turns quickly and goes into the kitchen.* PATSY *starts after him and then stops, standing in the middle of the room as if thinking to herself. Presently she breaks into a low nervous laugh, gazing around at the portraits and half whispering.*] Oh, you look mighty grand. But you don't scare me a bit, not a bit. [*Clenching her hands.*] All right, me against you, all of you.

GERALDINE *comes suddenly in from the right.*

GERALDINE [*frigidly*]. You wish to see someone?

PATSY [*embarrassed in spite of herself*]. No, thanky.

PATSY *looks at* GERALDINE *and smiles. Then before* GERALDINE's *proud haughtiness the strength seems to go out of her. She pulls the shawl up around her head and leaves through*

A still from Act II, Scene 2, performed by the Group Theatre on Broadway, 1931, featuring Ruth Nelson as Essie and Franchot Tone as Will Connelly (courtesy Paul Green Foundation).

the rear door. GERALDINE *moves about the room setting the chairs to rights.* WILL *comes in still carrying the empty glass in his hand.*

WILL. Oh—Geraldine—where's—Evelyn?

GERALDINE [*subtly mocking him*]. She put her shawl around her face and went out that way. *She turns and leaves the room. After a moment* WILL *pulls out his notebook and sits down by the table. Presently he begins rolling another cigarette. The Negro girl,* ESSIE, *comes in with a tray of dishes which she begins putting away in the corner cupboard. Now and then she looks slyly at him.*

ESSIE [*snickering*]. Sho' is a purty little woman.

WILL. Bring me a glass of whisky. *She fetches the whisky from the sideboard and stands by him as he drinks it.*

ESSIE. Sho' look at you with them bright eyes.

WILL [*peering at her over the glass—his harassed face gradually breaking into a low joking grin*]. Ha, yes, the way you look at Alec—eh?

ESSIE [*giggling*]. Lawd, Mr. Will. [*Scornfully.*] Pshaw, Alec!

WILL. Be married the first thing you know, won't you? How old are you?

ESSIE. 'Bout eighteen or nineteen.

WILL. Yeah, you'll be wearing his ring pretty soon—say, right on that finger there. You want a ring, you know. Yeah, all do. [*He touches her hand lightly and half-disgustedly with his finger.*]

ESSIE. I'd rather have a lavaliere.

WILL. Be tricky, you'll get that too.

ESSIE. I'd cook a long time for that, Mr. Will. [*With soft cunning.*] It'd make me look a lot prettier too. [*Making a gesture over her abundant bosom.*] Let it hang down there. You buy me one, Mr. Will.

WILL [*suddenly shouting and backing away from her*]. Get away from here! [*He crams his hat on his head and hurries out at the rear.*]

> ESSIE *snickers to herself and begins idly polishing the table, her eyes looking off in a dreamy stare.*
>
> *Fade-out.*

ACT II, SCENE 2

> *The same—a hot afternoon several months later. The Connellys have finished their lunch, and* GERALDINE *and* EVELYN, *now more houseworn and tired than before, are clearing away the dishes.* UNCLE BOB *with a book in his hand is lying on a cot before the screened fireplace and* MRS. CONNELLY *is sitting in a comfortable chair near the center of the room. They both are languidly fanning themselves with palm-leaf fans.* UNCLE BOB'S *face is more puffy and haggard than ever, and now and then his head sags over the edge of the cot in a doze. Through the open door at the rear the portico can be seen with half-parched vines climbing up it.*

UNCLE BOB [*rousing himself and reading aloud*].
>> *Regia Solis erat sublimibus alta columnis,*
>> *Clara micante auro flammasque imitante pyropo;*
>> *Cuius ebur nitidum fastigia summa tegebat,*
>> *Argenti bifores radiabant lumine valvae.*[16]

> *In the fields close by the* NEGRO LABORERS *are heard singing a low work song, their words mingled in a high harmony.*

NEGRO LABORERS. Say, my gal laid her head down,
Laid her head down and cried—
Tears fell on the cold groun',
Can't be satisfied.

EVELYN. The hotter it gets the more they sing about the girl and the gambling man. [*Blowing her breath out in a great sigh.*] Oh, it's so hot!

MRS. CONNELLY. Don't wash the dishes now. It will be cooler in the evening.

GERALDINE. We'll have to cook supper then, Mother.

EVELYN. The thermometer was a hundred in the shade at twelve, Uncle Bob. Excuse me, you are reading your book.

MRS. CONNELLY. It'll have to rain soon.

UNCLE BOB [*mumbling to himself*]. Rain! The sky stays like a sheet of glass. [*Sitting up and beating about him with a fan.*] These flies!

GERALDINE. Yes, the screens ought to be mended.

EVELYN [*stopping near the door to the kitchen and scrutinizing a roll of tanglefoot suspended from the wall*]. Look, Deenie, we're catching them fast.

GERALDINE *stands by her with her hands full of dishes. They watch their trap with the eager intent faces of little boys.*

GERALDINE. There goes another. GERALDINE *and* EVELYN *go into the kitchen and are heard washing the dishes.*

MRS. CONNELLY [*presently*]. Why doesn't Will come, Robert? [*Earnestly.*] Why doesn't he come?

UNCLE BOB. He will, Ellen.

MRS. CONNELLY. He's been gone all night. Something might have happened to him.

UNCLE BOB. He's stayed over in town before like this.

MRS. CONNELLY [*quavering for a moment like a childish old woman*]. He almost frightens me lately. I don't know him—he's not the same Will any more.

UNCLE BOB. Every man must have his fling.

MRS. CONNELLY. I can't wait up for him much longer.

UNCLE BOB. Yes, you'd better lie down. [*Creeping over to the door at the rear and looking out.*] Yonder's Patsy Tate hoeing away with them niggers in that boiling sun. Done had their dinner and back at it. What a woman! [*As if persecuted.*] Ha, there go the dry whirlwinds traipsing the fields again. [*He twists his head as if in pain, and then stands reading from his book.*]

"... O lux immensi publica mundi,
Phoebe pater, si das huius mihi nominis usum,
Nec falsa Clymene culpam sub imagine celat—"[17]

ESSIE [*outside*]. Howdy, Mr. Bob.

UNCLE BOB [*sharply*]. Howdy, Essie.

At the sound of her voice, MRS. CONNELLY *stops fanning.* ESSIE *comes in and stands near the door, sniggering and smirking with the faintest touch of familiar spitefulness. She is arrayed in cheap beribboned finery, topped off with a droopy wide-brimmed hat.*

MRS. CONNELLY. We don't need you any more, Essie.

ESSIE. Lor, I knowed that, Mis' Connelly. I just wanted to drop around again and say good-by.

MRS. CONNELLY. Good-by.

UNCLE BOB. Where you going?

ESSIE. You hadn't no sooner turn't me off this morning when I seed Alec, and I'm going with him towards Raleigh at a big meeting.

UNCLE BOB. Alec? Why, he can't leave his crops.

ESSIE. Says salvation calling and he got to go. I'll play the organ for him. [*Swinging nonchalantly over to the kitchen door.*] Good-by, Miss Evelyn. Orter have me to wash them dishes.

GERALDINE [*sharply, within*]. We don't need you, Essie.

ESSIE [*giggling*]. Reckon so. [*Turning back the way she came.*] Well, good-by, you all.

MRS. CONNELLY. Good-by, Essie.

ESSIE [*playing with the ornament around her neck*]. Reckon you ain't seen what I got from Sears, Roebuck?

MRS. CONNELLY [*calmly*]. Go along, Essie.

UNCLE BOB [*thundering*]. Get out o' here, you hussy.

With a foolish laugh, ESSIE *raises her hand in a queer gesture and goes out.*

MRS. CONNELLY. Oh, God!

UNCLE BOB. The lowest rung of iniquity has been reached and we hang pendulous there. [*Striking his oratorical attitude but with deep pain in it.*] Yea, to round out the story I should have got me idiot daughters and cried woe.

MRS. CONNELLY [*sharply*]. Don't speak like that any more, please.

UNCLE BOB. But always a coward before life and its responsibility. No matter. [*With strained jocularity.*] Evelyn was telling me you'd heard from Virginia this morning.

MRS. CONNELLY [*smiling at him wanly, strangely reminiscent of* WILL's *earlier timidity*]. Yes.

UNCLE BOB. She's marrying old Senator Warfield, I hear.

MRS. CONNELLY. Yes.

UNCLE BOB [*with cackling laughter*]. Ha-ha-ha—old enough for her father! [*He comes and sits down in a chair near* MRS. CONNELLY, *and for a long while they say nothing, both nodding now and then in drowsiness.*]

MRS. CONNELLY [*wearily and sleepily*]. She'll be entertained a great deal in Washington.

UNCLE BOB. In Washington, in Washington. [*Clearing his throat.*] *Certes ipso facto.*[18] [*Vacuously murmuring.*] When the almond tree shall flourish and fear shall be in the way. At last it's true. We're old. *In nomine Ecclesiastici.*[19]

MRS. CONNELLY [*after a long while—wistfully like a girl, her proud stateliness gone.*] It's all so strange now, sometimes it seems it's been a long time and then again just yesterday since— [*Shaking her head and smiling.*] since we were all so young, you with your hopes, me with mine.

UNCLE BOB [*sharply*]. My love and your hopes. [*Twisting in his chair and mopping his face.*] If life were but a dream man might hope to wake from its burden. [*He stops suddenly and sits staring before him.*]

MRS. CONNELLY [*patting her lace cap*]. And now tell me that joke about the Yankee beggar again.

UNCLE BOB [*not replying*]. Let the old tree die. [*Looking through the open door at the rear.*] There comes Patsy Tate.

MRS. CONNELLY [*agitated*]. I don't wish to see her. [*Raising herself on her crutch.*] Geraldine!

UNCLE BOB [*taking a glass of water from the table and draining it down*]. This to him and her, to us all, Ellen.

GERALDINE [*entering*]. Yes, Mother.

MRS. CONNELLY. Let me know when Will comes, Robert.

MRS. CONNELLY *and* GERALDINE *go out. Presently* PATSY *comes up on the porch outside.*

UNCLE BOB. Come in, Patsy. PATSY *enters, dressed in her working clothes, a cotton blouse, apron, and stout shoes. She carries a bonnet and field gloves in her hand and is harassed and tired.*

PATSY [*hurriedly*]. I want to speak to Will, Mr. Bob.

UNCLE BOB. He's not back from town yet.

PATSY. Not?

UNCLE BOB. Still trying to borrow some money, I reckon. Or spending it. What's the matter?

PATSY. When he comes tell him I want to see him.

UNCLE BOB. Trouble with the tenants again?

PATSY. No, I can manage them.

UNCLE BOB. Come on, tell your Uncle Robert. *He comes up to* PATSY *and apparently in self-perversity tries to put his arm around her.*

PATSY [*stepping away from him*]. I've got to see him myself.

UNCLE BOB [*now bitterly and without a shadow of jocularity*]. I can still raise that arm to its purpose. Truth remains extant—the entelechy of the shell. Ha-ha. *Eky ho anthropos ten physin apotetelesmenen.*[20]

PATSY. If you'd put your arms in the field with a hoe there'd be a lot more truth, whatever your words mean.

UNCLE BOB. I was saying how perfect is man, how like a god. Me the masterpiece of nature. [PATSY *starts out at the rear as* WILL *comes trampling in and almost collides with her. For a moment he stares at her and then goes to the table and sits down. He is dressed in his Sunday clothes, haggard and the worse for sleeplessness and drink. He has grown stouter and coarser.* UNCLE BOB *calls out cuttingly.*] Bless God, the prodigal! Well, here's the calf.

WILL. Had dinner?

UNCLE BOB. We have.

WILL [*shortly*]. Morning, Patsy.

PATSY. Good morning.

WILL [*calling*]. Essie, bring me some dinner!

UNCLE BOB. Fee-fi-fo-fum—

WILL. And what other bad news has made you happy?

UNCLE BOB. Call her again.

WILL. Essie, bring me something to eat! Where is she?

UNCLE BOB. Lavalieres have cost her her job.

WILL. So. Mother turned her off—anh? Well, we'll see.

> PATSY *with a funny mechanical smile on her face stands gazing at* WILL. *He turns and pours himself some water from the pitcher and drinks glass after glass.*

UNCLE BOB [*smiling and peering at him over his fan*]. Liver afire—hanh?

WILL. Can I do anything for you, Patsy?

UNCLE BOB. And water won't squench it?

PATSY. I don't know.

UNCLE BOB. I'll go tell your mother you're here. [*He starts out.*]

WILL. Your company's welcome, I guess.

UNCLE BOB. She wanted to know when you came.

WILL. How's Mother?

UNCLE BOB. The wayward son has not killed her yet. In time, in time. [*He bows and goes out.*]

WILL [*searching about the room.*] How is the chopping?

PATSY. We'll be finished today.

WILL. The old devil must have drunk it all. [*Opening the lower drawer to the cupboard.*] No. [*He takes out a bottle of whisky and pours himself a full glass, tosses it down and turns to her.*] Well?

PATSY [*gesturing at the glass*]. Why do you do that?

WILL. What?

PATSY. Listen, Will, Father's coming to see you.

WILL. Ha, you told him about you and me! I knew you would.

PATSY [*angrily*]. No!

A still from Act II, Scene 2, performed by the ReGroup Theatre, 2014, featuring Claire Buckingham as Patsy Tate and Logan James Hall as Will Connelly (photography by Mikiodo Media, courtesy of ReGroup Theatre Company, Inc.).

WILL. All right. I know I'm low-down. But who did it?

PATSY. He heard the two nigger women joking out there. He asked me and I said no. I'm afraid something might happen, Will.

WILL. Yes, something will happen.

PATSY. What do you mean by that?

WILL. Whatever you mean. [*They stand eying each other, the one as if calculating the strength of the other. At last a faint smile wreathes* PATSY's *lips again*] I don't understand you.

PATSY. Yes, you do.

WILL. I wish to God I did. It would be easier.

PATSY. You ought to if anybody does.

WILL. Well, I don't.

PATSY. Why not?

WILL [*sneering*]. All right! If you've the catechism give me a precept.

PATSY [*her face pale and pinched*]. I know what we ought to do. We ought to pull ourselves together and go on the way we planned and not let everything fall to pieces.

WILL. That's what I'm trying to do.

PATSY [*scornfully*]. You're not. Everybody in the neighborhood knows you're running around like a fool in town. Do you call that trying? Who has stuck in the fields day after day and tried to keep the tenants at work? Not you.

WILL. You've done it all, haven't you?

PATSY [*with growing feeling*]. Yes, I have. Oh, you started out with a great show making a speech and saying this and that, and then blow up when your mother won't consent to your marrying me.

WILL [*eying her*]. And who smiled so sweet and talked about life and was free with kisses? [*Triumphantly.*] And it was all a trap. I'll not be caught with that bait—ha-ha.

PATSY [*her lips trembling*]. I'm not begging you. I'm trying to reason with you. If you cared about the farm you'd understand.

WILL. Yes, you love the place and not me.

PATSY. I don't, but why shouldn't I? It's a sight more honest. The land never tricks you. Do your part and she'll do hers. But you—I did my part by you and what did you do? Tried to make a—whore out of me.

WILL [*helplessly*]. Ha-ha, you're the wise virgin, clairvoyant like God.

PATSY. I know what we ought to do, I know that. [*She hesitates and turns away.*]

WILL. Go on and say it again—get married—ha?

PATSY. I'd like to see you go on any other way. [WILL *sits down and drums on the table, saying nothing.* PATSY *comes softly up to him.*] You know I'm right, Will. [*Earnestly, her voice shaken.*] I take the blame on myself, but you've got to fight too. I'll help you—I'll do anything to help you. [*Putting her hand gently and now timidly on his shoulder*] There's no other way in the world for you nor for me.

WILL [*presently*]. Don't cry. For God's sake don't cry. I can't stand any more of that. [*He rubs his aching brow with both palms of his hands.*]

PATSY [*looking up, her eyes bright and tearless, full of pain and even fear now*]. I know you don't trust me.

WILL. Sometimes I do.

PATSY. And you must understand the person you love, must trust her. I understand you and trust you.

WILL. But you don't love me.

PATSY [*thinking*]. Sometimes I do.

WILL. That's not love.

PATSY. How do you know?

WILL. It's not the kind I want.

PATSY [*turning and seizing his hand*]. What kind do you want, Will? Tell me, I'll try to give it to you.

WILL. Stop that, Patsy.

PATSY [*with almost a cry*]. And what have I done? [*Excitedly.*] You didn't do it, I did it. You're right. I set a trap to catch you and it's caught me. [*She clutches his hand with both of hers.*]

WILL. What do you mean?

PATSY. You've got to believe it. All my people have wanted land, wanted land above everything. When we moved here I saw all this great plantation going to ruin. I wanted it, wanted to make something out of it. I loved you because you stood for all I wanted. I had never cared for any man. Never been interested in any man. I saw you liked me and I went on and on with you. [*She claps her hands together, rocking her shoulders like an old peasant woman grieving.*]

WILL [*starting to put his hand on her bowed head*]. Patsy— [*But he stops and drops his hand to his side.*]

PATSY. And I went on planning. All that mattered was the land, growing crops, great crops, that's all I could think of. And so—I went to you—that night—led you on. [*Shuddering.*] After that I was different. Something, a feeling for you. I think about the farm now and what we can do with it, but always there is something else there, you yourself. I want to belong to you. Then I think about you, and there's always the farm, and I want to rule over everything—make it great and beautiful! I'm all mixed up inside. I want to obey you, be your wife, have your children. I love you now, you yourself, Will. [*Beseechingly.*] You understand me, don't you? I swear it's the truth.

    PATSY *bows her head over on her knees again, her shoulders shaking in silent sobs. For a long while* WILL *says nothing but stands watching her in pained uncertainty.*

WILL [*mechanically*]. Please don't, don't do that.

PATSY. At night I get to thinking and I'm scared. I feel I've hurt something in me— [*Struggling for words and for thought.*] because I tried to get something my mind wanted—by— by— [*With heartsick eagerness*] and a woman can't do that, she must never do that, must she? And I'm afraid.

> *She sits looking up at* WILL *with tear-stained feverish eyes. He gazes back at her in astonishment. Presently he goes over and gets himself another drink of whisky.*

WILL. I don't understand you. [*With a loud shout.*] Go away and leave me!

> PATSY *stands quickly up, remaining still by her chair. After a while she turns on him with the slow dignity of her father,* TATE, *mastering her voice.*

PATSY. Yes. I'll go and leave you! I can't stay here any more. I'll let you run things a while. And you'll see what I've been doing these months. You've never had such a crop on this plantation, have you? Now I'll go away—and I'll wait till you come for me. You will come, won't you? I'll go away today.

WILL [*fiercely*]. No, you won't!

PATSY. Maybe that's the way for us. It'll be hard, but in the end it'll be right. Some day you'll realize how hard it is for me to leave—you'll come then.

> *She goes out.* WILL *sits down thinking, as if trying to sense the meaning of words that mystify him. Once or twice he makes a movement as if to rise and follow her.* UNCLE BOB *comes in.*

UNCLE BOB [*fanning and half singing, his eyes glinting with low malice*].
>> Drunk last night
>> And drunk the night before,
>> And if I ever see tomorrow night
>> I'm gonna get drunk some more.

Go your way, Will. How much it cost you last night in town? Stripped you like the lady in the Bible—unh?

WILL [*flinging out his arms*]. Ha-ha-ha, money? Love, she said.

UNCLE BOB. Lady-killer. These latter days they all love you, don't they? The crackling thorns! [*Mocking him.*] Ha-ha-ha. They know their business.

WILL [*after a moment, raising his harassed face*]. Yes, you're right—dirty, foul, crooked, all of 'em.

UNCLE BOB. Poor boy—sick. And when Jesse Tate finishes with you you'll be sicker than you are. Your mother wants to see you, Will.

WILL. Let him shoot, I can shoot too. Let him sue me, I'll pay if that's what he means.

UNCLE BOB [*earnestly*]. Look here, we're getting into enough trouble and you better fix things up. Throw everything to the devil and marry Patsy Tate. It's the thing for us all. You and your mother are wrong. You do it. [*Looking at him straight.*] This is the last time I'll ever give you any advice. You marry that girl.

WILL. You don't see what she is. [*Half to himself.*] She's queer. [*Vehemently.*] She's cunning, full of plans.

UNCLE BOB. That's a lie and you know it.

WILL. I can't get her out of my mind. Sometimes I want to catch her by that pretty throat and kill her.

He buries his face in his hands and bows over the table. MRS. CONNELLY, *helped along by* GERALDINE, *comes in. She sits down in her wide chair as before and begins fanning herself.*

MRS. CONNELLY [*gently*]. Would you like some dinner, Will?

WILL. No, Mother.

MRS. CONNELLY. I want to talk to you a moment.

WILL [*springing up*]. No, you needn't. I won't listen to you, Mother.

MRS. CONNELLY [*to those about her*]. Please leave us alone. UNCLE BOB *and* GERALDINE *start out.*

WILL. Stop! I'll talk to all of you! [MRS. CONNELLY *raises her hand as if to rebuke him and then sits still, gripping the arms of her chair.*] Where's Evelyn? [*Calling.*] Evelyn! [EVELYN *comes in from the kitchen.*] In the kitchen. Will must not have Essie around. Thank God for your help there!

GERALDINE *stares at him as if he had suddenly gone crazy.*

EVELYN. Well, what's the matter?

WILL [*with angry triumph*]. You all come to condemn me but I'll condemn first. [UNCLE BOB *reaches out for a chair and bends over as if to sit down but then straightens up again and stands fanning himself.* WILL *goes on with sweeping gestures, and* MRS. CONNELLY *gradually bows her head, saying nothing, as* WILL *fastens his eye upon her.*] I've waked out of my sleep to see it all. [*His voice high and strident.*] I'm down, whipped, beaten, as low as Uncle Bob there. See, two by two they go up the stairs. Let the cross-eyed woman pound on the organ. Rotten, rotten, I know it. Lamb of God, cut my throat and bury me in the garden with the others. No, bury me apart, with Uncle Bob.

UNCLE BOB *puts out a pleading hand.*

EVELYN [*childishly, as she throws her arms around* GERALDINE]. Please, Will.

UNCLE BOB. Go to bed and sleep— [*His tired eyes keep gazing about the room as if seeking a place to rest.*]

WILL [*still eying his mother's bowed head*]. Follow in the steps of my fathers. [*Gesturing at the portraits on the wall.*] The grand old Connellys—General William Hampton Connelly— [*Raising his glass aloft.*] in the vanguard of the brave—yea, a nigger wench in every fence-jamb.

GERALDINE [*springing before him, her hands clenched as if to strike him*]. Stop! You fool!

WILL [*pushing her back roughly*]. Down, down. Sister and brother, cats and dogs. [EVELYN *turns her head away.*] Sisters and brothers? [*As if calling to someone outside the door.*] You Duffy and Harvey and Jenny? All of you come in! Hist, let's set our flesh and blood at the table—a row of mulattoes. "Brother, sister, forgive us." Low? But lower still. And Essie, be seated close at my right. If there's horror we brought it into the world. Who wouldn't vomit and clean out his stomach?

GERALDINE [*bending over* MRS. CONNELLY]. Mother, stop him!

She gets down on her knees, peers up into her mother's face a moment, and then, rising, goes and stands before the fireplace, her back to them. EVELYN *moves over to her side.*

MRS. CONNELLY [*in a low voice*]. And now?

WILL [*imitating* UNCLE BOB'S *thin womanish voice*]. As the old family satyr says—
    Skip to my Lou, skip to my Lou,
    If you can't get a white gal
    A nigger'll do.
Give me a torch and I'll burn up the cursed old House of Connelly!

UNCLE BOB. Have some mercy!

WILL. Ha-ha, mercy. I'll cut into this sore. Let innocent Geraldine and Evelyn know the truth.

GERALDINE [*whirling upon him in a wild pleading, her pride and haughtiness gone*]. It's a lie, a lie! Say it is, Mother.

MRS. CONNELLY. Let him tell the truth if that's it.

GERALDINE *gazes at* MRS. CONNELLY *with pale face.*

GERALDINE [*whispering*]. Come on, Evelyn.

WILL. Run away? Can you run away from your body's blood? [*Like a child.*] No, sir, no, sir, you can't. [*Thinking.*] Then I would too. Somewhere I'll start all over again.

UNCLE BOB [*murmuring*]. Is that all now?

MRS. CONNELLY. Help me up, Geraldine.

WILL. Not all till you see the niggers thumbing their noses as you pass, you strutting barren peacock!

MRS. CONNELLY [*with an angry cry*]. Stop that!

UNCLE BOB *stands fanning himself mechanically, his face white and dead.*

WILL. I'm done now. [*Laying his head on the table.*] Patsy's right, we're all—rotten.

In the gap of silence the NEGRO LABORERS' *harmony outside is carried aloft.*

NEGRO LABORERS.
I put my little finger ring
On her little hand,
Feel her rolling, tumbling in my arms,
Loving up her gambling man.

MRS. CONNELLY [*gently, as she looks at* WILL]. There's nothing more to say. [*Softly—beggingly.*] Nothing, Robert? No. [*She stretches her hand out to* WILL. GERALDINE *and* EVELYN *stand with her, their hands dropped at their sides. She catches hold of them and they support her.*] Yes, something— [*Her strong mouth quivering as she struggles for words.*] of other things, Will—of sacrifice and forgiveness and human love. Your father—your father was a great man. He had a hard struggle, over himself and the world around him. He failed, struggled again, his face set upward—on— [*She sways with weakness and leans heavily on her daughters.*] No whining—no tears—of weakness. Now I'm old—weak. [*Smiling*] But do I weep? No. [*Sternly.*] Does Uncle Bob? What do you know of his life? [*Softly.*] I know. Go to him, if you are a man, and beg his forgiveness. [*Pleadingly.*] Do it, Will. You've said things too hard for him.

WILL [*in a muffled voice*]. No, no, no. Upward! Ha-ha—

MRS. CONNELLY. No? Yes— [*Softly.*] you will some day. Later we'll talk—I'm tired now. Come to my room.

WILL [*jerking his head up*]. I'll not come. It's the truth and you won't face it.

MRS. CONNELLY [*after a moment, quietly, as she sinks back into her seat again—struggling to keep from breaking down*]. I have faced it for forty years, Will. And yet I did my duty to your father.

WILL [*staring at her*]. The rottenness, the injustice?

MRS. CONNELLY [*softly with her head bowed*]. That, too, if you call it so.

WILL. And Uncle Bob and—oh, God!

MRS. CONNELLY [*whispering*]. Please, please—

UNCLE BOB. Ellen, Ellen. It's a lie!

WILL. Ha-ha, a lie! It's God's truth, and she knows it. You and your nigger young'uns!

> UNCLE BOB *bows his head and* EVELYN *and* GERALDINE *stand gazing speechlessly before them.* MRS. CONNELLY *goes on in a gasping broken voice.*

MRS. CONNELLY. And now you have your truth, Will. [*With sudden helplessness.*] I don't know what to say to him any more. The shame! The shame!

> GERALDINE *and* EVELYN *help their mother up and she goes out, leaning on them.* WILL *sits bent over the table and* UNCLE BOB *stands wrapped in his own thoughts, his fan going slower and slower.*

WILL. She talks to me. The first time in my life. Let that be good-by. [*To* UNCLE BOB.] Go ahead, it's your turn. [*But the old man says nothing for a long while, his fan gradually stopping until he has dropped it. Then as if breaking from a reverie he gives a violent gesture with his hand and begins to fasten up his shirt collar and adjust his tie. His face is set in an empty, desolate look which has appeared on it once or twice before during the scene. He picks up his coat from a chair and puts it on and then goes over to the mirror at the sideboard and stands gazing at himself.* WILL *goes on.*] I stood in the courthouse, a boy, and heard Father sentence poor Purvis, his own son, to—the gallows. You helped prosecute him. [*In a low voice, to himself.*] There in the robes of justice he rose up, the power of the law. Why didn't he strip himself and say, "I am the guilty one, judge me"? [*Clenching his fist.*] True! True! There's something right behind all this. [*Triumphantly, as if making a discovery.*] But he didn't, the coward, and now I'm a coward. [*Thinking, a note of awe finally coming into his voice.*] There's something to search for—find it—a way to act right and know it's right. Father and Grandfather didn't do it, and we're paying for it. All the old Connellys have doomed us to die. Our character's gone. We're paying for their sins. [*Flinging up his hands.*] Words—words— [*He shakes his head in weariness, his mind growing foggy and losing its short trail. Turning, he pours himself another glass of whisky, drinks it, and stands looking at* UNCLE BOB.] Dressing for a party? Well, by God, he will have his joke.

UNCLE BOB. Today's the day. Nothing more to be said. She's said it all. My time to speak. Hear her defend me? Forty years she's done so—knowing—knowing what I am— [*His voice breaks off.*]

WILL [*starting up and rubbing the back of his head as if to wipe out an aching there*]. I leave it all to them—to you. I've got enough for my ticket to Texas. Let everything be sold and pay the debts, the rest divided. You're a lawyer, you'll execute. Ha-ha. And tell the pretty girls all hello for me. Tell 'em I'll not be riding out any more. Ha-ha.

UNCLE BOB [*still smoothing his beard and hair*]. I will if I see them. And so—good-by.

WILL. I'm not leaving till the morning train.

UNCLE BOB [*surveying himself*]. Not much of a garb for a far traveler.

WILL. Where you going?

UNCLE BOB [*opens the cupboard drawer and puts a pistol in his pocket*]. Try another shot at that hawk in the cypress tree.

WILL. You've never hit him and never will.

UNCLE BOB. In my ancient primer Ben Franklin said, "If at first you don't succeed—" [*He stands silent as if trying to recall something to mind. Presently he goes on in the same dulled voice.*] Marry Patsy Tate, Will. [*Murmuring to himself.*] For the proud days are ended. [*He pours himself a drink of whisky, looks at it a moment, and then raises his glass to the portraits on the wall.*] Ladies, gentlemen, *ave, vos alutamus*.[21] [*He touches the glass to his lips and then sets it down without drinking.*] *Facilis descensus Averno—quis—quamquam—mea memoria—nemo—mei—mnemisc*[22]—I cannot remember.

WILL [*chuckling*]. Good, good. An apt joke. A dead language.

UNCLE BOB. Very good and apt. [*As if suddenly full of glee* WILL *pounds on the table*. UNCLE BOB *goes out quietly at the rear.*

> WILL *watches him out with a scornful questioning smile, then he sits down and takes a roll of bills from his pocket and counts them and marks in a notebook. The single report of a pistol sounds in the garden.*

WILL [*jerks his thumb in that direction.*] Valedictorian, silver-tongued orator, most lately nothing. He shoots at a hawk and away flies—well—ambition. [*He drinks*. BIG SIS *and* BIG SUE *burst in at the rear door, grunting and waving their arms. They throw their aprons over their heads and walk up and down the room, moaning.* WILL *goes to the door and looks out—with a shout that dies in his throat.*] Great—

> *Presently* TATE *and* DUFFY *come hurrying up the portico and into the room, bearing the body of* UNCLE BOB. WILL *starts back and stands staring at them with open mouth as they lay him on the cot. Then he runs forward to help them.*

TATE. Have mercy on him! Here, some towels. *Spying the open sideboard drawer,* TATE *drags out a cloth and stuffs it against* UNCLE BOB's *side. All the while* WILL *stands speechless.*

DUFFY [*bobbing his head up and down foolishly*]. The pistol was in his hand, Mr. Will. He done it hisself. [*Flinging himself down by the cot and wringing his hands.*] Mr. Bob. I ain't to blame. Don't let the Great Moster hold it against me. Many times I prayed sump'n happen to you 'cause you done my po' mammy wrong! Now he answer me. I repents, I repents. White folks, help me, don't let it be writ against me in that Great Book! Mercy, mercy! Pappy! Pappy! [DUFFY *fumbles around him, gets his hat, and runs out of the room.*]

TATE. He's dead. [*He mutters to himself.*]

WILL [*murmuring as if in a dream*]. Dead? [*Mopping his head foolishly.*] He's dead! [*He runs out of the room to the right*]

TATE [*to the Negro women*]. Stay here. [TATE *goes out at the rear with his hat in his hand.*]

The Negro women stand by the cot with their aprons still over their heads. Raising their arms and letting them fall, they set up a low melodious moaning.

WILL [*in the hall outside*]. Come back! Don't go in there.

MRS. CONNELLY. Leave me alone! [*She opens the door and makes her way in on her crutch. After tottering across the room she stands near the cot, saying nothing.* EVELYN *and* GERALDINE *are seen weeping in the hall.* MRS. CONNELLY *cries out brokenly*] I failed you.[23] [*With a low convulsive moan that ends in a high shrieking gasp.*] Forgive me! *She crumples down on her knees on the floor.* BIG SIS *and* BIG SUE *go on moaning, and far off in the fields the* NEGRO LABORERS *raise their song.*

WILL [*loudly*]. Geraldine!

BIG SIS *and* BIG SUE *now fall on their knees by* MRS. CONNELLY's *motionless form and let loose their loud lamentations.*

Fade-out.

ACT II, GREEN'S ORIGINAL SCENE 3

Christmas evening in the Connelly dining room several months later. The fire is burning low on the hearth. BIG SUE *squats hunched over before it, stirring the ashes and blowing on the coals as she mouths and mumbles to herself.*

BIG SUE [*blowing*]. Open them eyes, fire coals, lemme see you. That's right. [*She stares forward, then starts back with a sharp grunt, stretching her mouth in a wide toothless smile.*] Unh-unh! *The door at the right opens and* BIG SIS *comes in with two heavily stuffed and shabby suitcases which she sets down on the floor.*

BIG SIS. Reading the signs again?

BIG SUE. Yeh, and get the same message. Come here, look. [BIG SIS *goes over and stares down into the fire.*] See?

BIG SIS. Can't see 'em yet.

BIG SUE [*stirring the ashes and blowing*]. Look way down in the blue flame.

BIG SIS [*putting her arm around her sister's shoulder*]. What's in there, honey?

BIG SUE [*spitting into the fire*]. See there.

BIG SIS. Yeh—yeh—do—now—the long black coffin.

BIG SUE. And woe, woe to the transgressor.

BIG SIS [*jubilantly*]. And all up above her the wind do mourn— [*In a room far off at the right* EVELYN *is heard sobbing.* BIG SIS *jerks her hand in that direction.*] Poor Miss Evelyn, her little heart done broke in two.

The Negro women moan and wipe their eyes.

BIG SUE. Good-by forever—uhm—

BIG SIS [*sputtering with anger*]. Yeh, say so. [*Fiercely.*] That gal put a spell on Mr. Will Connelly and run him crazy.

BIG SUE [*sighing*]. Poor Mr. Will.

BIG SIS. Poor fool.

BIG SUE. Walking down in the dark valley.

BIG SIS [*scornfully*]. Yeh.

BIG SUE. This morning he say the truth done come to him and he gwine follow it.

BIG SIS. The truth wrapped up in the shape of a purty woman—all hot and hongry-mouthed. Ah, Lord. [*She throws up her hands.*]

BIG SUE. Eigh Lord, the House of Connelly is fell like the Great Temple.

BIG SIS [*harshly, her lips near her sister's ear*]. And only you and me to build it back.

BIG SUE. Done said, yeh, done said.

> GERALDINE *and* EVELYN *come in from the right dressed in deep mourning, hats and veils, and with cloaks on their arms, which they lay on the table. A few months of grief and change and broken ties have aged the two sisters more than a few months should. The feminine spring and go that once enlivened* EVELYN'S *form are almost gone.* GERALDINE'S *hair is much grayer and the primness and gentility of her nature have grown more hard and bitter with the disappointments that have been her life. As they enter the two Negro women stop their moaning and stand quickly up.* BIG SUE *hurries and lights the lamp on the sideboard.*

BIG SIS [*speaking angrily into the air*]. Poor little turtledoves, you hafter fly from your home.

GERALDINE. Ask Duffy to bring the buggy around to the back drive. Tell him to hurry.

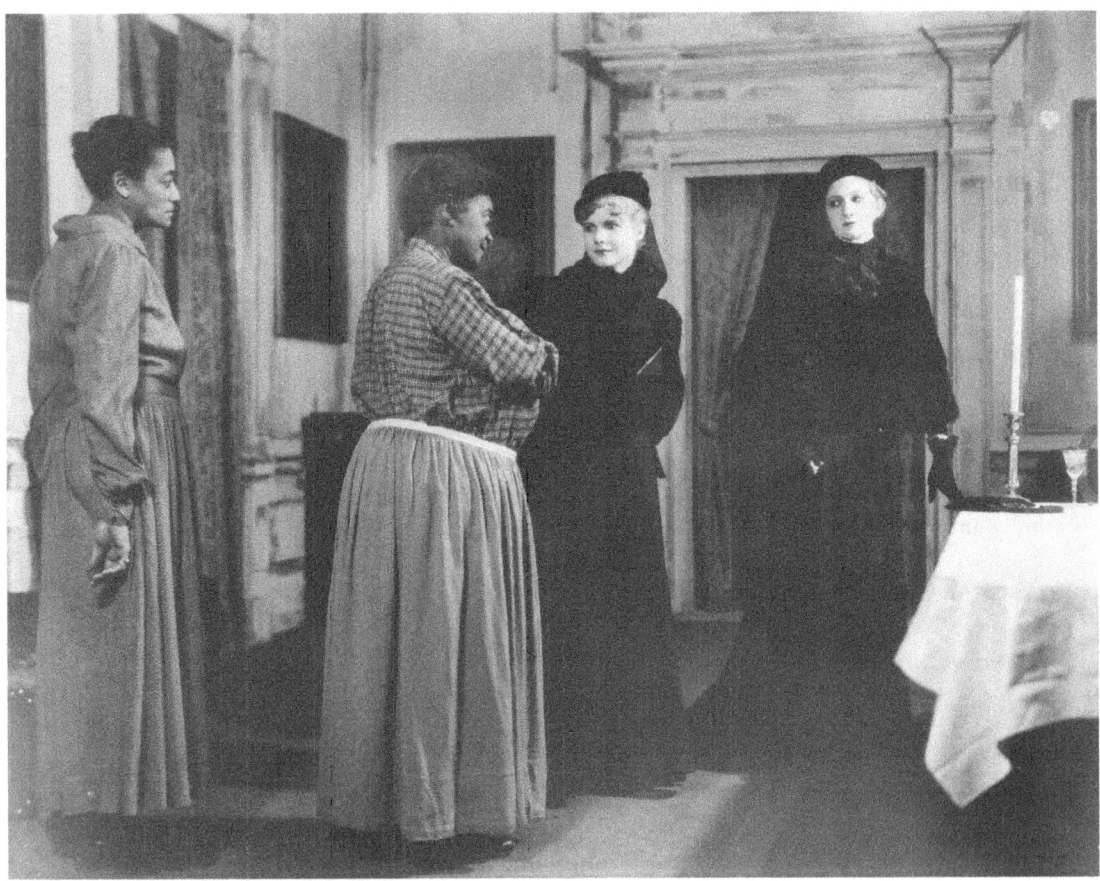

A still from Act II, Scene 2, performed by the Group Theatre on Broadway, 1931, featuring Rose McClendon as Big Sue, Fanny deKnight as Big Sis, Eunice Stockard as Evelyn Connelly, and Stella Adler as Geraldine Connelly (courtesy Paul Green Foundation).

BIG SIS. Yes'm. Go with me out there, Sue.

BIG SUE. That gyarden look skeery—hee-hee?

> *Muttering, they go out at the rear.* GERALDINE *and* EVELYN *stand motionless in the room. And in the words and actions which follow there is a vague indirect hollowness as if something unspeakable and oppressive weighed them down.*

EVELYN. Wonder what they think of our going, poor things?

GERALDINE [*at the fire*]. Come warm yourself. It'll be cold on the way to the station.

EVELYN. What'll Will think?

GERALDINE [*taking the broom and mechanically sweeping the hearth*]. He knows he's choosing between us. He chooses her.

EVELYN. But he's never thought we'd leave. I don't believe he has.

GERALDINE. What else could he expect and he bringing her here as his wife? It's a blessing Mother's not here to see it. [*She shudders. With the broom handle she unloops the Confederate flag and lets it drop down, hiding the General's face.*]

EVELYN [*at the sideboard*]. Let's drink some wine. [*Looking up.*] Why do you do that?

GERALDINE [*smiling*]. Just an idea. [*Her words seeming to come only from her lips.*] Grandmother made that flag.

EVELYN. They never do such fancy work these days, do they?

GERALDINE. No. [*In a voice like her mother's.*] The Lord knows we've tried to be good to Will—sympathize with him—talk to him. [EVELYN *pours herself a glass of wine and stands sipping it. They are both silent.* GERALDINE *goes on, with a deep hidden jealousy.*] He has somebody to talk to now. [*She keeps moving about the room as if unable to remain still. At the sideboard her hands take hold of the candlesticks and she wanders with them over to the table.*]

EVELYN. What are you doing?

GERALDINE. Bring the plates.

EVELYN. Are you setting the table for them?

GERALDINE [*as if suddenly realizing what she is doing*]. Yes.

EVELYN [*taking the plates in her hands where she stands—with a sob*]. I always loved these gold plates. [*Breaking out.*] And to leave all this to her!

GERALDINE. We'll remember it as it's always been.

EVELYN. She'll sell everything and put it in the farm—the boxwoods, the antiques—

GERALDINE. We shan't see it. [*Gazing about the room.*] It will always be this way to me, the way I've known it.

EVELYN [*bursting into tears*]. I can't do it. Don't make me go. *A buggy is heard driving up at the side portico.*

GERALDINE. I hear the buggy. [*Handing* EVELYN *her coat.*] Evelyn!

    BIG SIS *and* BIG SUE *re-enter.*

EVELYN. Yes, yes.

BIG SIS. Duffy's out there waiting.

BIG SUE. And the snow just pouring down.

EVELYN [*putting her coat on, a mournful smile with a touch of joy in it shutting around her lips*]. Remember we wanted it to snow last Christmas— [*She suddenly stops.*]

BIG SIS. And them serenaders is down there at the front already waiting for Mr. Will—and the wedding party.

EVELYN [*running up to the two Negro women*]. Good-by!

BIG SIS *and* BIG SUE [*covering her hands with kisses*]. Don't forget us way where you gwine.

EVELYN *and* GERALDINE. No, oh, no, we shan't.

BIG SIS. Maybe you be coming back.

BIG SUE. Yeah, maybe you get the message to come back.

EVELYN. Message?

GERALDINE. No, we're never coming back. [*Drawing on her gloves.*] Give Mr. Will our message—we're gone—and stay here till they come. Keep the fire going.

BIG SIS. Oh yes'm, us meet 'em stylish.

BIG SUE. Oh yes'm, us take care of everything for you.

BIG SIS. Till you come again.

EVELYN [*starting out*]. Bring the suitcases, Sis. [*Now as if anxious to be going.*] Hurry, Deenie!

> BIG SIS *takes up the suitcases and follows after her.* GERALDINE *gives a long look around the room. She notices the table centerpiece a bit awry and straightens it. Then she follows* EVELYN. BIG SUE *goes to the fire and stirs it as before. She seems to see something in the fire that pleases her, for she stretches her mouth in a wide toothless grin and cuts a few steps of joy about the room. A moment later the buggy is heard driving away.* BIG SIS *re-enters, drying her eyes with her apron.*

BIG SIS. Their little hands cold and still like ice.

BIG SUE [*sighing again*]. And nobody in the great world to warm 'em. [*Gesturing.*] Can still see it.

BIG SIS [*grinning*]. Still read it, right?

BIG SUE. Yeh. [*She picks up the gong stick and strikes the gong.*] Ooh!

BIG SIS [*punching the fire and sending the sparks upward*]. Make merry for the bride and groom!

She spies the bottle of wine and in braggadocio takes several gulps and passes it on to BIG SUE *who drains it empty. They stand in the middle of the room eying each other.*

BIG SUE. Everything so quiet and still.

BIG SIS [*sighing also*]. Hear the snow falling 'gainst the windows.

BIG SUE. And on the houses and fields and trees and on the poor graves.

BIG SIS. And on the grave of Missus, wrapping up this world in its soft blanket.

BIG SUE [*sighing once more*]. And the dead rest safe under it in their deep sleep.

BIG SIS. But old Missus lies all restless there.

BIG SUE. Uhm—

BIG SIS. Uhm—

BIG SUE [*closing her eyes and again spreading her mouth in a wide toothless grimace*]. Soon she gwine rest in peace.

Far down in the garden outside rises the noise of fiddles, horns, and guitars, interrupted now and then with shouts and high cries.

BIG SIS [*angrily*]. White trash make merry 'cause her got him at last.

BIG SUE [*bitterly*]. Yeh, she got everything. Got Mr. Will, got the House of Connelly, got all.

BIG SIS. Ain't got you and me.

BIG SUE. You done said. [*Merrily piling wood on the fire.*] Poor little bride, her'll be cold.

BIG SIS. Somp'n maybe keep her warm.

BIG SUE. Won't be the hunter neither.

BIG SIS [*winking at her sister*]. Hee—hee—

BIG SUE [*winking back*]. Hee—hee—

They slip away into the kitchen as the door at the right opens and WILL *and* PATSY *enter dressed up snug for the cold. A light sprinkle of snow covers their shoulders.* WILL *is well dressed in a dark overcoat, dark suit, hat, and gloves. There is something stronger and more manly in his bearing than before, and though his face shows the harassed signs of what he has been through, there is a certain satisfaction in him of one victorious in the struggle with himself. He carries a package in his hand.* PATSY *is dressed in an attractive brown coat-suit with a lace collar showing above it, hat, and gloves. Her cheeks are pink and her eyes bright from the cold.* WILL *puts the package on the table and helps her off with her wraps.*

WILL. We are home now.

PATSY [*looking up at him*]. Home.

WILL *lays their wraps and things on the cot and, turning, puts his hand on her shoulders and stands looking down into her eyes. The serenaders come up under the portico outside, stamping, singing, and ringing their bells. Their shouts and calls are loud and joyous and no longer marked with the teasing and derision of the Christmas before. The musicians begin playing the ballad of "The Brown Girl and Fair Elinor."* WILL *kisses* PATSY *and then they both go over and open the door.*

WILL *and* PATSY. Howdy, howdy, everybody!

Voices. There they are!

Other Voices. There's Patsy. Gimme a kiss. Ain't she pretty. Hey, Patsy. Hey, Missus.

Several of the serenaders, dressed in their outlandish garbs, come inside the room, throwing their arms and bodies rhythmically about.

MACK LUCAS [*loudly and gravely as he poises his fiddle bow in mid-air*]. A speech!

OTHERS. A speech from the bride—no, a kiss from her!

The music dies down and they crowd farther forward into the room, some of them removing their dough-faces and masks to see and hear better.

WILL [*a bit uncertainly and hesitatingly*]. I'm glad to see you all having a good time. We thank you for coming over here—and meeting us— [*Stopping.*] That's about all now. Yes, let today mark a new start for us. I've made mistakes— [*As if with determination he catches* PATSY *by the arm.*] we both have. But we're trying to wipe out our mistakes.

A YOUTH [*wearing a bucket over his head, with eyes and a mouth cut in it*]. That's all right, Mr. Will.

OTHERS. Sure, that's all right.

WILL [*stammering*]. We'll all do better now. We're going to build up everything, won't we, Patsy?

PATSY. Yes.

WILL. Let her talk to you. I'm no good at a speech.

A Voice [*half in mockery*]. You're a good speaker, Mr. Will.

Voices. That he is! [*They clap their hands to applaud him.*]

Patsy [*stepping before them, her eyes bright with high elation*]. We both thank you for your welcome. We appreciate it from the bottom of our hearts. Mr. Will wants me to tell you that he knows how hard it's been on you all this last year. Everything's been turned upside down. But it won't be any more. And everything that's been promised you you'll have, won't they, Will?

Will [*murmuring*]. We've had death and trouble, you know. But that's past.

Patsy. And after trouble comes the good things.

Voices. That's right, that's so. Everything'll be all right. Hooray for Mr. and Mrs. Connelly!

Other Voices. Hooray!

Patsy [*smiling*]. I hope you have a grand time serenading the neighborhood tonight. Don't scare Ike Messer too bad.

A Boy. Go with us, Miss Patsy.

Another Boy. Foolish, they've just got married.

Patsy. I will next time.

Will [*smiling at them*]. Next Christmas we'll have a real party maybe. And now good night to everybody.

> Will *steps forward and shakes hands with the serenaders. The* Idiot Boy *waddles out, takes his hand, and then runs back among the others.* Patsy *shakes hands with them also, and several of the girls kiss her and whisper, giggling, in her ear. The* Youth *with the bucket takes his headgear off and, giving her a quick kiss, tears laughing and yelling out at the rear.* Mack Lucas *has already set his fiddle going again and now leads them out. Finally they are all gone, their gay music dying down the lane.* Will *closes the door and stands abstractedly by the fire.*

Patsy [*watching him*]. They seem so glad about it, Will.

Will. Yes, they won't go hungry any more with you here.

Patsy [*with strange gentleness and almost in a low whisper as she comes over and leans her head against his shoulder*]. I was like a person dead, away from the farm and you. Now I'm alive. Now I am alive again. I knew you'd come some day and I kept working and waiting there in that city factory. But you were so long—the weeks and the days so long!

WILL [*after a moment*]. It took me a long time to see it the way you said— [*Stopping and staring over her shoulder.*] and the way Uncle Bob said. It gives me a sort of peace now. We're doing what's right.

PATSY. You'll learn to love me, won't you?

WILL. And you me maybe. [*Gazing at her.*] How beautiful you are.

PATSY. Kiss me. [*He kisses her.*] I do love you, Will. [*After a moment turning about the room in a high burst of spirits.*] Think of all we have to do!

WILL [*gives her a fleeting glance and then turns to the fire again, warming himself*]. And I'll follow the leader the best I can.

PATSY. It'll be together. [*With humble archfulness.*] Forget your distrust now.

WILL [*smiling*]. And you forget it.

PATSY. And the others will forgive and forget, won't they?

WILL. Yes. [*Going to the door at the right and calling.*] Geraldine, Evelyn. [*His voice echoes through the house, and the two stand a while listening.*]

PATSY. They'll come in a minute.

WILL [*glancing over at the package on the table*]. I'll give them their Christmas presents then.

A voice calls beyond the rear door, and TATE *sticks his head in.*

PATSY [*in a mixture of pleasure and displeasure*]. Father!

WILL. Good evening, Mr. Tate.

TATE [*pulling off his hat*]. Good evening. [*Coming up to them and shaking their hands.*] I wanted to come and say bless you and then go away again.

WILL [*kindly*]. Thank you, Mr. Tate.

TATE. You've both took the right step and the Lord will prosper you forever. [*In sound good humor.*] Yes, he will.

WILL. Talk to Patsy a moment. I'll be right back. [*He goes out at the right.*]

TATE *stands looking around the room. Presently he puts on his hat.*

TATE. Well, Patsy.

PATSY. Yes.

TATE. Well, be a good girl—yes, be a good wife to him.

PATSY. I will.

TATE [*tapping his hands together*]. We'll miss you at home.

PATSY. I thought you'd got used to that.

> *The door to the kitchen opens slightly and the roving eyes of* BIG SIS *and* BIG SUE *are seen gleaming in from the darkness beyond.*

TATE. Come over and cook me some biscuits now and then, won't you?

PATSY [*taking his arm and standing by the table*]. Will can sit there at the head. I'll sit here. [*In a low voice.*] You there— [*Pointing.*] the boys—so—and so. [*She turns and eyes her father in a sort of naïve triumph.*]

TATE [*looking at her in astonishment*]. I'll be plagued!

PATSY. And they'll have rooms of their own to sleep in now.

TATE [*with a prideful glance about him*]. Think of that. [*He chuckles, but immediately the stern look returns to his face as he gazes at her.*] I dunno—maybe everything'll be all right. God bless you.

PATSY. And that makes me happier than all the rest. There comes Will now.

TATE. Good night. [*He touches her gruffly on the shoulder and goes out just as* WILL *re-enters.*]

WILL [*calling after* TATE]. Good night, Mr. Tate. Thank you for coming.

TATE [*calling back*]. A happy Christmas to all.

WILL [*to* PATSY]. They're not in their rooms, Patsy.

PATSY [*gazing up at the portrait*]. Maybe they're upstairs. I'll get supper and we'll all sit down together.

WILL [*following her glance*]. What's happened to that picture?

PATSY. Maybe the flag fell down.

WILL [*murmuring*]. Geraldine! [*He looks from the portrait to the table—then fiercely, to himself.*] They'll see it like I've tried to show 'em.

PATSY [*taking the broom handle and pushing the flag back*]. Maybe so—yes, that's what happened. It fell down.

 BIG SIS *enters from the kitchen.*

BIG SIS. Us been waiting here for you all.

 PATSY *looks at her narrowly and goes over to the fire.*

WILL. Where are Miss Evelyn and Miss Geraldine?

BIG SIS [*rolling her eyes*]. Lord, they done gone from here.

WILL [*with a shout*]. What!

BIG SIS. They packed their little things and went to the train. Said give Mr. Will the message they wouldn't be coming back no more.

WILL. Great Scott! You hear that, Patsy? You better not joke with me, Sis.

 BIG SUE *enters from the kitchen. She carries a tow sack wadded in her hand.*

BIG SIS. Tell 'em, Sue.

BIG SUE [*casting up her eyes*]. They cried a little bit and wiped their eyes and said good-by to everything. They've gone to Richmond to live with Cousin Vera. [BIG SUE *looks over at* BIG SIS *who gives a low whickering laugh.*]

WILL [*angrily*]. Stop that laughing! When did they go?

BIG SIS. Duffy took 'em over jus' 'fore you all come. They's a letter in the hall for you, they said. WILL *hurries out at the right.* PATSY *gets the broom and begins sweeping the hearth. The two Negro women move up softly and stand near her. She glances at them.*

BIG SUE. And you the Missus now. [*She massages the sack in her hands.*]

PATSY [*smiling at the two, friendly but firmly*]. And I'll try to be a good one too.

BIG SUE. Hear that, Sister?

BIG SIS. Can't hear it.

BIG SUE. How come!

BIG SIS. The dead folks cries so loud down in the gyarden.

PATSY [*strongly*]. Go build a fire in the kitchen, Sis.

WILL *comes hurrying in, opening a letter as he enters. He goes to the lamp and reads it. The Negro women remain where they are.*

WILL [*dropping down in a chair*]. I've run them from their own home. [*Springing up excitedly.*] They've got to come back. [*He starts toward the rear door as if to go after them.*]

PATSY *runs across the room to him. The two Negro women stand watching them.*

PATSY [*with almost an angry cry*]. No, no, you haven't done it!

WILL [*with half a shout as he stops*]. We've both done it, then.

PATSY [*clinging to him*]. They know their own minds, Will. Please, please—listen—

WILL [*harshly, to himself*]. They must have hated me. [*Bursting out and trying to move from* PATSY'S *arms.*] My God, the cruelty of it! [*His voice dies out of him with a gasp, and he stands staring at the floor an instant, his face harassed and torn.*]

BIG SIS [*in a sudden burst of tearful pleading, coming up to him*]. Please, sir, Mr. Will, git 'em to come back. Ketch up wid 'em, Mr. Will.

BIG SUE [*likewise*]. They ain't gone but a little ways.

PATSY [*hugging* WILL *tightly to her as she searches for words to help him*]. It is cruel, Will, all this suffering and—

WILL [*with a cry*]. And I thought we were done with death and suffering.

PATSY. But we'll stand it, stand it together—whatever pain and suffering there is. [*Vehemently, her words rushing on now.*] That's the way it has to be, Will. To grow and live and be something in this world, you've got to be cruel—you've got to push other things aside. [*Fiercely.*] The dead and the proud have to give way to us—to us the living. [*Her face close against his, her voice intense and vibrant.*] We have our life to live and we'll fight for it to the end. Nothing shall take that away from us. [*She bows her head against his breast, her shoulders shaking. Then she goes on more quietly but with firm and steadfast voice.*] Right now we have to decide it, Will. Let them go. It's our life or theirs. It can't be both—they knew it. That's why they went away. [*She stops and stands up straight and waiting, looking at* WILL'S *struggling face.*]

BIG SIS. Oh, they moaned at leaving their home and their little hearts are breaking.

BIG SUE. And the salt tears falling from their burning eyes.

BIG SIS. Please'm—please, suh, Mr. Will.

BIG SUE. Please, suh, Mr. Will.

WILL [*in sudden anger*]. This is their home, their home, Patsy! [*Loudly.*] And I'll not run them from it. [*He flings her away from him, grabs up his overcoat, and hurries out at the rear.* PATSY *stands an instant, gazing before her.*]

PATSY [*to* BIG SIS]. Go build a fire in the stove like I told you.

BIG SIS [*begins piling wood on the fire, singing in her deep bass voice*].
        They grabble his eye, they work in his head,
        Man don't feel 'em, three days dead.

BIG SUE [*adding her melodious alto*].
        And all up above him the wind do mourn—
        Pity poor man ever was born.

PATSY [*staring at them*]. That's right, build up the fire then. Heap it up. They'll be cold.

BIG SIS. [*winking at her sister*]. Hee-hee, cold. Cold, Missus.

PATSY. What's that?

BIG SIS. [*speaking into the air*]. Gimme some motion, gimme some sound—

BIG SUE. Death gwine take her, church-wedding bound.

BIG SIS. Poor dead Missus, walking in the gyarden. Her can't sleep, her can't rest in her grave.

BIG SUE. Her done speak and say—a sacrifice. [*Lifting her open tow bag toward* PATSY.] This here hold many a good sassafras root, honey.

BIG SIS. Yeh, do tell, sweetie pie. [*Singing softly.*]
        The sporrer sot with her head in her wing,
        The snake crope up and 'gun to sing.

PATSY [*hotly*]. You heard what I said! I'm Missus here now and you'll do what I tell you to do. [*She turns suddenly and grabs up the poker from the hearth, but* BIG SIS *is quick as a cat and snatches it from her and throws it out of the way.* PATSY *stares at them, her eyes beginning to widen with a touch of fear.*] You stop that!

BIG SUE [*holding the mouth of the sack open before her*]. Look in there, Miss Patsy, us bring you a wedding present.

PATSY [*almost ragingly, as she summons all her strength against the two demonic creatures*]. Did you hear me! Go in the kitchen!

BIG SIS [*rocking with laughter*]. That's right, that's a wedding present from us, a wedding present in the sack. *At* BIG SIS'S *gesture the two women fling themselves upon* PATSY.

PATSY [*crying out*]. Wait, wait! Will! Will!

But they crush her down onto the floor and smother her, shrieking, in the sack. They continue to choke her with their bone-crushing great hands. Her struggles finally stop. Then the two women lay her on the couch and stand looking piteously down at her, their aprons stuffed to their eyes.

BIG SUE [*softly*]. Purty like a baby—

BIG SIS [*whispering and making her stroking motion in the air*]. Flesh soft same like feathers—

BIG SUE. Smooth like a snake—

BIG SIS [*as if about to weep*]. Poor little scrushed lily.

BIG SUE [*likewise*]. Little rose of Sharon.

BIG SIS [*suddenly spitting at the still figure*]. But they got her safe now, and them snake eyes done shining.

BIG SUE. Got her safe there where Purvis is.

BIG SIS. And with the Old Man and the Missus and Uncle Bob. They all sleep safe now.

BIG SUE. Till the trumpet sound and rise 'em up.

BIG SIS [*singing in her man's voice, to which* BIG SUE's *rich alto rises again*].
>   In the cold earth the sinful clay
>   Wropped in a sheet is laid away.
>   Rock to the hills to the trees do mourn,
>   Pity poor man ever was born.

They place the candles on the floor at the dead girl's head and feet and go softly out at the rear, moaning as they go, their aprons to their eyes. The door is left open, and the wind-laden snow blows in from the portico, fluttering the candle flame about. Far across the field the serenaders are heard carrying on their song.

Fade-out.

ACT II, SCENE 3, revised ending for the Group Theatre

CHRISTMAS *evening in the Connelly dining room, several months later. The fire is burning low on the hearth, and for a moment the scene is empty. Then* BIG SIS *and* BIG SUE *come in from the right with two suitcases, which they set down, muttering and growling to themselves.*

BIG SIS [*speaking angrily into the air*]. Ain't no mo' use begging, dey gwine leave heah.

BIG SUE. Yah, po' little turkle-doves dey fly away from deir own home. [*They remain silent a moment wiping their eyes with their aprons.*]

BIG SIS. Po' Miss Evelyn, her little heart done broke in two.

In a room far off at the right EVELYN *is heard sobbing. The Negro women moan and wipe their eyes.*

BIG SUE. Goodbye fohever—uhm.

BIG SIS [*sputtering with anger*]. Yah, say so. [*Fiercely.*] Dat Mr. Will Connelly done must gone crazy!

BIG SUE [*sighing*]. Po' Mr. Will.

BIG SIS. Po' fool!

BIG SUE. Walking down in de dark valley.

BIG SIS [*scornfully*]. Yah!

BIG SUE. Dis morning he say de truf done come to him and he gwine follow it.

BIG SIS. Patsy Tate de truf he gwine follow! [*Spitting bitterly at the fireplace, and half-moaning.*] And dis heah de end now. Eigh, Lawd, de House o' Connelly is fell lak de Great Temple.

BIG SUE. Lawd, Lawd, ha' muhcy!

GERALDINE *and* EVELYN *come in from the right. They are dressed in deep mourning, hats and veils, and with cloaks on their arms, which they lay on the cot. A few months of grief and change and broken ties have aged the two sisters more than a few months should. The feminine spring and go that once enlivened* EVELYN's *form are almost gone;* GERALDINE's *hair is much grayer, and the primness and gentility of her nature have grown more hard and bitter with the disappointments that have been her life. As they enter, the two Negro women gradually stop their swaying and moaning.*

GERALDINE. Ask Jerry to bring the buggy around to the back drive.[24] Tell him to hurry.

BIG SIS. Yes'm. Go wid me out dere, Sue.

BIG SUE [*bitterly*]. Dat gyarden look skeery—hee-hee?

> *Muttering, they go out at the rear.* GERALDINE *and* EVELYN *stand motionless in the room. And in their words and actions which follow, there is a vague, indirect hollowness as if something unspeakable and oppressive weighed them down.*

EVELYN. Wonder what they think of our going, poor things?

GERALDINE. Warm yourself. It'll be cold on the way.

EVELYN. What'll Will think?

GERALDINE [*taking the broom and mechanically sweeping the hearth*]. He knows he's choosing between us. He chooses her.

EVELYN. But he's never thought we'd leave. I don't believe he has.

GERALDINE. What else could he expect and he bringing her here? [*With the broom handle she unloops the Confederate flag and lets it drop down hiding the General's face.*]

EVELYN [*at the sideboard*]. Let's drink some wine. [*Looking up.*] Why do you do that?

GERALDINE [*smiling*]. Just an idea. [*Her words seeming to come only from her lips.*] Grandmother made that flag.

EVELYN. They never do such fancy work these days, do they?

GERALDINE. No. [*In a voice like her Mother's.*] The Lord knows we've tried to be good to Will—sympathize with him—talk to him. [EVELYN *pours herself a glass of wine and stands sipping it. They are both silent.* GERALDINE *goes on with a deep hidden jealousy.*] He has somebody to talk to now! [*She keeps moving about the room as if unable to remain still. At the sideboard her hands take hold of the candlesticks and she wanders with them over to the table.*]

EVELYN. What are you doing?

GERALDINE. Bring the plates.

EVELYN. Are you setting the table for them?

GERALDINE [*as if suddenly realizing what she is doing*]. Yes.

EVELYN [*taking the plates in her hands where she stands—with a sob*]. I always loved these gold plates. [*Breaking out.*] And to leave all this to her!

GERALDINE. We'll remember it as it's always been.

EVELYN. She'll sell everything and put it in the farm.

GERALDINE. We shan't see it. [*Gazing around the room.*] It will always be this way to me, the way I've known it.

EVELYN [*bursting into tears*]. I can't do it! Don't make me go!

>   *A buggy is heard driving up at the side portico outside, and* BIG SIS *and* BIG SUE *re-enter.*

GERALDINE [*handing* EVELYN *her coat*]. Evelyn.

EVELYN. Yes, yes.

BIG SIS. Jerry's out dere waiting.

BIG SUE. And de snow des' pouring down.

EVELYN [*pulling on her coat, a mournful smile with a touch of joy in it shutting around her lips*]. Remember we wanted it to snow last Christmas— [*She suddenly stops.*]

BIG SIS. And dem serenaders is down dere at de front already waiting foh Mr. Will—and de wedding party.

EVELYN [*running up to the two Negro women*]. Good-bye!

BIG SIS and BIG SUE [*covering her hands with kisses*]. Don't fohgit us way whah you gwine.

GERALDINE and EVELYN. No, oh no, we shan't.

GERALDINE [*drawing on her gloves*]. Stay here till they come. Keep the fire going.

BIG SIS. Oh, yes'm, us meet um stylish.

EVELYN [*starting out*]. Bring the suitcases, Sis. [*Now as if anxious to be gone.*] Hurry, Deenie!

>   *The Negro women pick the suitcases up and follow after her.* GERALDINE *gives a long look around the room. She notices the table centerpiece a bit awry and straightens it. Then she follows after* EVELYN. *A moment later the buggy is heard driving away.* BIG SIS *and* BIG SUE *re-enter with their aprons to their eyes.*

BIG SIS [*presently*]. Deir liddle hands cold and still lak ice.

BIG SUE [*sighing*]. And nobody in dis great world to warm um.

>   *They move restlessly about the room.*

BIG SIS [*punching the fire*]. Mek merry foh de bride and groom!

BIG SUE. Yah! [*She picks up the gong stick and strikes the gong—shuddering.*] Ooh!

BIG SIS *spies the bottle of wine and in braggadocio freedom takes several gulps and passes it on to* BIG SUE *who drains it empty. Then they stand in the middle of the room eyeing each other.*

BIG SIS [*sighing*]. Everything so still.

BIG SUE. Heah de snow falling 'gin de windows.

BIG SIS. And on de houses and de fields and on de po' graves.

BIG SUE [*sighing likewise*]. And de dead rest soft under it in deir deep sleep.

BIG SIS [*stretching her mouth in a wide bitter grimace*]. Po' old Missus lie onrestless dere.

BIG SUE. Uhm—

BIG SIS. Uhm—

> *From down in the garden outside rises the sound of fiddles, horns, and guitars, interrupted now and then with shouts and high cries.*

BIG SUE. Dere—

BIG SIS [*angrily*]. White trash mek merry 'cause her got him at last. [*Bitterly.*] Yeh, she got everything—got Mr. Will, got de House of Connelly—got all.

BIG SUE. Ain't got you and me.

BIG SIS. Not yit nohow.

> *They slip away into the kitchen as the door at the right opens and* WILL *and* PATSY *enter dressed up snug from the cold. A light sprinkle of snow covers their shoulders.* WILL *is well-dressed in a dark suit, overcoat, hat and gloves. There is something stronger and more manly in his bearing than before; and though his face shows the harassed signs of what he has been through, there is a certain satisfaction in him of one victorious in a struggle with himself.* PATSY *is dressed in an attractive brown coat-suit, with a lace collar showing above it, hat and gloves. Her cheeks are pink and her eyes bright from the cold.*

WILL [*helping her off with her wraps*]. We're home now.

PATSY [*looking up at him*]. Home.

> WILL *lays their wraps and things on the cot and turning puts his hands on her shoulders and stands looking down into her eyes. The serenaders come up under the portico outside,*

stamping, singing, and ringing their bells. Their shouts and calls are loud and joyous and no longer marked with the teasing and derision of the Christmas before. WILL *kisses* PATSY *and then they both go over and open the door.*

WILL and PATSY. Howdy, howdy, everybody!

VOICES. There they are!

OTHER VOICES. There's Patsy! Gimme a kiss! Ain't she pretty? Heigh, Patsy! Heigh, Missus!

Several of the serenaders, dressed in their outlandish garbs, come inside the room throwing their arms and bodies rhythmically about. Old TATE *comes heavily and shyly in, embraces* PATSY *and shakes hands with* WILL *without a word.*

MACK LUCAS [*loudly and gravely as he poises his bow in mid-air*]. A speech!

OTHERS. A speech from the bride! No, a kiss from her! [*The music dies down and they crowd further into the room, some of them removing their dough-faces and masks to hear better.*]

WILL [*a bit uncertainly and hesitating*]. I'm glad to see you all having a good time. We thank you for coming over here—and—meeting us. [*He puts his arm around* PATSY.]

A YOUTH [*wearing a bucket over his head with eyes and a mouth cut in it*]. Hooray for Mr. Will!

OTHERS. Hooray!

WILL [*stammering*]. Let—let Patsy talk to you. I'm no good at a speech.

A VOICE. You're a good speaker, Mr. Will.

VOICES. That he is. [*They clap their hands and cheer him.*]

PATSY [*stepping before them, her eyes shining*]. We both thank you for your welcome. We appreciate it from the bottom of our hearts. Mr. Will wants me to tell you he knows how hard it's been on you all this last year. But it won't be any more. You'll have what's been promised you. Won't they, Will?

WILL. We've had death and trouble—you know. But that's past, and now—

PATSY [*to all around her*]. After trouble comes the good things!

VOICES. That's so. Every thing'll be all right. Hooray for Mr. and Mrs. Connelly!

OTHER VOICES. Hooray!

PATSY. I hope you have a grand time serenading the neighborhood tonight. Don't scare Ike Messer too bad.

A Boy. Go with us, Miss Patsy.

Another Boy. Foolish, they've just got married.

Patsy. I will another time.

Will [*smiling at them*]. Next Christmas we'll have a real party maybe. And now goodnight to everybody. [*He steps forward and shakes hands with them.*]

> The Idiot Boy *waddles out, takes his hand and then runs back among the* Others. Patsy *shakes hands with them also, and several of the girls kiss her and whisper giggling in her ear. The youth with the bucket takes his head-gear off, and giving her a quick kiss, tears laughing and yelling out at the rear.* Mack Lucas *with his fiddle going again now leads them out. Finally they are all gone, their gay music dying down the lane.*]

Patsy [*turning back into the room and closing the door*]. They seem so glad about it, Will.

Will. Yes. They won't go hungry any more with you here.

Patsy [*with strange gentleness and almost in a low whisper as she comes over and leans her head against his shoulder*]. I was like a person dead away from the farm and you. Now I am alive again. I knew you'd come some day, and I kept working and waiting. But you were so long.

Will [*after a moment*]. It took me a long time to see it the way you said [*Stopping and staring off over her shoulder.*] and the way Uncle Bob said. It gives me a sort of peace now. We're doing what's right.

Patsy. You'll learn to love me, won't you?

Will. And you me maybe? [*Gazing at her.*] How beautiful you are!

Patsy. Kiss me. [*He kisses her.*] I do love you, Will. [*After a moment turning about the room in a high burst of spirits.*] Think of all we have to do!

Will [*glancing at her*]. Yes. [*Going to the door at the right and calling.*] Evelyn! Geraldine! [*His voice echoes through the house, and they stand listening.*]

Patsy. Maybe they're upstairs. I'll get supper and we'll all sit down together. [*Her gaze sweeps around the room and she stops and stands staring at the General's covered portrait.*]

Will [*turning back, and following her gaze upward—then starting*]. What's happened to that picture? Ah—

Patsy. Maybe the flag fell down.

WILL [*murmuring*]. Geraldine— [*He looks from the portrait to the table—then fiercely to himself.*] They'll see it like I've tried to show 'em! [*He turns and goes hurriedly out at the right.*]

> PATSY *remains still in the middle of the room as if thinking to herself. Far off outside the serenaders are heard singing.*

PATSY [*as if accepting some hidden challenge*]. All right then—

BIG SIS [*coming in from the kitchen, followed by* BIG SUE]. Us been waiting heah foh you all.

PATSY [*moving to the sideboard*]. Glad you did. [*Now briskly.*] Build a fire in the stove and bring in some wood.

> *They eye her with malevolent sassiness.*

BIG SIS. And you de Missus now?

PATSY [*smiling at them friendly but firmly*]. And I'll try to be a good one too.

BIG SIS. Heah dat, sister?

BIG SUE. Naw, cain't heah um.

BIG SIS. How come?

BIG SUE. De dead folks cry so loud down in de gyarden.

BIG SIS [*moaning and watching* PATSY]. De old man and de Missus and Uncle Bob—all dere whah Purvis is.

BIG SUE. 'Twell de trumpet sound and rise um up.

PATSY [*staring straight at them*]. Did you hear me? [*They snicker disrespectfully and move ominously towards her.*] I'm missus here now and you'll do what I say.

BIG SIS [*in sassy and mock alarm*]. Uh—uh!

BIG SUE [*likewise*]. Uh—uh!

PATSY [*whirling towards the fireplace and snatching up the heavy poker—furiously, her eyes blazing*]. You do it or by God I'll— [*She springs at them, the poker uplifted.*]

BIG SIS and BIG SUE [*their eyes rolling in amazement and fear as they back hurriedly into the kitchen*]. Don't, Miss Patsy—please'm—yeb'm—yeb'm!

> *The door swings behind them and they are heard clattering at the stove. Presently* PATSY *picks up the broom, and lifts back the flag from the General's face.*

WILL [*hurrying in*]. They're not here. [*Calling.*] Sis! [*The two Negro women enter again and stand just inside the door.*]

BIG SIS [*meekly*]. Yessuh.

WILL. Where are Miss Evelyn and Geraldine?

BIG SIS. Lawd, Mr. Will, dey done gone from heah.

WILL. What!

BIG SIS. Dey packed deir little things and went to de train. Said give Mr. Will de message dey wouldn't be coming back no mo'.

WILL. You hear that, Patsy!

BIG SIS. Tell um, Sue.

BIG SUE [*casting up her eyes*]. Dey cried a little bit and wiped deir eyes and said goodbye to everything. Dey gone to Richmond to live wid Cousin Vera.

WILL. Stop that!—When did they go?

BIG SIS. Jerry took 'em over jest 'fo' you all come.

WILL [*dropping down in a chair*]. I've run them from their own home! [*Springing up excitedly.*] They've got to come back! [*He starts toward the rear door as if to go after them.* PATSY *runs across the room to him.*]

PATSY [*with almost an angry cry*]. No! No! You haven't done it.

WILL [*with half a shout, as he stops*]. We've both done it then.

PATSY [*clinging to him*]. They know their own minds, Will. Please—please—listen—

WILL [*fiercely—to himself*]. They must have hated me. [*Bursting out and trying to move from* PATSY's *arms.*] My God, the cruelty of it! [*His voice dies out of him with a gasp, and he stands staring at the floor, his face harassed and torn.*]

PATSY [*hugging him tightly to her as she searches for words to help him*]. It is cruel, Will—all this suffering—and—

WILL [*with a cry*]. And I thought we were done with death and suffering.

PATSY. But we'll stand it—stand it together—whatever pain and suffering there is. [*Vehemently, her words rushing on now.*] That's the way it has to be, Will. To grow and live and be something in this world you've got to be cruel—you've got to push other things aside.

A still from Act II, Scene 3, performed by the Group Theatre on Broadway, 1931, featuring Rose McClendon as Big Sue, Fanny deKnight as Big Sis, Margaret Barker as Patsy Tate Connelly, and Franchot Tone as Will Connelly (courtesy Paul Green Foundation).

The dead and the proud have to give way to us—to us the living. [*Her face close against his, her voice fierce and vibrant.*] We have our life to live and we'll fight for it to the end. Nothing shall take that away from us. [*She bows her head against his breast, her shoulders shaking. Then after a moment she goes on more quietly but with a firm and steadfast voice.*] Right now we have to decide it, Will. It's our life or theirs. It can't be both. They knew it—that's why they went away. [*She stops and stands up straight and waiting, looking at* WILL's *struggling face.*]

WILL [*presently clinging to her, suddenly and almost like a child*]. Yes—yes—Help me—ah I need you so, Patsy.

PATSY [*after a moment*]. And I'll always be here to help you when you need me.

WILL [*brokenly*]. Aye, you will—you will. [*He searches her face with hungry intensity. Suddenly and with loud vehemence.*] Yes, let them go. Let the past die. It's our life now—our house!

[*He stands staring out before him as if defiant of the portraits on the wall. The two Negro women who have been looking on bow their heads over on their breast in a sort of hopeless resignation.*]

PATSY [*after a moment quietly to* BIG SIS *and* BIG SUE]. Go on back to the kitchen.

> *But they remain standing where they are, full of a sullen moroseness. Presently* WILL *looks up, his mind echoing* PATSY's *command.*

WILL. Miss Patsy's my wife now.

BIG SIS and BIG SUE [*hesitating*]. Yessuh.

WILL [*loudly*]. Then you do what she tells you!

BIG SIS and BIG SUE [*as they take each other by the hand and go into the kitchen*]. Yessuh, Mr. Will.

WILL [*suddenly sweeping* PATSY *into his arms, his voice grim and eager*]. And with you I'll go on—I'll go on!

> *They stand wrapped in each other's embrace. Across the fields the serenaders are heard playing and singing about Fair Elinor.*

PATSY [*her voice shaking as she tries to keep from breaking down*]. Think of it, you've had no supper. [*She gently moves away from his arms and begins lighting the candles.*]

> *Fade out.*

Paul Green's *The House of Connelly*, a Play (and Playwright) "worth bothering about"

A SCENE-BY-SCENE ANALYSIS

by MARGARET D. BAUER

"I paid a visit one day many years ago to a ruined old Southern place in eastern North Carolina—a rambling two-story house with a driveway lined by storm- and sleet-broken cedars leading up to it.... A wrinkled, blear-eyed woman was sitting in a rockingchair in the desolate, shadowed wide hall of the old house, her palm-leaf fan leisurely moving back and forth sweeping away the flies.... We had some talk about the past days, the proud days, the good days. There she sat waiting for final death."—Paul Green, letter to Cheryl Crawford, 22 April 1975 (Avery 682–83)

North Carolina's preeminent playwright Paul Green is best known today as the author of the longest running (and first of its kind) outdoor symphonic drama *The Lost Colony* and as the creator of the genre itself. However, two of Green's more traditional plays, *In Abraham's Bosom* and *The House of Connelly*, are, as plays, better works—I would argue his best. The latter even rivals the best work of Tennessee Williams. In *The History of Southern Drama*, Charles S. Watson calls Green "[t]he leader of the new drama in the South ... the central, indispensable figure in the development of southern drama" (101), and yet, in contrast to the internationally renowned Tennessee Williams, whose work continues to enjoy revivals, Paul Green, along with his short folk plays and full-length plays, has been largely forgotten beyond the playwright's home state. Comparing Green with the South's most successful playwright, one might consider the possibility that one cause of Green's historical obscurity, by contrast to Williams's continued popularity, is that while both men's work addresses Southern themes and conflicts, Green's plays explore the more controversial and discomforting issue of miscegenation.[1] And his plays were written and performed before William Faulkner's perhaps most fully developed exposé of this issue in *Absalom, Absalom!*. It is interesting that Green's *In Abraham's Bosom*, which won the Pulitzer Prize in 1927, has *never* been performed in the South, and very few people have ever heard of *The House of Connelly*, although it was the debut Broadway production (in 1931) of New York's highly respected Group Theatre. It remains to be seen what effect the Re:Group Theatre's 2014 revival of this play in New York will have.

A poster created for the final performances of the ReGroup Theatre's 2014 production of the play, featuring Selena C. Dukes as Big Sue and Sheila Simmons as Big Sis (photography by Mikiodo Media, courtesy of ReGroup Theatre Company, Inc.).

The House of Connelly from Script to Stage

The production history of *The House of Connelly* is fascinating. As it was originally written, the play is even more provocative than the reviewer for the *New York Sun* could have known when he wrote, "It is a play to provoke argument and rouse thought and the power to do these things is essential in plays worth bothering about" (Lockridge). The violent ending that Paul Green wrote initially is among the most challenging and disturbing endings of a work of literature that I can think of: in the final scene, two black women smother to death the white female lead, a tenant farmer's daughter and the play's symbol of hope, who has just married the owner of the plantation on which they all live and work in turn-of-the-century North Carolina.

Upon completing *The House of Connelly*, Green sent it to his friend Barrett Clark, who passed it on to the Theatre Guild in New York. The Guild optioned it, and then some time later the Group Theatre, many of the members of which had participated in Theatre Guild productions, selected it to be the first play they would produce. The Group's decision to have Green revise the violent ending (as will be recounted within the discussion of the final scene) cost them: the Guild board threatened to cut their financial support in half (from $10,000 to $5,000) if Green's original ending was not restored.[2] But then Eugene O'Neill visited Cheryl Crawford, one of the play's co-directors, and when she told him of this loss, he contributed a thousand dollars toward going on with the show with the new ending, thus inspiring Crawford to seek the rest of the money they needed from the publication house of Samuel French, who published much of Green's work (Crawford 55). The revised play opened on September 28, 1931, at the Martin Beck Theatre on West Forty-fifth Street in New York.

Reviewers of the Broadway premiere of *The House of Connelly* praised the freshness of Green's poetic vision, even as they acknowledged that there was little new about the themes or plot of the play (the *Saturday Review of Literature* published its positive review under the headline "New Plays on Old Plots"). More than one reviewer noted poetic elements in the play. Writing for the *New York Times*, for example, J. Brooks Atkinson called the play a "prose poem" ("Play" 22), and in a follow-up review he praises Green's "splendid characters" ("October Nights" 107). Franchot Tone was broadly commended for his performance of Will Connelly, but reviewers' highest praise went to the non–Group Theatre actors Fanny DeKnight and Rose McClendon, who played Big Sis and Big Sue, respectively, the two black women who serve in this version more as the play's chorus than the Fates they would have played if the play had ended as Green originally intended. In spite of their diminished roles in the revised play, *The Chicago Defender* called them "the stars of the play" ("House" 5).

Several reviewers compared *The House of Connelly* to Chekhov's plays, but even with overwhelmingly positive reviews, the play closed in December after only ninety-one performances. According to Alma A. Ilacqua, although *The House of Connelly* "brought fame to the Group Theatre ... the play did not become a commercial Broadway success" (81). Paul Green called it "a sort of so-so success in New York" (*Plough* 53). Ultimately, *The House of Connelly* went the way of all of Green's plays (with the exception of *The Lost Colony*)—indeed, the way of most drama—largely overlooked and forgotten within decades of their production.

The House of Connelly takes place, according to the play's front matter, in "the early years of the twentieth century" on "an old aristocratic plantation somewhere in the southern part of the United States." As many of the play's reviewers noted, neither the decline of an Old

Paul Green working with the author Richard Wright on the campus of the University of North Carolina in Chapel Hill, where they adapted Wright's novel *Native Son* for the stage (courtesy Paul Green Foundation).

Southern family, nor the love story between an aristocratic man and the daughter of a tenant farmer is new dramatic material.[3] So why does Green's story development feel fresh, even over eighty years after its first production? Commonly found in Southern literature, here again are the consequences of adulterous miscegenation and guilt over this and other crimes of slavery. What is so different about Green's story? For one thing, the original ending, but of course the reviewers did not see that ending, so that could not be why they saw *The House of Connelly* as innovative. I propose that the originality of this dramatic depiction of the turn-of-the-century South is Green's raw exploration of class issues, in addition to the more familiar race issues. The class conflict is evident in the scenes featuring Big Sis and Big Sue, two former slaves, now servants on the plantation, and Patsy Tate, the ambitious daughter of a tenant farmer on Connelly land. Once Will Connelly shows an interest in this young woman, she is perceived by the two black women to be some kind of threat—though whether to their traditional way of life or to something else in the post–Reconstruction/pre–Modern South is left ambiguous, giving the audience much to think about after the curtains close. This violent tension between the black and white working women anticipates a central conflict in much of the fiction of Louisiana author Ernest J. Gaines, who explores the tensions between the Cajun tenant farmers, overseers, and merchants on one side and the African American field hands and domestic workers on the other. Poor whites were allowed more upward mobility than the descendants of slaves; consequently, Gaines shows in his fiction, resentment developed when these whites were given better options on land as plantations were divided than the blacks who had long worked that land for the plantation owners. Green addressed this class conflict in *The House of Connelly* a generation before Gaines began writing.

Reconsidering this most provocative and powerful of all of Paul Green's plays—indeed, in its original, tragic form, perhaps one of the most powerful plays in Southern literature, the audience is led to wonder what to make of the violence enacted against a woman who, if not entirely innocent, is certainly not guilty of any crime against the two black women who kill her. What could Paul Green have been thinking to write such an ending? Liberal-minded for his day, Green was a man who used his literary fame to challenge capital punishment in North Carolina, his home state, largely because he recognized that the death penalty was perpetuated more often against the poor than the rich, that black criminals were more likely than white to receive the death penalty, and that blacks and poor whites were more likely than upper class white men and women not to receive a fair trial before conviction.[4] In Green's heyday as a Broadway playwright, he was praised for his sympathetic, understanding, and realistic depictions of African American characters and culture, which was why Richard Wright picked him to adapt *Native Son* for the stage.[5] What then is Green suggesting in the original conclusion to *The House of Connelly*, in which two black women kill a lower class white woman whose only "crime" was to marry above herself? What threats did Patsy *Connelly* pose to Big Sis and Big Sue? One answer may be the injustice of white tenant farmers having more opportunities than blacks for upward mobility in the early twentieth-century South. The two black women, for example, could not marry up the social or racial stratum. But I suggest too that Patsy also threatens the imminent *end* of the Connelly family, which the two black women could see coming, until Patsy, with her plan for how to revive the Connelly farm, marries Will. Consider how the revised ending allows for hope that a new, stronger generation of Connellys will be born from the union between Patsy Tate and Will Connelly. Prior to this union, Sis and Sue had reason to believe they would live to see the end of the family that once enslaved them, and I propose that they kill Patsy to make sure that they will still do so.

Patsy's ambitious plans for herself and the Connelly land are a threat to the status quo, which may not be very prosperous for anyone, including at this point the Connellys themselves, but is familiar and thus less frightening to those who witnessed the violent treatment of some freed slaves during the Reconstruction era. *The House of Connelly* does seem to dramatize the resistance to change of some black as well as white Southerners. Change, of course, brought new dangers to freed slaves just after the Civil War. For example, a freed slave trying to leave behind the bonds that continued for African Americans even after Emancipation still had to escape from slave catchers-turned-Klansmen, and the vigilantes who might run them down were no longer constrained by the idea of these people as the property of men with power. Anger and outrage over the destruction of the South during the Civil War was often taken out on those blamed for that war, the former slaves whose desire for freedom was a motivating factor in the war. Consequently, the plantations on which they were raised were often safe havens from the violence enacted against members of their race who tried a new way of life after their emancipation. Thus, many freed slaves stayed put (with the devil they knew) after the Civil War, and were still living on plantations like the Connellys' at the turn of the century.

Subsisting on their former plantation with white as well as black tenants, the Connellys continue to feel obligated to provide for the progeny of former slave property. Times are hard on Connelly land, but on Christmas Eve, when Duffy, a black man who works for the Connellys, appears to request meat for his large family (in Act I, Scene 2), Will asks him how much he needs and Mrs. Connelly tells Will to give Duffy "whatever's there.... He has to eat."[6] Although Mrs. Connelly does not, until Will pushes the issue later in the play (in Act II, Scene 2), overtly acknowledge the probable familial connection between her children and the mulattoes on the farm, she is apparently aware of it, and as the current matriarch of the place, she accepts responsibility for the offspring, black as well as white, of the deceased patriarch and his brother. Later in the play, weeping over the corpse of Bob Connelly, Duffy will call him "Pappy." Duffy, then, is a mulatto first cousin of Will, Evelyn, and Geraldine. Ironically, while in the earlier scene Mrs. Connelly seems to feel obligated to feed Duffy's family, Bob is resentful of Duffy's presumptuous request for meat and, perhaps even more ironic, he is enraged by Duffy's numerous children: "*Raising his pudgy fist aloft, his voice full of sudden anger,*" he says that in an earlier time, he would "step in and give Duffy's old woman the worst beating she'd ever had. I'd say, get out of that bed, you old whelp, and get to work, you and your puppies. And then I'd fall in on Duffy, and then I'd stretch three or four of his young'uns out cold." Note here that Bob is talking about killing his own grandchildren, though he apparently only thinks of these children as additional mouths to feed. No one is sufficiently outraged by such a violent outburst. Evelyn merely responds with the reminder, "It's not slave days any more, Uncle Bob." It may not be "slave days any more," but it is the Jim Crow South, and race relations do not seem to have changed very much in the turn-of-the-century South of this play. Yet the necessity of change is the truth Patsy tries to bring to the rest of the people on this dying plantation: the Connellys must change—both the way they farm and their continued belief in a caste system—or they will die out.

Act I, Scene 1

The House of Connelly opens on Christmas Eve with a set description that emphasizes the current barren condition of the property: "A rail fence grown up with an unkempt hedgerow of dead fennel weeds, poke stalks, and sassafras bushes crosses the foreground, rotten and spraddled with a disused stile near the center.... The decaying stalks and weeded hedge exude the rot of death into the air, and the mood of a heavy loneliness is over the earth." In the background, Green describes "three stack-poles, now empty and gaunt, stand[ing] up like black gallows trees," presumably alluding to the three crosses on Calvary. The audience wonders who has or who will be sacrificed on this land—and whether that sacrifice will result in redemption and resurrection or a wasted loss that emphasizes the nihilism of the Modern world in which World War I veteran Paul Green wrote.

The play's action begins with the entrance of Big Sis and Big Sue. In spite of the indication that they are "*old*," they are described in direct contrast to the barren landscape: "*sexual and fertile.... The mark of ancient strength and procreation still remains in their protuberant breasts and bulging hips*." In spite of these references to their sexuality, Green describes their faces as "*smooth and hairless as a baby's*," a simile that Will Connelly will shortly echo when he refers to them as "[h]elpless as children." The twenty-first century audience, new to the play but not to the Mammy stereotype in literature of that era, might be more likely to note how Green's physical description of the two black women anticipates Scarlett O'Hara's Mammy in *Gone with the Wind*, published five years after the first production of this play. Yet anyone who knows of *The House of Connelly*'s original ending would note the irony of imagery suggesting the childlike innocence of these two women.

In their opening conversation, Big Sis and Big Sue provide one suggestion of who has already been sacrificed on the "Calvary" in the background setting as they recall "nigger Purvis," "Poor Purvis," the black son of General Connelly, who did nothing to stop the execution of his own son. Indeed, as Will says more directly in the climactic scene much later in the play, General Connelly pronounced the sentence for whatever crime Purvis committed, which is, significantly, not identified. The point is not Purvis's crime but the crime against Purvis. Reminding his family of this event from their past, Will notes in Act II, Scene 2, "There in the robes of justice he [General/Judge Connelly, Will's father] rose up, the power of the law." Then Will asks, "Why didn't he strip himself and say, 'I am the guilty one, judge me?'" But the General has never been held accountable for his crimes. Rather, we learn very early in the play that he is still mourned and revered by his widow, who holds him up to their children as a model of gentility—even though she indicates during the play that she knew of his sexual relations with women other than herself. General Connelly is also praised by his brother, Robert (Uncle Bob), who, in Act I's second scene, during the family's Christmas Eve dinner, offers a toast to the memory of his deceased brother, praising General Connelly's Civil War heroism. Robert Connelly, Will later reveals, also enjoyed sexual relations with black women and also participated in the convicting and sentencing of Purvis, his nephew, the general's son and Will's half-brother. The other Connelly family members have turned their own faces from these men's behavior and the procreative consequences, just as General Connelly turned away when Purvis was being taken to his death. However, Will Connelly is apparently haunted by the knowledge of his father's sins and the memory of his half-brother's suffering.

In spite of the tone of the black sisters' recollection of poor Purvis's fate, Big Sue also recalls General Connelly in fond terms: "He were good though—in the heart. The Old Man were good. When us wanted *meat* he give it to us" (emphasis added). This first reference to meat in the play reflects the fear of going hungry in the not too distant future, which likely inspires the tension between these women and Patsy Tate. Right after this example of the "Old Man's goodness"—in providing meat, now apparently rare—Big Sue observes "that new tenant gal." Whereas the two black women have expressed regret over the loss of General Connelly even as they recognize his sinfulness and acknowledge his mistreatment of Purvis, they are not so generously understanding or forgiving in their response to this white tenant woman. They seem to admire jovially the General's sexual shenanigans, implicitly contrasting his apparent prowess with his white son's suggested impotence as they find Will's poor marksmanship hilarious. Will can't hit the doves he shoots at, which at this point they merely mock as reflective of his unmanliness, in contrast to his father. In the next scene, when Duffy asks for meat for his family and we discover how little meat there is, the missed birds take on more serious connotations. Coming home empty-handed from hunting could mean no meat on the Connelly dinner table some time soon. For now, given that Will tells Patsy, "let them be" after she takes his gun and shoots down two birds, one might wonder what meat, if any, Patsy and her family will have for dinner. She did, however, note exactly where they fell, so there is no stopping her from picking them up after he is gone, and one can imagine the practical Patsy doing just that.

Backtracking to the scene before Will enters, the two black women are in a surprisingly good humor, even about their former master, until their attention turns to Patsy, and their tone turns bitter, not playfully mocking, as they talk about her. They notice Patsy watching them "snatching firewood" out of an old fence rather than going a little farther to find wood that does not destroy property. "Poor white trash," Big Sue says. Big Sis concurs, her words reflecting perhaps the hostility between these black women and poor whites like Patsy: "Like all of 'em—scrouging and a-gouging—Poor white trash!" Then Big Sue elaborates, suggesting the source of this animosity in the unfairness of the upward mobility of poor whites in contrast to poor blacks: "Pushing up in the world—reaching and a-grabbing at the high place of the quality and the cover over *our* heads!" (emphasis added). They clearly perceive Patsy's ambition as a threat to them or their way of life. One might consider freed slaves' experiences of poor whites, the class from which "patterollers" and overseers were often drawn, to understand the context of their distrust.

When Patsy enters, chastising Big Sis and Big Sue for the fence destruction that might allow hogs to escape, except for her contrasting youth, the description of her is in terms more comparable to the description of Big Sis and Big Sue than to the subsequent scene's description of the two Connelly sisters. Patsy is "full-figured," suggesting the procreative capability of her body, as was noted in the physical description of Big Sis and Big Sue. And as the two black sisters are paradoxically procreative and ultimately destructive, Patsy's countenance is both "pink"-cheeked and "hard"-eyed. Life has not been easy for this ambitious young woman, whose father seems to accept his station, content to "die the other fellow's man," while his daughter longs for more and assures her father that he will "have [his] own farm yet." Finding little to laugh at around her, Patsy is disconcerted by these giggling women. She wonders why they are "feeling good," but they only respond by changing their demeanor in mocking willingness to suit her: "Us feel bad, feel lonesome then with nobody to love us." When they offer to tell Patsy's fortune, the young woman brightens a bit but is still wary. Big Sue responds "*mammy-like*," according to the stage directions, to put Patsy at ease as they prepare to prophesy her future husband. But when Will Connelly arrives on the scene just after they chant, "Who she gonna keep warm with in bed?," their demeanor becomes menacing: "Death gwine take her church-wedding bound," Big Sue says, and Big Sis adds threateningly, "Mought's well take your mind off'n him," before they both recompose themselves into a subservient, seemingly guileless pose for Will.

The audience may be disturbed by Green's depiction of lazy black women intimidating a fellow tenant woman while playing the fool for the white patron they do not admire. Was Paul Green contributing to the stereotype so often found in traditional plantation literature? Clearly Green did not share Will Connelly's patronizing view of these women as childish. Indeed, in the original ending of the play, Big Sis and Big Sue are certainly not so harmless as Will believes. Their destruction of the dilapidated fence in this first scene of the play can therefore be interpreted, not as being too lazy to go farther to get wood but rather as reflecting their contempt for the place where their people were once enslaved. They may also feel a sense of entitlement to this property as former slaves who worked for so long for no wages. Moreover, as (possibly) illegitimate Connelly offspring who are not recognized by their white relations, they will certainly not inherit the land they have worked, while their white relations, who *will* inherit, benefited from that work. The current sterility of this former plantation might be traced back to such injustice. The present state of the Connelly place reminds the audience of the consequences of slavery and miscegenation in William Faulkner's *Absalom, Absalom!* The pending end of the Connelly line may also remind readers of Faulkner's Compson family in *The Sound and the Fury*. In contrast to Faulkner's Dilsey and Roskus, who may be the only reason the Compsons have lasted so long as they have, Big Sis and Big Sue may not be so devoted to their white family. They are more succubi than nurturers. And as Green's drama plays out, one comes to understand how such monsters (Big Sis, Big Sue, Faulkner's violent Joe Christmas in *Light in August*) evolved from the sins of the (white) father against his (black) children and their mothers and against all the enslaved people.

Green began work on *The House of Connelly* in 1927, and it was first produced on stage in 1931, less than two years after *The Sound and the Fury* (1929) was published, five years before *Absalom, Absalom!* (1936). Green's play is comparable to both of these Southern literary classics by Green's contemporary: Patsy Tate receives the same kind of condemnation for her untraditional behavior as Caddy Compson; Will Connelly suffers the white male guilt and related sense of impotence that Faulkner explores with Quentin Compson and Henry Sutpen. As noted previously, before Will enters the scene, Big Sis and Big Sue mock him, implicitly for his lack of prowess. Patsy then shows Will up, taking his gun and killing two birds with two shots. When Will exits, humiliated and shaken, Patsy's father repeats the black women's point of contrast between Will and General Connelly, and also like the two black women, Jesse Tate acknowledges that the older Mr. Connelly was a sinful man. Mr. Tate believes that Will's weakness is a consequence of that sinfulness: "I reckon the world evens up somehow," he says, pondering the difference between father and son: "He's no more like his father than black is white," an interesting analogy given the racial dynamics here. The consequences of General Connelly's behavior, as Faulkner would expand upon in *Absalom, Absalom!*'s "house of Sutpen," is ultimately the sterility around them all, not just in the land, but in the three unmarried, childless Connelly heirs. Tate, in fact, notes that "a man old as [Will] ought to have a family and be making things go along," but what he says next anticipates the conflict that will arise when Will's family perceives Will's interest in Tate's daughter: "there's nobody good enough for him, and never will be, according to his mother—and sisters. Never was anybody good enough for a Connelly."

Act I, Scene 2

The stage directions for Act I, Scene 2 emphasize the sterility of the *house* of Connelly. This second scene takes place inside the house, and the indoor setting is described as

> *pretentious but now falling to decay. The walls ... yellowed and cracked, and the portraits of the Connelly ancestors hang mouldering in their frames.... The furniture is falling to pieces, the brass candlesticks on the walls and the useless chandelier hanging over the table are cankered and green. The ivory wood trimmings are peeling off ... and great gaping cracks run leeringly across the plastered ceiling. The dead Connellys erect in their frames wait for the end.*

One recalls how the signs of the procreative past of the black women was emphasized in stark *contrast* to the decaying outdoors in the previous scene's stage directions. In this second scene, the two white women are described in terms similar to rather than different from their surroundings: "*The two surviving daughters of Connelly Hall [are] late-middle-aged spinsters.... GERALDINE is tall and somewhat prim, with pallid aristocratic features; EVELYN is a few years younger and less austere.*" Paralleling the stage directions, which contrast the past "*hospitality*" with the present sense of isolation, as the Connelly sisters set the table for Christmas Eve dinner, Evelyn talks wistfully of past Christmases, with orchestras and dancing, again reminiscent of the tone of plantation fiction in which the white aristocracy laments the post Civil War losses of their wealth and status.

The sisters call the family to Christmas Eve dinner, and the audience is introduced to Uncle Bob and his sister-in-law, Mrs. Connelly, mother of Will, Geraldine, and Evelyn. The scene reveals Robert Connelly, once an attorney and a legislator, as well as a Civil War veteran, to be a drunk who punctuates his pontificating with pretentious Latin and Greek phrases one minute, but then might make a sound suggestion. For example, in this scene he advises Will to "[t]urn the farm over to old man Tate and his gal, Patsy." Before Mrs. Connelly enters, her daughters imply in their references to their mother that she is an invalid, and upon her entry, dressed in mourning black, Green describes her as "*near Uncle Bob's age but appear[ing] much older, a shell of a woman, but with something of the dignity and strength of the matriarch yet remaining to her. Her head dodders with palsy, but her mouth is firm, even stern at times, and her eyes are alert. She is crippled and walks with the aid of a crutch.*" Mrs. Connelly's infirmity, like Uncle Bob's dissipation, reflects the decline of the Old South that they both represent. Indeed, writing about his original inspiration for this play, Green tells the story of a woman he met once when he was "poking around ... in Eastern North Carolina" and came across "an old house on a hill ... a fine old house but decrepit. And there was an old lady ... [with] a terrible sore on her face" (*Plough* 42). Green decided the sore was "symbolic of the sick region," and as he left, he determined to "write a play about the old South" (*Plough* 43).

After the surviving Connellys gather around the dinner table, Duffy enters with his plea for meat to feed his numerous children. He underscores a significant point of contrast with the implicit barrenness of the white Connellys. Their lack of progeny is due to their devotion to a past tradition that insists upon appropriate class matches, which have evidently not yet happened for any of the three younger Connellys. As Mrs. Connelly prays before dinner, "Teach us to *hold sacred* ... the memory of our fathers" (emphasis added), one might be reminded of Jesse Tate's earlier reference to the Connellys' sense of superiority. In Scene Two, then, when Evelyn opens a gift, "*a flashy toilet set*," that Will has brought to her from Sid Shepherd, a neighbor who has apparently prospered financially in recent years, she remarks upon the "nice" gesture but criticizes the man's "taste." In the previously quoted passage from the stage directions, one might note that Green has distinguished Evelyn from her sister ("*a few years younger and less austere*"). Sid Shepherd's evident interest in Evelyn suggests that there is still hope for her to have a family, as there is for Will, too. As a man, Will has more time to have a family, but here and elsewhere when Sid Shepherd is mentioned, his interest in Evelyn is not taken seriously. He may have money now, as both Will and Uncle Bob point out, but Mr. Shepherd is still not of their class, so Evelyn does not seem inclined to encourage his interest in her. Will, in contrast, does say "Sid Shepherd's all right—if he did grow up from poor-white folks," reflecting his own lesser concern about social station. But just as Evelyn rejects the idea of this man as a suitor, so too would she not consider Patsy Tate to be suitable for Will, though Will is soon clearly attracted to Patsy, and their affair becomes the source of the play's central conflict as Mrs. Connelly and her daughters disapprove of Patsy and instead push Will in the direction of Virginia Buchanan.

When Will rejects the notion of Virginia Buchanan as a potential wife (saying, "Virginia Buchanan—and I beg her pardon—never had a thought but for blue blood and the Confederate flag and something she think her folks did on the battlefields of Virginia"), Uncle Bob intuits what has possibly attracted his attention away from Virginia and reports that he saw his nephew with Patsy earlier that day—"Sweet, ain't she?" he asks, but Will ignores him. As if on cue, Patsy and the other festive "serenaders" are then heard outside. The playwright here brings into this more traditional, more fully developed of his plays an element of the folk culture of the many one-act plays of his Carolina Playmakers days. The youthful tenants who arrive at the door are dressed for carnival-like festivities, and they sing folk songs rather than Christmas carols. At one point Patsy is cajoled into *"a sort of crude gipsy dance."*

When Mrs. Connelly, who left the table when tempers flared during dinner, rejoins the family to find out what the ruckus is, Uncle Bob disrupts the festivities with an incongruous soberly intoned toast to his deceased brother:

> To the blessed memory of a gallant soldier and a great gentleman—the dead husband of our dear lady and erstwhile master of this house.... To him we drink who in the face of death mounted the Stars and Bars above the rampart of the enemy; the first at Manassas, last at Appomattox, furthest at Gettysburg—to thee we lift this cup—(*As if addressing a living person.*) To thee, suh, jurist, patriot, soldier, citizen, we drink—General William Hampton Connelly of Connelly Hall.... Ah, we shall not look upon his like again.... And may this, thy son, wear the mantle of his father, with profit and renown. May he become conscious of the name he bears.

Addressing his deceased brother with the formal "thee" and referring to "thy son," Uncle Bob sounds like he is praying to a god, which bodes ill for "the son of [this] god" in this largely Christian region, especially given the three crosses imagery in the backdrop of the first scene. The audience may therefore wonder if it is Will Connelly who is to be sacrificed in the course of the play, as foreshadowed in the opening imagery. Certainly his mother and sisters will ask Will to sacrifice his own desire for Patsy and marry Virginia—but in order to bring back the past, not to start a new way of life.

Uncle Bob abruptly ends his apostrophic Christmas Eve toast and sits down, overwhelmed and worn out, it seems, by his memory of the past, particularly in light of the much reduced circumstances of their present. The revelers again take their cue, this time to leave. Patsy invites the Connellys to join the merrymaking, but only Uncle Bob expresses interest, and it is clearly the younger Connellys who are being invited. Before departing, Patsy asks, "Why're you all so—so solemn?" It's Christmas, and ironically those who can recall a prosperous past are burdened while those who have never known prosperity are enjoying the spirit of the season. Drawn to this much brighter tone, Will, after his mother and sisters go upstairs, makes up an excuse to go outside, refusing to confirm his uncle's guess that he is going to catch up with the other young people. While his sister may be reticent to enjoy Sid Shepherd's attentions, Will is apparently not so put off by the class difference between himself and these revelers.

Act I, Scene 3

After the two winter scenes, Scene 3 of Act I takes place in spring—significant once Patsy steps on stage and the romance between the two young leads begins. But first, once again the scene opens with Big Sis and Big Sue serving as a chorus to let the audience in on what is going on: Virginia Buchanan has arrived for a visit, and in spite of their poverty the Connellys are hosting a ball to set the stage for a courtship between Will and Virginia. Once again too, the black women both mock Will and express hostility toward Patsy, who has been invited to the festivities. First, they express what a wasted effort "Miss Virginia" is making: "Sashay her tail off, do her no good with Mr. Will," who is clearly interested in Patsy Tate. From Virginia, whom they call "a queen," they turn their attention to Patsy, "that huzzy bitch," expressing again their animosity toward the latter, as well as revealing that they see no threat in the notion of Virginia joining the family. In that eventuality, status quo would likely continue, whereas Patsy, they seem to realize, would bring change, and change is frightening to them.

After setting the stage, so to speak, for the events to follow, the black women exit, and Will and Virginia enter. Their conversation is most revealing. Telling Will how much she has enjoyed his garden, Virginia notes that she "read *Lorna Doone* half through" sitting out there the previous day. Later in the conversation, she mentions another literary romance, Longfellow's "Excelsior," and in between she quotes poetry by Coleridge, a third romantic writer, thus establishing her as a foil for uneducated and pragmatic Patsy. It appears that Virginia is amenable to the Connelly women's plans for her and Will. But Will is in a contrary mood: "I'm not very well up on poetry and the moon" and "I'm not a true Southern gentleman," he tells his guest. Virginia remarks upon Will's angst: "You seem worried all the time," an interesting echo of Patsy's parting remark on the solemnity of the Connellys at the end of Scene Two. Virginia's observation is also provocative in that if she is interested in romantic novels and poetry, one can see the appeal to her of the disconsolate Will: his brooding moroseness fits the characterization of the romantic hero in the tradition of Byron and Werther. Virginia might do well to remember that these romantic heroes' ideals were often tragically consequential to the women who loved them. Virginia should feel fortunate that Will is so clearly uninterested in her, and the audience should be concerned about Patsy as we recognize Will's attention in her direction.

Virginia may actually detect the source of Will's lack of interest, for she turns their talk to Patsy, asking Will who "that country girl" is and then, when Will reports that Patsy Tate lives there and Virginia discerns that this means Patsy is "a tenant girl," the visitor wonders aloud, "What's she doing at the dance?" Virginia is evidently as much a snob as Evelyn and Geraldine. Turning the conversation back to her own interests in the romantic "stage" around them, Virginia notes the ladies' beautiful white dresses and then, shortly after, Patsy's "outlandish dress," which we soon learn is black. Thus, Green employs the stark contrast that so many romantic writers use to set up young female rivals as dark and light foils for each other. But again like Patsy, Virginia asks Will about making improvements on the property. Her ideas, like the Connelly women's, hearken back to the past: "Do you ever think of getting [the old race track] in shape again?" she asks him. Echoing Will's sisters, Virginia is recalling parties from the Connellys' halcyon days, but here Will directs her attention to what his family has tried to mask since her arrival, asking bluntly, "Does this place look like there's any money to spend on race tracks, Miss Virginia?"

Will's formality prompts Virginia to remind him that they go back a long way, that her father once courted "Cousin Geraldine" and to recount to Will that her mother used to "tease [her father] about the aristocratic Miss Geraldine." Mrs. Buchanan's teasing might be perceived to imply that Mr. Buchanan ultimately married beneath his own class, and one may wonder then if his less aristocratic wife might be a factor in the Buchanans' continued prosperity. Patsy could also bring new vitality to the Connelly family, but this tenant farmer's daughter is not considered suitable for Will by anyone but Uncle Bob, who recognizes early on that she and her father's work ethic would be beneficial to the place, perhaps as assuredly as—and more permanently than, as Will later argues—Virginia's actual wealth. Annoyed by Virginia's reminder of his family's reputation, Will lashes out: "your little moon shines on the tombstones. That's the poetry of it.... And all the great past that comes to dust.... The great Connellys are all dead. The fools and the weak are left alive." But Virginia is not cowed by Will's morbid candor, and she chastises her host before going inside to dance with another man: "Silly boy, you're not the only one that's had bitter thoughts."

Left to stew in his annoyance and perhaps humiliation, Will lashes out next at Uncle Bob, who has enticed Patsy to follow him outside with the promise that he has something to tell her. Clearly, one motive is to seduce her: "You've put new life in this old hulk," Uncle Bob tells Patsy, followed shortly by "Forty-odd years ago I sot here on a bench and made love to another gal.... Still going strong—unh?" he asks, but Patsy resists his advances and Bob chastises her for leading him on and assaults her, prompting Will to emerge from the shadows to come to her defense. Bob does not think the usually meek Will poses much of a threat, and when he realizes differently, he turns his condemning mockery upon his nephew, repeating the earlier suggestions from Big Sis and Big Sue and also Jesse Tate that Will isn't much of a man: "Hah, you happen to knock an old man down and it turns your stomach. Now take her, see'f there's any blood in you, sissy!" On the one hand, Uncle Bob here recalls a past when the plantation women were his and his brother's for the "*taking*," but on the other, one might wonder if Uncle Bob has lured Patsy out here to bait Will into action. As noted, he has previously pointed out to Will the value of the Tates' work ethic; later he will urge Will to marry Patsy.

Will is unsettled by his own violent eruption, and Patsy takes advantage of his distress, first complimenting him and then offering to help him with the farm. Will expresses his doubts: "I'm numbed, cold, empty. I've stayed in this old house too long." Patsy replies, "you must live—live! Wipe away all these gullies and broomstraw patches—and waste—waste" (190). As she talks, the two black sisters creep in from the shadows to listen. Patsy asserts that she loves Will, and Will believes her and responds, "Yes! Out of this death and darkness—into the light!" Will and Patsy exit, and the two black women, reminiscent of Shakespeare's Weird Sisters (indeed, Green had referred to them as "*sibyl-like*" in the opening scene description), chant in echoes of Will's last remarks:

BIG SIS. This darkness, bless God!
BIG SUE. That light, hallelujah!
BIG SIS. Ehp, her don't know that Connelly blood her messing with mebbe.... Water can turn to blood.

Again the sisters' tone toward Patsy is threatening. Once the drama plays out to its tragic end, the audience realizes that Patsy was coming between Big Sis and Big Sue and their plans for the (white) Connellys. One explanation of their motivation to kill Patsy, besides her being a threat to the status quo, is because the possibility of her marrying Will is a threat to the sterility of the Connelly heirs. This theory suggests that the murder is at least in part an act of vengeance against Will's father for his crimes against his former slaves. Killing Patsy before she can produce a new generation of Connellys cuts off the Connelly bloodline.

A still from Act I, Scene 3, performed by the ReGroup Theatre, 2014, featuring Selena C. Dukes as Big Sue, Anthony Laciura as Uncle Bob Connelly, and Sheila Simmons as Big Sis (photography by Mikiodo Media, courtesy of ReGroup Theatre Company, Inc.).

Uncle Bob's behavior toward the two black sisters when he steps back into the scene after Will and Patsy exit suggests the possibility that he (and thus perhaps, too, his brother, General Connelly) has had sexual relations with one or both of these women. Uncle Bob calls to the moon with a mocking "Cock-a-doodle-do! He *"flaps his harms up and down ... [and] cuts a goatish step before them."* Big Sis and Big Sue join in with Uncle Bob, and the three dance together, the women becoming more bawdy in their movements, Uncle Bob soon lying down on the ground *"and peering at their huge flashing legs and joggling bodies."* He prays blasphemously, "Our Father who art in heaven, hallowed be the sin which now doth flourish forth to salvation," referring perhaps to what he would be up to with Patsy if he were Will and hoping perhaps for a new generation of Connellys after Will's presumed affair. He then turns back to the women dancing above him and encourages them to continue: "Ecch, set to it, old cows, we'll all go home at milking time." He claps for a bit longer and then, foreshadowing his death in the next act, *"he stretches himself out flat on the ground,"* presumably passed out from drink.

Act II, Scene 1

Act II opens *"a few days later"* with Will preparing to meet with the tenant farmers about how things are going to change on the plantation. Essie, a mulatto servant, remarks knowingly, it seems, upon Will's hearty appetite and his having missed saying goodbye to Virginia, whom his sisters have gone with to the train station. Green's use of "mulatto" as a signifier suggests that Essie could be a daughter of General Connelly or Uncle Bob and at any rate reminds the reader of miscegenation on the place.[7]

Uncle Bob enters just before the tenant farmers arrive. Like Essie, he notes Will's renewed energy "under the sign of Venus." There is evident animosity between the two men. It is no wonder: they have fought over a woman, and Will was clearly the victor. And now Will is finally taking over his father's role without consulting his uncle about his plans.

Jesse Tate leads the tenant farmers into the dining room. The black men stand behind the white men as they gather, revealing the racial hierarchy among men doing the same kind of work. Green describes the "*scurvy, nondescript crew*" in terms reminiscent of plantation fiction, reflecting perhaps what Will and Uncle Bob see when they look at these men:

> *Three or four ancient ebony darkies with faces wizened as aged monkeys beneath their flaring white hair stand respectfully near the table.... There are a few middle-aged white men with ragged moustaches and beards, thin gaunt fellows, hollow-eyed and hopeless, their faces burnt like leather by the wind and sun. Some of the Negroes are middle-aged, tattered and mournful like* DUFFY. *And the others are younger, more greasy and merry, with bold gleaming eyes that roll in their sockets as they take in the splendor of the room.*

Two other details in the stage directions are worth noting: "*Most of the Negroes are mulattoes,*" which reminds us that many are likely related to Will, half-brothers and cousins of his, perhaps. Also, as the men enter and greet Will, some do so "*with little or no respect in their voices,*" suggesting that they share the black sisters' opinion of him.

While Will "*looks around ... nervously,*" Uncle Bob "*goes around among them,*" with personal greetings to the men, all of whom he seems to know by name. When he remarks to one man that he is "[m]ore like your mammy every day," the stage directions indicate "*giggling and snickering*" from the group. One wonders again about possible innuendo here: how well does Uncle Bob know this man's mother? Could Uncle Bob be his father? Uncle Bob asks another, a white man, about his wife, who has apparently been unwell; Uncle Bob suggests she take Pluto water or swamp root for her stomach—is she perhaps pregnant—could the baby be Uncle Bob's? Does he still engage in sexual relations with women who work his family's land? White as well as black? (Recall his efforts to seduce Patsy.) Green leaves all of this ambiguous. It is not something that would be discussed openly. However, as Green did with the men's interactions with Will, he also included a hint as to how some of these men feel about Uncle Bob in the stage directions: as Uncle Bob approaches two of the oldest men in the group, "*They rise and shake his hand with a dignity that hides all their knowledge of his sins and meannesses.*"

Uncle Bob wraps up his greetings and exits, leaving the men to Will's business, though he does heckle a bit from offstage as Will explains his plans for the changes that will take place for all who work on his land, including calling their attention to his own change of clothes and the fact that this is likely the first time they have seen him wearing work clothes. Will tries vainly to get the men to speak to him freely about what has gone wrong on the land, but the men are hesitant to respond honestly to their employer, so Will answers himself: "We ain't been working. Year after year we've lived from hand to mouth. We've let the soil wash away, bushes grow up in the fields, half-plowed the land." He concludes by taking responsibility for this behavior and its effect upon the land: "I've been a damn poor manager." He then continues, "Maybe I been too good to you, good and no backbone. But that's not all the trouble. We sleep too much on this place." One of the black men denies this *"as if in alarm,"* and the audience is reminded of why Big Sis and Big Sue see Patsy as a threat when she commented on their laziness in pulling wood from a fence rather than going into the woods for firewood.

Will notes that the current state of affairs on Connelly land has resulted in younger men leaving home to work in factories: "They couldn't stand this dead place.... We got no life here," he says, recalling the description of the setting in the play's opening stage notes. He wraps up as he began, noting that when he says that "Everybody's got to work," he also means "I'm going to work." He then adds what is likely that which Big Sis and Big Sue are so worried about: "And everybody works will get rations. I'm going to start a commissary to furnish you. And I'll see who deserves to eat *and who don't*" (emphasis added). The implication is that there will be no more obligatory handouts. By planning to work alongside the men who farm his family's land, Will can lay down the burden of the past (guilt) and not feel so compelled to make up for his father's and uncle's sins against these men and their women. When prompted by Will to respond (as the rest seem reluctant to speak), Tate assures Will that there is nothing wrong with the land that cannot be addressed by this plan, and a couple of the black men there assure Will that they "don't mind work." Will informs them that he will make his rounds to make sure "everybody that works gets his rations" but also that any who "don't, don't eat, and he don't stay on this land." The threatening tone reminds us that he is still (or is finally) the patriarch here—some things have not changed.

The men exit and Mrs. Connelly enters with Uncle Bob. When Will comes back in from seeing his workers out, she chastises her son for his failure in his duty to the family during Virginia's visit. It isn't too late, Mrs. Connelly notes, since Virginia has invited Will to go to visit her during the fall hunting season. But Will tells his mother he will be harvesting then. He tries to explain that *he* must save the Connelly land, not marry Virginia and use her money to save it: "Because I'd go on being the same kind of weakling I've always been. It would be her money that did everything, not me. I want to do something." But Mrs. Connelly does not have faith in her son's abilities, and she suspects what—or rather who—is motivating him, cruelly pointing out to him that he may not want to use Virginia's money, but he is still not the one masterminding the new work plan.

Mrs. Connelly believes (or at least suggests to Will) that Patsy has "set out in cold blood to become mistress of Connelly Hall." Such blind hypocrisy is completely missed by both of them as they duel toward their respective corners of suspicion. She encourages Will to woo the wealthy Virginia for the sake of the Connelly land, but finds it whorish of Patsy to seduce Will for the same land. The audience sees what Will quickly begins losing sight of: Patsy may not have money to invest in their land, but she clearly brings the backbone and work ethic that Will has noted missing among the workers and his family, especially himself. Will tries to insist to his mother that Patsy loves him, but realizing that his certainty means he has been intimate with Patsy, Mrs. Connelly tells Will, "It proves everything I've said if she's gone as far as that.... Only selfishness and greed would make a woman violate herself." And to prove her point she adds, "Big Sis and Big Sue have heard [Patsy] scheming in the fields with her father."

Will should take note that Big Sis and Big Sue have thus proven to be the menace that Patsy suspected them to be (but that he dismissed), but he does not remark upon Mrs. Connelly's revelation that the two black women have been spying on Patsy and reporting to the Connelly women. It is not long before the audience recognizes that, rather than becoming suspicious of these conspiring women, Will is instead troubled by Mrs. Connelly's suspicions about Patsy, which have penetrated the fragile new self-confidence Patsy's interest in him had previously inspired. So when Patsy enters after Mrs. Connelly exits, Will questions the motives behind her latest plans and her love. Patsy does not know what to make of his harsh, changed tone or his attempts to fondle her, more Uncle Bob–like than she is comfortable with in the middle of the Connelly house. She pushes him away, and he exits. Left alone, she looks around at the Connelly portraits and asserts, "you don't scare me a bit, not a bit.... All right, me against you, all of you," but then Geraldine enters and Patsy sheepishly exits.

When Will reenters, he orders Essie to bring him whiskey, and his subsequent teasing exchange with the young black woman may remind the audience of his uncle's behavior toward the two black sisters at the end of the first act. Will asks about Essie's relationship with the preacher/tenant farmer Alec and suggests that she will "be wearing his ring pretty soon." Probably alluding to his mother's suggestions of Patsy's intentions for him, he adds, "You want a ring, you know. Yea, all do," but Essie responds, "I'd rather have a lavaliere," adding soon after, "You buy me one, Mr. Will," perhaps suggesting her willingness to be involved in some kind of committed relationship to Will, who of course cannot ever be engaged to her, as a ring would imply. Lavalieres, as symbols of pre-engagement in some social circles, might symbolize for Essie a kind of plaçage relationship, which would be one means of moving up on the limited social ladder for people of her race.[8] Of course, one might wonder what advantages Essie thinks she will enjoy, given how poor the Connellys now are. Still, she teases Will with vague suggestions of what she would do for a lavaliere from Will rather than an engagement ring from her black suitor. Will is, for the moment at least, disgusted by another woman willing to trade herself to him, and he sends her away, but in the next scene, as will be discussed, Essie is conspicuously "*playing with the ornament around her neck.*" Is it from the beau Will teased her about? Uncle Bob perhaps? Or did Will succumb to the temptation Essie offered, maybe in part, to push Patsy away? Once again, Green keeps the (probable) sexual activity offstage and somewhat ambiguous.

Act II, Scene 2

Act II, Scene 2 takes place "*several months later,*" and in his description of the scene's opening setting, Green notes that the Connelly sisters look "*more houseworn and tired than before,*" and "Uncle Bob's *face is more puffy and haggard than ever.*" We find out too that Will is "not the same Will any more," and it is not a positive improvement as a result of participating in the land revitalization as he said he would. Rather, he has taken to drinking in town, leaving Patsy to lead the work force without him. As the other family members remark upon Will's staying out the whole previous night, they observe Patsy working in the field alongside the farmers. It is also revealed during the family's conversation at the beginning of this scene that Essie has just been discharged, for reasons related to Will's recent behavior, it seems. She comes in to say good-bye and, "*sniggering and smirking, with the faintest touch of familiar spitefulness,*" flaunts a new necklace, as noted previously. There is a slight possibility that it is Uncle Bob who bought her the necklace. Uncle Bob quite openly remarks upon her departure, "The lowest rung of iniquity has been reached and we hang pendulous there.... Yea, to round out the story I should have got me idiot daughters and cried woe." Could he be suggesting that a child resulting from his union with Essie, possibly his own daughter or niece, or of Will's union with a woman who may be his sister or first cousin would be mentally impaired? But the giver of the necklace, if there was one—Essie claims to have bought it for herself "from Sears-Roebuck"—is left ambiguous. Perhaps both men gave her money, which emphasizes how Will is now behaving more like his father and uncle. In any case, the Connelly women have fired Essie. When Will returns and calls for Essie to bring him his dinner, Uncle Bob reports that "Lavalieres have cost her her job," and Will responds, "So Mother turned her off—anh? Well, we'll see," suggesting that he might assert his patriarchal rights as ruler of this household and rehire Essie—for his further enjoyment—again behaving like his father and uncle. Though the specifics are left ambiguous, the implications are pretty clear.

Seeing that Will is home, Patsy has come to talk with him, and once again we learn that Big Sis and Big Sue have been telling tales on Patsy, this time to Patsy's father, who is coming to see Will. Will sees Patsy's warning about her father as further evidence that Patsy has set a trap for him, but Patsy just wants to continue on with their plans, even though she knows what he has been up to—at least in town, if not with Essie. They accuse each other of duplicitous behavior—Patsy telling Will his big talk with the farmers was all boast with no follow through and Will accusing Patsy of seducing him to get his land. The audience recognizes that Patsy is the more honest of the two, for she does not lie to Will when he observes that she "love[s] the place and not [him]": "why shouldn't I? [she responds.] It's a sight more honest. The land never tricks you. Do your part and she'll do hers.... I did my part by you and what did you do? Tried to make a—whore out of me."

Patsy is a pragmatist. She believes they should marry, not because she has been ruined or disgraced, but for the sake of the "ruined" land. She also accepts that Will cannot love her because he does not trust her, and she admits that she has difficulty separating her feelings for Will from her love of the land. This play is no traditional romance, for the wronged woman is no innocent victim. Patsy admits honestly, "I set a trap to catch you and it's caught me," but begs Will to understand her motivation:

> All my people have wanted land, wanted land above everything. When we moved here I saw all this great plantation going to ruin. I wanted it, wanted to make something out of it. I loved you because you stood for all I wanted. I had never cared for any man. I saw you liked me and I went on and on with you.... All that mattered was the land, growing crops, great crops, that's all I could think of. And so—I went to you—that night—led you on.

Patsy exits, asserting her belief that once Will sees a crop unlike any he's seen before, he will come to get her, believing too, perhaps, that in her absence he will have to run things and so will be forced to change his behavior.

Uncle Bob enters, teasing Will about his recent prowess among the women in town and warning Will about Patsy's father looking for him. The audience might smile at Will's response—"Let him shoot, I can shoot too"—recalling from the play's opening scene that he is actually not a good shot, except that his words could also reflect a subconscious death wish. Perhaps Bob recognizes Will's defeatist attitude. He does seem, in this scene, to be more intuitive than one might give him credit for through most of the play. Here, he encourages Will to marry Patsy, defending Patsy against Will's accusations about Patsy's manipulations. Foreshadowing Patsy's death in the original ending to the play, Will admits to Uncle Bob that sometimes he wants to strangle her in order to get her out of his head. It is interesting to note here that earlier in this scene, Uncle Bob had commented upon Will's vain efforts to quench his thirst, recognizing that Will is hung over. And perhaps Uncle Bob recognizes that Will's drinking, as well as his sexual exploits in town and at Connelly Hall, show that he is turning into his uncle. Advising Will to marry Patsy may be as much an effort to help Will as to save the Connelly name and land. In what follows in this scene, Will certainly does not return Uncle Bob's commiseration in kind. Rather than displaying empathy, with his father out of reach, Will turns his wrath upon his uncle.

When Mrs. Connelly enters, having called the family together to confront Will about his recent behavior, Will takes charge of the "intervention" (as it might be considered in today's parlance), readily admitting that he is "as low as Uncle Bob." Again recalling the Calvary imagery of the play's opening scene, Will calls to the "Lamb of God [to] cut my throat and ... bury me apart with Uncle Bob." Horrifying his sisters, he points out too that his actions "[f]ollow in the steps of my fathers ... a nigger wench in every fence-jamb." In a preaching mode, he continues, "Sister and brother," the significance of which terms suddenly seems to strike him, so he calls out to "Duffy and Harvey and Jenny ... let's set our flesh and blood at the table—a row of mulattoes. 'Brother, sister, forgive us.' ... And Essie, be seated close at my right. If there's horror we brought it into the world.... Skip to my Lou, ... / If you can't get a white gal / A nigger'll do." He concludes, "Give me a torch and I'll burn up the cursed old House of Connelly." Uncle Bob, distressed to have his sins broadcast before Mrs. Connelly, whom he idolizes, begs for "mercy," but Will takes one more shot at his uncle, who is getting the brunt of the rage Will is really feeling toward himself and his deceased father. When Uncle Bob asks if that is all he has to say, Will responds, "Not all till you see the niggers thumbing their noses as you pass, you strutting barren peacock!" Mrs. Connelly intervenes then, and Will concludes, "I'm done now.... Patsy's right, we're all—rotten."

Mrs. Connelly asks Uncle Bob if he would like to respond, reaching out kindly to her brother-in-law. Receiving no response, she speaks herself, on "sacrifice and forgiveness and human love," and is finally sympathetically human (though one might say also too forgiving of her late husband):

> Your father ... was a great man. He had a hard struggle, over himself and the world around him. He failed, struggled again, his face set upward.... No whining—no tears—of weakness. Now I'm old—weak... But do I weep? No.... Does Uncle Bob? What do you know of his life? ... Go to him, if you are a man, and beg his forgiveness.... You've said things too hard for him.

Will believes his mother is refusing to see the truth, but she responds, "I have faced it for forty years, Will. And yet I did my duty to your father." Uncle Bob tries to assert that Will is lying, but Will turns on him again: "It's God's truth, and she knows it. You and your nigger young'uns!" This is when Will reminds Uncle Bob that he and his brother, Will's father, stood by when Purvis was executed, neither ever admitting their guilt toward their black children, these children's mothers, and in General Connelly's case, betraying his wife. Will believes the Connellys' current state of affairs is "pay[ment] for their sins." So rather than try to save the House of Connelly, Will announces his intent to leave.

Devastated by having his sins aired publicly, particularly in front of Mrs. Connelly, Uncle Bob exits, and subsequently a shot sounds from off stage. The two black sisters enter in great distress, followed by Jesse Tate and Duffy carrying Bob's lifeless body, Duffy urgently telling Will, "He done it hisself.... I ain't to blame." The black man, so often scapegoated to take the blame for a crime, is also in this case distraught for having "prayed sump'n bad happen" to this man since his role in Purvis's hanging. Significantly, Duffy here calls Uncle Bob "Pappy," his rage at Uncle Bob thus paralleling Will's rage at his own father. With Uncle Bob's death, it seems, the sacrifice foreshadowed in the opening scene's Calvary-like backdrop has come to pass. Paul Green referred to Uncle Bob's suicide in an interview with Billy E. Barnes as "wiping out the Old South" (Barnes 42).

Winifred L. Dusenbury, in probably the earliest scholarly discussion of this play, views Uncle Bob's suicide as a sacrifice of his own life for Will's: "he does not shoot himself in despair, but with recognition that his action might save Will," that "the last of the Connellys can be saved," but not with Will threatening to leave. Therefore, Uncle Bob "gives his own life to prevent Will's running away" (152): Uncle Bob knows Will won't leave his mother and sisters with no man in the house with them. And to encourage a next generation, before he left the room to take his life outside, Uncle Bob tells Will again to "Marry Patsy.... The proud days are ended"—presumably now that Will has exposed the sins of the Connelly men. Dusenbury's analysis of *The House of Connelly* is in her book *The Theme of Loneliness in American Drama*, copyright 1960, a year before the original ending of the play was ever published, which would explain the critic's unqualified perception of a "happy conclusion," which Dusenbury contrasts with the endings to Tennessee Williams's *The Glass Menagerie* and Lillian Hellman's *Another Part of the Forest*, both of which also have at their center "young men of fallen Southern families," neither of whom, "escapes from the loneliness of failure and of being the last of the males of his line." But Dusenbury's point of contrast in "the successful union [of] Will and Patsy" (154) in the play's final scene does not hold when one considers the original Scene 3 that Paul Green wrote, in which Uncle Bob's death is only the first of two sacrifices to follow the earlier sacrifice of Purvis. The final violent murder of Patsy, which follows Uncle Bob's suicide in the original final scene, does not suggest the possibility of redemption.

Act II, Scene 3

Several months pass between Scenes 2 and 3 of Act II. It is Christmas Eve again in the play's final scene, bringing the drama full circle, the sense of which is also reflected in the scene opening with Big Sis and Big Sue in their chorus role. Their conversation fills us in on what has transpired between scenes: in particular, Mrs. Connelly has died, removing the major voice of opposition to Will's interest in Patsy. He has just married Patsy, in fact, and he is bringing her home to live in the House of Connelly. The original final scene of the play opens with Big Sue trying to read the future in the glowing coals of the fireplace; she shows her sister a "long black coffin," saying, "woe to the transgressor." They still see Patsy as a villain, a threat to the House of Connelly, "And only you and me to build it back," Big Sis tells Big Sue, a line that seems to suggest that their motive for the murder of Patsy is to preserve rather than end the Connelly line, but as will be noted, such an idea is paradoxical, as the latest generation of Connellys (at least those bearing the name Connelly) would, without Patsy, probably be the last.

In this scene's opening conversation (in both versions), Big Sis and Big Sue also let the audience know that, unbeknownst to Will, his sisters are preparing to move out of the House of Connelly, intending to be gone before he arrives with his bride. The white sisters believe that Patsy will taint their home, and they will not live under the same roof with her. Apparently, they do not agree with Uncle Bob that "the proud days are ended." It is likely Will's "revelation" was no more a surprise to them than it was to their mother (beyond the shock of hearing it spoken aloud), and we have seen how the Connelly women have not applied their standards for behavior to their own family. They still cannot see that, given the past behavior of Uncle Bob and General Connelly (and the recent behavior of Will), it is not Patsy who is the tainted one in this pair of lovers. Aristocracy or wealth are still the only standards that determine the appropriateness of a match for a Connelly, even after all that has been exposed about them.

Geraldine and Evelyn enter, and the playwright indicates that their appearance between scenes has further degenerated: "*The feminine spring and go that once enlivened* EVELYN's *form are almost gone.* GERALDINE's *hair is much grayer and the primness and gentility of her nature have grown more hard and bitter.*" As they talk about Will bringing Patsy to live here, Geraldine uses a broom to reach up and pull a Confederate flag down so that it is fully visible—though oddly thereby blocking the portrait of General Connelly. She offers no explanation. Is she hoping to remind Will that the South is more important than his issues with their father? Is she hiding the sight of the new Mrs. Connelly from their father? The audience is left to ponder the significance of this gesture. Whatever the intent, Will seems to understand, for when he notices it later, he mutters to himself (in both versions of the final scene), "Geraldine." It is interesting that earlier in the play it was Evelyn, not Geraldine, who kept bringing up past Christmases—from better days. Now, Geraldine seems to be directing attention to the past. And just as the sisters were doing when they first appeared on stage, Christmas Eve a year before, Geraldine begins setting the table, until Evelyn calls her attention to the person she is setting it for. They look around at what they are leaving behind, which they believe Patsy is likely to sell in order to have money to invest in the farm, and Geraldine notes that since they will not be here to see the place change, they will always remember Connelly Hall as it was.

Soon after the white sisters' departure, the black sisters exit behind them, still muttering about Patsy to each other—still calling her "white trash" and threatening, "Soon she gwine rest in peace." Although the revised final scene follows almost the same plot line, some of this kind of threatening dialogue between the two black women is cut from the first half of the revised scene. For example, when Big Sis and Big Sue enter to tell Geraldine and Evelyn that Duffy has the carriage ready for them,[9] in the original version of this scene, the black women reference the possibility that the Connelly women will return:

BIG SIS. Maybe you be coming back.
BIG SUE. Yeah, maybe you get the message to come back.
EVELYN. Message?
GERALDINE. No, we're never coming back.... Give Mr. Will our message—we're gone—and stay
   here till they come. Keep the fire going.
BIG SIS. Oh yes'm, us meet 'em stylish.
BIG SUE. Oh yes'm, us take care of everything for you.
BIG SIS. Till you come again.

These references to some message the white women will get is left out of the revised scene.

Will and Patsy enter, Will, in contrast to his sisters' decline, described as "*stronger and more manly in his bearing than before.*" Others from the farm gather to welcome the bride and groom, and the tone, for a while, is hopeful, as it was when Will gathered the tenant farmers in his house earlier in the play, as well as merry, reminiscent of when the serenading tenant workers visited on Christmas Eve the year before. Will credits Patsy with the tenant farmers' good cheer: "they won't go hungry any more with you here." His explanation reminds the audience of the various earlier allusions to eating (and not eating) in the play. The subsequent dialogue between Will and Patsy fills us in on what else we have missed in the months since Uncle Bob's death. Patsy left to work in a factory, believing (correctly) that Will would eventually come to get her. "I was like a person dead away from the farm and you. Now I am alive again," she tells her new husband. The play maintains its untraditional, non-romantic marriage plot: the newlyweds talk about "learn[ing] to love" each other, but they are hopeful about the future until Will calls for his sisters and is told by Sis and Sue that they have moved out.

In the original ending to the play, before Will learns of his sisters' departure, Mr. Tate enters to give his blessings, and Will leaves father and daughter for a few moments to look for his sisters. In Will's absence, Mr. Tate tells his daughter to "be a good girl [and] a good wife" and asks her to come cook for him every now and then, and she reveals her plans to move him and her brothers into the Connelly house. This brief section of the final scene is cut from the revised ending, perhaps to shorten the play or maybe to avoid the suggestion that there was some truth to Big Sis and Big Sue's reports of Patsy plotting with her father. In any case, this exchange reminds us of Green's complex character development—again, atypical of a more romantic plot.

In both endings to the play, Will responds to the news of his sisters' departure by declaring his intent to convince them to come back home. In the original ending that Green wrote, when Will steps out of the room to retrieve the letter Big Sis tells him his sisters left for him, Big Sis and Big Sue approach Patsy menacingly.[10] Big Sue acknowledges in both endings, "you the Missus now" (a statement in the original ending, as a question in the revision), but when Patsy smiles and responds, "I'll try to be a good one," Sis says she can't hear Patsy over "[t]he dead folks cr[ying] so loud down in the gyarden" (in both versions). Unnerved, Patsy asserts her new authority, ordering Sis to go make a fire in the kitchen. Will reenters, blaming himself for making his family unhappy, and determines to go right after Evelyn and Geraldine, which Big Sis and Big Sue encourage him to do. Patsy tries to convince him that

> To grow and live and be something in this world, you've got to be cruel—you've got to push other things aside.... The dead and the proud have to give way to us—to us the living.... We have our life to live and we'll fight for it to the end.... Right now we have to decide it, Will. Let them go. It's our life or theirs. It can't be both—they knew it. That's why they went away.

From this point on, the two endings distinguish themselves dramatically.

Act II, Scene 3, the original ending

In Green's original ending, Patsy's words, followed by Big Sis and Big Sue's descriptions of the Connelly sisters' tearful departure, anger Will, and "*He flings* PATSY *away from him*" and exits. Patsy tries to regain her composure by repeating her order to Big Sis to build a fire in the kitchen, but Big Sis instead starts building the fire where they are, in the dining room, and the sisters start chanting about hearing voices from the family graveyard outside, including Mrs. Connelly, calling for "a sacrifice." Patsy tries once more to assert herself as "Missus here now ... *grab[bing] up the poker from the hearth*," but Big Sis takes it from her, and the two black women (referred to as "*demonic creatures*" in the stage directions here) approach, again threateningly, this time pouncing on Patsy. Patsy cries out for Will, but he has chosen the old Connellys over the newest one—and any future generation—so her screams are unheard. He has gone to retrieve his sisters.

The black sisters smother Patsy with a tow sack that Big Sue carries (only in the original ending), perhaps planning to raid the house of valuables, which Will would believe his sisters had taken with them. An intent to steal from the Connellys would undermine the notion of their loyalty to the family, and neither should one read their murder of Patsy as indicative of some kind of loyalty to Mrs. Connelly's disapproval of this marriage. They do refer to "Poor Missus" who "can't rest," before they kill Patsy, but when Patsy stops struggling and lies dead at their feet, the women are finally able to look at her "*piteously*": "Purty like a baby," Big Sue observes; "Poor little scrushed lily," says Big Sis. Big Sis also compares Patsy to a snake, but here too the connotation is not entirely negative: perhaps the reference is to the temptation Patsy offered to see what the New South would be like with a new kind of mistress, who did not hand out food out of some sense of obligation but did know how to grow it.

Big Sue also remarks provocatively that Patsy is now "safe ... where Purvis is," and Big Sis adds, "And with the Old Man and the Missus and Uncle Bob. They all sleep safe now." So, although early in the scene Big Sis had suggested that she and Big Sue had to "build ... back" the House of Connelly, one might still wonder if what Patsy threatened was not the Connelly family but the possibility of witnessing the *end* to this family. Patsy, newlywed to Will Connelly, heir to what's left of the Connelly plantation, would have likely allowed for a new generation of the family that once enslaved these women. Could that perhaps be what they resented, even more so than the hard work that is now required of anyone living on this land to be provided with food? By killing Patsy, are they actually intending to ensure the fall of the House of Connelly? Back at the opening scene of the play, upon hearing Will's gunfire, the two women "*point their forefingers in the direction of the sound and make a falling-hammer motion with their thumbs, after which they break into a peal of laughter.*" This gesture and laughter foreshadow their ultimate vengeance upon the Connellys through the murder of Patsy and thus likely ending the possibility of another generation of (legitimate) Connellys.

Paul Green himself might have argued against such an interpretation of these women's motive for killing Patsy, for in one response to questions about this play, he called the two black women "protectors of the old way of life and enemies to the new" (Avery 504). Whatever Green's intent, the hypothesis that the murder is motivated by vengeance is more credible than the idea that the women would sacrifice themselves for the sake of the family that once enslaved them. The consequences of killing a white woman in the South will be their own execution. Would they give up their lives for the sake of the Connellys?

While he was working on the *The House of Connelly*, Green's June 17, 1928, diary entry includes the following: "Patsy should die at end — error in judgement and in deed aesthetically demands it, but —."[11] That's all there is to this entry, no further explanation as to whose "error in judgement and in deed," but Green was not so far removed in time from the tradition of writers killing off female characters who engage in sexual activity outside of marriage, often as much to punish the male protagonist as the fallen woman. One wonders if Green is suggesting that Patsy's manipulative and unchaste behavior cannot be rewarded. He did refuse to include sex scenes in the screenplays he wrote and voiced his disgruntlement when they were added by other writers who contributed to a script after him, all of which suggests his somewhat Puritanical attitude about sex, at least in the arts. But whatever his intention, Patsy's "bad" behavior in this play certainly pales by comparison to the sexual skeletons in the Connelly closet, and at least she ultimately admits to what she has done. The playwright himself may have been punishing Patsy (consciously or not), but she is likely to be viewed by the audience as another victim of the Connelly men.

Also troubling is Green's stated perception of the two black women carrying out a death sentence upon a woman who threatened the (false) purity of a white aristocratic family. Consider the consequences to two black women for killing a white woman in the early twentieth-century South: Big Sis and Big Sue would inevitably follow in the footsteps of Purvis to be executed themselves. Recall that these women's animosity toward Patsy seems to be related to their own fear of change, knowing as they did how change in the South often resulted in more violence against people of their race. So why would they risk their own lives for the Connellys, except perhaps as a sacrifice for others of their race? Such is more believable than two black women sacrificing themselves for a white family that once enslaved them.

Whatever the playwright's intent regarding the black women's motivation for killing the new, untraditional Mrs. Connelly, the death of Patsy effectively kills off the Connelly line, and bringing about the end of that line is the most convincing reason that Big Sis and Big Sue would risk their own necks. We have already witnessed Will's fragility, from the very beginning of the play. A man so distressed by the "cruelty" he perceives in having driven his sisters from their home that he runs after them, leaving his bride on their wedding night, is likely to be irreparably devastated by discovering that his desertion of his new wife resulted in her death. If one agrees with Winifred Dusenbury's suggestion that "Uncle Bob is a representation of what Will is likely to become" (152), one might even wonder if, in contrast to Dusenbury's hopeful reading of Uncle Bob's suicide as sacrificing himself to force Will to stay and make something of the Connelly land,[12] the Connelly heir will follow his uncle's example, either in a slow suicide by drink or with a suicidal gunshot. This possible future scenario is supported by Will's earlier heavy drinking in response to his mother's distrust of Patsy and lack of faith in his abilities. Uncle Bob, of course, drinks heavily throughout the play, and he never married, never fathered legitimate heirs. The death of Patsy will likely mean that Will's future will be comparable to his uncle's. Harold Clurman rightfully interprets the two women's role in Green's play, then, as "Fates, *Macbeth*-fashion" (47), but Clurman, as well as the other two Group Theatre directors, Lee Strasberg and Cheryl Crawford, preferred a more hopeful ending. According to Helen Krich Chinoy in *The Group Theatre: Passion, Politics, and Performance in the Depression Era*, "they wanted Patsy's lower-class, earthy vitality and love to rejuvenate the weak Connelly heir and the land" (50).

Act II, Scene 3, the revised ending

According to Crawford, during the rehearsal for the first production of this play in 1931, the three directors "became concerned about the way the play ended" (55). In a 1975 letter to Crawford, Green associates the "communist ideology" of the members of the Group Theatre with their dissatisfaction with the ending he had originally written for this play (Avery 680). Such an ending, Crawford suggests in her writing about the play, "said that the South had no future. But we didn't believe that," and she didn't believe Green did either (55). Crawford and her colleagues wanted poor white Patsy to be successful in breaking through class barriers, to be rewarded for her willingness to work hard for land that Will Connelly had inherited rather than earned. Chinoy reports that "the three directors invited Green to join them in Brookfield in order to convince him to rewrite the ending." She continues, "Although Green saw his drama as tragic, he believed a positive ending could be justified historically. Giving in to their pressure, even thinking that their point of view might be interesting to explore, he wrote the alternate close the directors requested" (50).

In the new ending, Big Sis and Big Sue cower when Patsy grabs up the poker after they do not follow her orders while Will is out of the room looking for his sisters. Then, after

Patsy's speech to Will about making a choice, "our life or theirs," instead of leaving to go after his sisters, Will "cling[s] to her ... almost like a child." The two black women look on, resignedly, until Patsy looks up and *"quietly"* orders them back to the kitchen. When they resist, Will asserts, "Miss Patsy's my wife now ... you do what she tells you!" This ending seems to address Clurman's summary of how the play should end: "The resistance of the black servants was something that had to be overcome through Patsy's firmness rather than yielded to through a memory of the function of Fates in literary drama" (48). One might perceive a kind of racism reflected in this statement, which suggests that Clurman supports a white/black hierarchy, even as he rejects a social hierarchy within the white race. Here one might note that none of the Group Theatre actors was black. Note, too, the line Green adds a bit earlier in the scene as Big Sis and Big Sue wait for Will and Patsy's entrance: in both versions, Big Sue says *"bitterly"* of Patsy, "she got everything. Got Mr. Will, got the House of Connelly, got all," to which Big Sis responds, "Ain't got you and me." In the original Big Sue agrees, "You done said," but in the revised version, Big Sue says instead, "Not yet nohow." Big Sue knows that Patsy's rise in station is not a possibility for everyone on the place. As Will notes at the end of the revised scene, Big Sis and Big Sue will be expected to work for the new Mrs. Connelly in the same capacity as they worked for the previous one. Green describes the two black women at the end of the revised final scene as being "in a sort of hopeless resignation," while the white tenants outside "are heard playing and singing" in celebration, according to Big Sue's comment earlier, of one of their own moving up in the world.

The revised ending in which Patsy (now Mrs. Will Connelly) triumphantly (and without violent consequence to herself) asserts herself to the black women as their new mistress of the House of Connelly may not be as powerful as the tragic ending, with its more ambiguous, less proletariat-friendly final scene, but Green ultimately defended the verisimilitude of this performed ending in a letter to Doris Falk, "a teacher and scholar of modern drama":

> The tragic ending I once planned for *The House of Connelly* was cued out of life.... God knows this sort of killing off of good and new movements below the Mason and Dixon line has occurred often enough.... The ending I used [the revised ending for the Group Theatre] was also cued out of life. Often in the [S]outh new ways have taken hold and produced new and better conditions [Avery 504].

In an essay about the Group Theatre, for example, he noted, "More than once I had seen a so-called poor-white family burst its way up and into the new South and become the Dukes of Duke University or the Reynoldses of the Reynolds Tobacco Company and Wake Forest College" (*Plough* 49). Similarly, in another letter about rewriting the ending, Green told Crawford that "actually in life the new South (Patsy Tate represented this) rose dynamically out of and above the ruined life (Will Connelly and the Connelly family stood for this). So let life take over, I agreed" (Avery 680–81). One sees, therefore, that Green was ultimately not entirely unhappy with the ending the Group Theatre elected to perform. But he still wrote in his essay on the Group Theatre that his original ending was "for me preferable" (*Plough* 49).

Two Endings, One Theme: The Need for Change

Provocatively, the review of the Group Theatre's production of the play in the *Saturday Review of Literature* concludes, "The play, and not the ending is the thing" ("New Plays"

202). To those aware that the play has two endings, this point of praise resonates beyond the reviewer's intent. The reviewer is praising *The House of Connelly*, as it was performed (Patsy still standing in the end), for not having a clear winner and loser in the conflict between the Old and New South in the play. One might apply the reviewer's line about the ending to the argument that with either ending, the central theme of the play, the necessity for change, remains consistent. The hope for the South after the Civil War and Reconstruction did lie in people's willingness to change. Those who resist change would eventually die out: Uncle Bob and Mrs. Connelly die before the end of the play; the two Connelly sisters are childless spinsters. In the original ending, the Connelly line ends because of resistance to Patsy's efforts to make changes.

Like Eve, Patsy tempts her lover to practice his free *will* (hence, perhaps, Green's choice of name for his male protagonist) and embrace change with her even if it means having to let go of the false Eden of the Old South. In one version of the play, Will forsakes "Eve" to go after his sisters, and in his absence Eve/Patsy dies—but so shall Will, eventually, for without his wife, he is likely to leave no progeny when he dies—at least no progeny that will continue the Connelly name (even if he follows in the tradition of his uncle and father and engages in sexual relations with black women). As noted before, it is unlikely that Will would ever remarry after Patsy's death in the original version. In the version performed by the Group Theatre, Will, like Milton's Adam, decides that he is better off with Eve, no matter where they must go when they are kicked out of Eden. Adam and Eve, because they elect to stay together, are not just the first man and woman but also the first parents. They eventually die, as they were warned would happen, but their progeny would live indefinitely in the numerous generations to come after them. Mr. and Mrs. Will Connelly, the revised ending implies, will bring new generations into the House of Connelly. Thus, the message regarding the connection between change and survival is consistent regardless of which way the play ends.

But for thirty years, the original ending remained obscure—until John Gassner, "longtime play reader for the Theatre Guild, anthologist, and teacher of drama," learned that the play had another ending besides the one he'd read in Green's *The House of Connelly and Other Plays* (published in 1931 with the ending written for the Group Theatre).[13] Gassner wrote to Green to ask about the other ending he had heard about, and Green sent him a copy of "the script used at the University of Iowa in July 1939 (the first production of the play with the original tragic ending)." Gassner responded that he found the original ending "tremendously effective" (Avery 534), as had the audience of that 1939 production: Green wrote in his diary on July 22, 1939, "Mabie announced the group would play the play with two endings. Audience to vote its preference. Almost unanimous for original ending which had just been produced for first time" (Diary). Gassner published both endings when he included the play in his 1961 anthology *Best American Plays: Supplementary Volume, 1918–1953*. Then when he edited Green's *Five Plays of the South* (1963), he included the tragic ending *rather than* the originally performed and previously published ending.

In his chapter on the Group Theatre, Gerald Rabkin discusses the play only considering its revised ending (citing its original 1931 publication in *The House of Connelly and Other Plays*). Rabkin's book, *Drama and Commitment: Politics in the American Theatre of the Thirties*, was published in 1964, and therefore, Rabkin very likely did not know that another ending of the play existed when he submitted his manuscript to his publisher. Rabkin contrasts Green's vision with that of preeminent Southern playwright Tennessee Williams:

Now were Tennessee Williams proceeding with the play, the old aristocracy, however decadent, would still be preferable to the new forces of change. After all, is there not virtue in the posture of gallantry? Surely there could be no rapprochement between the old order and the new....

The premise that resides at the heart of *House of Connelly* is that decadence is a fact of institutions and classes; in the work of Tennessee Williams corruption is existential. The first premise [Green's] makes the concept of social action meaningful, the second [Williams's] declares all social gestures essentially irrelevant [85].

Perhaps Rabkin is thinking here of such Williams plays as *A Streetcar Named Desire* (he does not refer specifically to any particular Williams play in his comments). Blanche Dubois does ultimately emerge as "prefer[able]" to the brutish Stanley Kowalski who defeats and destroys her. But one might actually *compare* the fate of Green's poor white Patsy Tate in the play's original ending to Chance Wayne's eminent violent end as the curtains close on Williams's *Sweet Bird of Youth*. Like Patsy, Chance dares to aspire toward the Big House, via his relationship with the daughter of an aristocrat, and in that case Williams is certainly not suggesting that Boss Finley's Old South politics are preferable to Chance Wayne's ambitions, but these ambitions are thwarted, and Chance Wayne is presumably castrated, if not killed.

Writing about *The House of Connelly* based only on the performed ending, Rabkin (like Dusenbury's 1960 reading, mentioned previously) perceives at least a less fatalistic vision from Green, in contrast to Williams. Interviewing Paul Green in 1975, over a decade after the publication of editions featuring the original ending of the play, Jacquelyn Hall asked the playwright about changing the ending and then restoring the original. She tells Green about Rabkin's idea that the more positive ending first performed and published distinguishes him from Williams, suggesting as it does that Green "see[s] corruption as a function of institutions and classes and therefore potentially changeable, whereas Williams sees it as existential or irrational, something like original sin." (This distinction may be another reason for the reviewers' praise of the play's freshness in spite of familiar themes.) Thus, when Green changed the play back to its original ending, "with the tenant girl being smothered," Hall asks, "does that put you back in Williams's camp?" (Hall 11). Green responds at some length, beginning by criticizing himself for not revising the whole play when he revised the ending for the Group Theatre:

> That is very interesting. You structure something, let's say a play or a novel (or a house), you structure it and pretty soon you see the intent, which is the direction in which it is going. So, when the Group Theatre persuaded me to come out with a "yea saying" ending then to do the right work of art, I should have gone back to the very first and intended it so. It was a spurious and a sinful thing to do, to turn loose a half-baked product. So, if I was going to go part hog, I should have gone whole hog, but I didn't have time and I was persuaded. You know how it is [Hall 11–12].

Green goes on to suggest again that either ending could be true to life:

> I could see that ... life provided either way.... Actually out of the old South came the Reynoldses and the Cones and the John Sprunt Hill, Watts Hill; all of that came out of the old South. They set up their own factories.... "Why send this stuff to Massachusetts to be processed? We'll build our own factories right here, and we've got our own cheap labor and we won't have any unions." So, they set up and then this union business, out of which came the Burlington Dynamite Case and also the Gastonia rioting and so on [Hall 12].[14]

Ultimately, Green seems to be suggesting in these musings, violence would follow regardless of how the play ended—if not against Patsy by those beneath her station who felt threatened by the changes she was bringing to their world (as Green himself seems to have interpreted Big Sis and Big Sue's motivations), still violence would—did—ensue as the South changed from agricultural to industrial. The audience might note that while Patsy waited for Will to accept her vision for a new kind of plantation, she worked in a factory. And work conditions at many factories during this period—not unlike the worst times of slavery—resulted in strikes and violence, as Green recalled to his interviewer.

"So, it [the ending of his play] can go either way," Green concluded, but then added, "but you can't let life control your art form." He explains, "I am inclined to think that the richest civilization is one in which the art form controls the life action, or helps to control it" (Hall 12). Here he implies that the effect of the play upon an audience is ultimately what is most important: "A story is an arrangement on the part of the artist of the actions and the raw material of life shaped into an art form in which the participants, the readers, the spectators, the auditors, they can come and see that and get enriched. It's part of the process of humanistic growth" (Hall 13). Like his reviewer, quoted earlier, he too seems to be agreeing with Hamlet's assertion that "the play's the thing" that will reveal the truth about humanity's transgressions and encourage better behavior in the audience after witnessing the consequences of bad behavior on stage. Will Paul Green's play, with either or both endings, inspire recognition of culpability and insight about how to effect change in a positive way? As shown here, both endings reflect the necessity of change if the South is to survive. But as Green reminds us with his reference to the industrialization that arose during this same period, not all change is necessarily good—indeed, not all change is really change at all. The same greed that resisted efforts to end slavery in the South prompted factories that supported a different kind of slavery, a kind of indentured servitude, throughout all industrial areas of the U.S.

In the revised ending that the Group Theatre performed, I wonder, too, how different is the new Mrs. Connelly, from the old? Notice how in the "triumphant" ending Patsy immediately asserts her authority over the two black women, commanding them to "Build a fire in the stove and bring in some wood" as soon as Will steps out of the room to call for his sisters. When they do not follow her instructions, she asserts, "I'm missus here now and you'll do what I say," and in the revision, Patsy picks up a poker from the hearth, *"furiously, eyes blazing"*—not to defend herself but to threaten them. Although this revised ending, in which Will stays with Patsy instead of leaving her alone with the two black women to go after his sisters, provides hope for the continuation of the Connelly family line through the children this couple will have, still one may find that Patsy's behavior toward these black women does not bode well for change. Her first command echoes the last order the Connelly sisters gave, to "Keep the fire going." So perhaps (as Tennessee Williams often did when coerced to provide a different ending when his plays were adapted for film), Green did not change the play as much as the directors thought he did. He suggests even in his revised, supposedly more hopeful ending that the Old Southern way of life is so ingrained that it can corrupt this representative of a New South just that easily: as soon as Patsy Tate becomes Mrs. Connelly, the mistress of the house, she begins to transform into a "proper" Mrs. Connelly, the matriarch of an Old Southern family in that she asserts her dominance over the black women who work in *her* kitchen.

From Stage to Screen: *Carolina*

WYNN: What was your evaluation of the final film which Reginald Berkeley did from your [play]?
GREEN: Oh, it was pitiful, I thought. Rather pitiful. They called it *Carolina* [Wynn].

On July 1, 1926, Paul Green wrote to his wife from the MacDowell writers' colony in New Hampshire, and in this letter, he talks unenthusiastically about what he is currently writing:

> I am on my second play now, wrote twenty pages today.... It is not much, a good idea, but my poor head is slow to dig up plots. What I have in mind is a Southern family—the Connellys, related to the Connellys in Virginia, one of whom has been a supreme court justice—worn down and out, two prim and dried up old maids, a younger brother, about 35, living in the old Connelly country home, going to ruins, the brother trying to farm and making no success, the tenants taking everything to run them, gradually going down and down. This brother falls in love with a tenant farm girl, the very vital blood his effete strain needs. But his pride and the pride of his sisters keeps [*sic*] his better impulses down. The girl loves him. A liaison is established. The father of the girl, a very devout patriarchal man, drives her from home when he finds she is going to have a baby. She has begged the Connelly man to marry her. He has wanted to, hesitated, sunk his best nature below his pride and let matters go on. The girl terrified and distraught over her condition—having been raised up on the Bible and the law of Moses—staggers off and makes her way to town and in a boarding house gives birth to her child and tries to kill herself. The news is brought to the Connelly home, the young man in a passion of contrition stands up before his family and curses himself and them, owns up that the little baby boy is his and he has loved her all the time and rushes away to see her. To his surprise the old maids want the girl brought in, having concluded that their way of living is empty. He marries the girl, and the whole plot has something to live for in the child. I am not sure that is the way I shall end it [Avery 129–30].

One can easily see all the elements from this original concept that the playwright changed as he developed this melodramatic plot into the tragic drama he originally wrote. Even when he revised the ending to suit the Group Theatre's desire for a triumphant end for Patsy, he did not, as he had indicated he would in this letter, allow the Connelly sisters to have a change of heart about their brother's mistress-turned-wife. Such is the stuff of melodrama, and, unfortunately, such is the kind of melodramatic ending the screenwriter would create when adapting this play into a movie.

In her book chapter "Dixie on Film," Karen L. Cox traces the popularity of the Old South in 1920s-era films, adding, "Even when a film was set in the contemporary South, the region was still portrayed as being ensconced in the [Old South] past" (85–86). In the next decade, the decade that saw the adaptation of Green's *The House of Connelly* into the film *Carolina*, certainly a film depicting Southerners "still wedded to their antebellum past and liv[ing] in isolation from the changes that were taking place outside of the region," the number of movies about the South increased, according to Cox, "but the story of the region remained the same" (86–87).[15] The loose adaptation of Green's play participates in the romanticizing of the Old South much more so than does *The House of Connelly*. In *The Celluloid South: Hollywood and the Southern Myth*, Edward D.C. Campbell, Jr. notes that although "[t]he romantic films of the Old South during the 1930s did not, of course, ameliorate the low spirits of numerous viewers" (it was, after all, the time of the Great Depression), their "contribution towards such an end was evident," and movies that "praised the fortitude of the South furnished a popular example of recovery from adversity." Therefore, Campbell concludes, "movies of the 30s verified legend and presented an apologia more sweeping than any the section had constructed." He correctly reminds us, however, that these movies' "stories were simply the studios' reflection of popular tastes which craved films of romance and flair" (140). *Carolina* was released on February 2, 1934[16]; according to Cox, 1935 "was an especially productive year for Hollywood films about the South, which became some of the most successful the industry produced that year" (87–88).

In early October 1933, Paul Green wrote his wife from Hollywood, California, where he was consulting on *Carolina*. He was only a consultant, not the screenwriter for this movie. Laurence Avery explains that Green remained in Hollywood into November, revising the script, mainly for "verisimilitude" in the details regarding, for example, what tobacco looks like (222). What is particularly odd about the role of tobacco in the movie is the suggestion in the film that it would be a novelty to bring tobacco to this plantation, as though tobacco was not already a common crop in North Carolina. The tobacco plot reflects how little the movie's screenwriter knew about Paul Green's North Carolina. Green himself took issue with the ending's "suggest[ion] that the [Connelly] family has gone into tobacco *manufacturing*, whereas the burden of the story is the regeneration of the farm itself" (qtd. in Avery 223; emphasis added).[17] According to Avery, the playwright was also not happy with the changed title, although given how different the movie is from the play, he may have eventually been glad of the different title, which would not attract Green aficionados' attention unless they were looking specifically for the film.

While Green had not been very enamored with the film industry since working in it as a screenwriter, watching his own work adapted into this particular movie may have prompted a section of an essay he wrote called "The Theatre and the Screen." This essay was originally published (under a different title) in the *New York Times* in early February 1934, just a couple of weeks after *Carolina*'s January 24 premiere in Charlotte, North Carolina, which Green had been coerced into attending.[18] In this essay, Green talks about the potential cultural value of movies, their powerful and affective influence, which he believed was not being exploited enough. He recalls from his childhood his first viewing of an animated picture, which had so impressed him, and then his experience as a young man watching the film *The Birth of a Nation* in 1915. He had been struck by the strong reaction to D.W. Griffith's film, which he observed from the theatre audience. While he concedes that the audience he sat among watching this pro–Old South classic (before it was a classic, of course) was Southern, he also notes the international popularity of this movie.[19] Given the white supremacist perspective in the film, its appeal to audiences of the day is disturbing but all the more attests to the power of film, which Green remarks upon in an interview with James R. Spence: "I've never seen art used with more fervent result than that picture.... He had a great picture, unfortunately" (qtd. in Spence 158).[20] Perhaps to make his point with a more positive film example than this racist movie, Green turns in his essay from the popularity of *The Birth of a Nation* to the "loud appreciation" of audiences for Charlie Chaplin (*Drama* 87).

Recognizing the potential of such a medium to reach the broadest audience a playwright could imagine, Green was excited by the opportunity to work as a Hollywood screenwriter, but his enthusiasm about this well-paying job did not last through the first picture he worked on, *Cabin in the Cotton*, in which Bette Davis would play the first of her many roles as a vixen. Green writes in "The Theatre and the Screen," "For several weeks I labored on a script, *trying to measure up in some degree to the camera which was to express the story I had to tell*"

(*Drama* 88; emphasis added). One can see Green's high regard for film reflected in this statement. He certainly was no literary snob about movies. But Green often complained about how his first screenplay was changed by others—cheapened, he felt, so that it was unrecognizable to him, beyond "a bit here, a bit there" (*Drama* 89). He was disgusted by the wasted time on his part and by the explanation from another screenwriter: "this is a business out here, not an art" (*Drama* 90). He saw this attitude as resulting in a missed opportunity to reach the masses—literate and illiterate—with art through movies.

Although Green does not mention *Carolina* specifically in "The Theatre and the Screen," the essay's initial publication at the same time as the movie's release is likely not coincidental. One can imagine what Green must have been thinking after viewing *Carolina*. It is certainly no wonder that seeing how his own play was adapted into a film full of false, at worst, and over-used, at best, clichés prompted him to write about his disappointment with the whole industry. And his summary complaint is right on target with the problem with *Carolina* (and so many other movies):

> The studios have a product to sell to the masses of the world, and in order to sell to everybody they think they must strike a common denominator of general illiteracy and bad taste. Their pictures are standardized by what they consider to be the intelligence quotient of the majority of people in the small villages and crossroad places. For there are many times more 14-year-old minds in the world than 30-year-old minds—and a dime is a dime no matter whose it is, and the best picture from the Hollywood point of view is the picture that attracts the most dimes [*Drama* 91].

Hollywood's perception of the South, as it is depicted on screen in *Carolina*, is simplistic and offensive, to say the least. And yet, the *New York Times* reviewer would praise the movie: "There is no straining for effect, no extravagantly depicted incidents, which one might expect in the filming of such a tale, and the settings are realistic" (Mordaunt Hall 17). Characterizing it as "realistic" probably reflects the reviewer's ignorance about the actual (rather than Hollywood) South, given such anachronisms as black field hands being called to a turn-of-the-century Southern home to serenade the family and their visitor, Virginia Buchanan, as they might have been summoned to do in the time of slavery. They sing Negro spirituals in the moonlight and magnolia tradition of romance novels.[21] Lost is the play's scene of the (white) tenant youths costumed on Christmas Eve to go serenading around the county, a scene that illustrates the heterogeneity of the South, with folk traditions varying from state to state and county to county. The scene in the film employs a more familiar tableau of a more homogenous Southern culture.

Numerous film critics on the subject have discussed Hollywood's sentimental attitude toward the plantation South. Such romanticizing leaves little room for references to sexual relations between master and slave, the consequences of which *The House of Connelly* explores. Miscegenation was also prohibited by the Motion Picture Production Code, although, as Karen Cox points out, numerous films included mixed-race protagonists.[22] Cox concludes that the head of the Production Code Association, Joseph Breen, "was far more interested in covering cleavage, limiting kisses, and excising scenes of childbirth than in issues of race" (41). So one cannot be sure why the screenwriter of *Carolina* made the changes that took the issue of miscegenation out of the film. Perhaps the reason is related to the film being billed as a comedy and its evident intent to be an uplifting Horatio Alger story. Whatever the reason for basing a film on a play and then leaving out the source of the major conflict in that play, since miscegenation is not alluded to in the film, the references to Purvis, are (not surprisingly) absent, but so is Duffy, with his numerous children to feed (and only a vague, easily deleted reference to the identity of his white father). Rather than the play's two black male characters, the tragic figure (Purvis) and a common working man (Duffy), the filmmakers have inserted a stereotypical African American male character named Scipio, played by Stepin Fetchit doing his usual performance as a lazy and slow-witted, bumbling and practically incoherent servant (what an African American had to do, it seems, to become the highest paid black actor of his day). In a 1944 seminal article on Negroes in films, Lawrence Reddick writes of Stepin Fetchit, "His great art was used to drive in deeper than ever the stereotype of the lazy Negro good-for-nothing" (11). One can assume that Green, the man Richard Wright chose to adapt *Native Son* for the stage because of his sensitive and insightful depictions of black characters in his own plays, was horrified by Stepin Fetchit's performance in a film adapted from one of his works.

In most films of the 1930s, Reddick explains, "the Negro is exploited chiefly for comic relief. He is the clown ... a buffoon ... a servant" (4–5). Among the typical qualities Reddick lists for such characters on screen are several that apply to Stepin Fetchit's role in *Carolina*: "ignorance ... laziness, clumsiness." Reddick does note that there may be "excellent acting," but there is also a "ceiling above which the Negro on the screen is seldom, if ever, permitted to rise," and that ceiling "is lower than the ceiling for the Negro in American life itself" (5). In a 1948 article, similarly critical of the character type Stepin Fetchit portrayed, Peter Noble lists *Carolina* among the "dozens of films" in which "Fetchit portrayed the lazy, ignorant, good for nothing colored servants" and points out that "so successful was his contemptible impersonation of this type of part that Fox Studios [which is the studio that produced *Carolina*] signed him to a fat contract, so that his biased characterizations might be continued" (254). In *Toms, Coons, Mulattoes, Mammies, & Bucks*, Donald Bogle, who discusses Stepin Fetchit at some length, notes that "special scenes were often written into pictures for him" (39). Bogle is more generous than Noble in his discussion of this actor, believing that "at least on a subconscious level, no one knew better than Fetchit the injustices and cruelties of the 'benevolent' white masters in his films. Fetchit's great gift was in rendering his coons as such thoroughly illiterate figures that they did not have to respond when demeaned because they were always unaware of what was being done" (43). That description can most definitely be applied to the character Scipio in *Carolina*, but Bogle's discussion of the actor's role in *Carolina* does not fully apply, leaving the reader to wonder if he actually saw the movie or just found a reference to it among the actor's credits:

> By the time Fetchit appeared in *Carolina* ... his characters had become integral parts of the household, involved in the affairs and troubles of the ruling families. They were still used for crude comic relief but at heart they were harmless creatures who, during crucial moments, would "come through." ... Between Fetchit's master and himself there were a spirit of good will and much mutual affection [42–43].

Stepin Fetchit's role in *Carolina* is pointless except as comic relief (to those, that is, who found his antics humorous). This is not a movie involving a beloved family servant, and Scipio certainly plays no role in resolving the movie's conflict.

Noble, on the other hand, does seem familiar with the movie *Carolina* but was probably not familiar with the play on which it is based, for if he were, he might not have said that he "is *not* suggest[ing] that the studio deliberately 'wrote in' anti–Negro parts in their films, but since Fetchit's popularity with mass movie audiences was founded upon these unfair portrayals, Hollywood, notorious for its system of type casting, continued to allot him similar roles, especially in films dealing with the Southern States" (254; emphasis added).

Scipio *is* "written into" this film adaptation as assuredly as is Uncle Bob's long lost love Barbara, who turns out to be the grandmother of the new tenant farmer's daughter, as will be discussed later. It is disappointing to read in the movie's reviews of audiences enjoying such a demeaning performance, for Stepin Fetchit's character in this film tries the patience of a contemporary audience as much as he tries Mrs. Connelly's, to the point that keeping him on the payroll seems a very generous thing for her to do—perhaps this is the screenwriter's interpretation of Mrs. Connelly's sense of obligation toward Duffy and his family in the play. Scipio may have been added to contribute to the conversion of a realistic play (as performed on Broadway, tragic if one considers the original ending) into a romantic comedy, but today's audience—and any audience familiar with Green's original play and with the more dignified black characters of many of Green's plays—is more likely to be offended than amused by Stepin Fetchit's ridiculous and pointless antics. Surprisingly and sadly, repeating the baffling praise of the *New York Times* reviewer who believed the movie was "realistic," when the local *News & Observer* printed a story on the film's 1934 screening in Raleigh, North Carolina, the reviewer reported, "Stepin Fetchit, a Southern Negro who achieved fame several years ago with the advent of the talkies as *an able portrayer of Southern Negroes*, makes his comeback in 'Carolina' after several years' absence from films" ("Paul" 7; emphasis added). This praise would certainly be easier to dismiss as merely ignorant if it were not in a Southern newspaper, indeed, a newspaper from the playwright's own native North Carolina. Again, one can imagine Paul Green's disgust.

In *Slow Fade to Black: The Negro in American Film, 1900–1942*, Thomas Cripps is certainly more critical of Stepin Fetchit's role in this film, though he mentions it only briefly and in doing so mistakenly refers to the movie as "Paul Green's *Carolina*" (just as the headline for the *News & Observer* review of the film had mistakenly called it "Paul Green's Play, *Carolina*." In the context of noting that "a few new Negro roles appeared" during the Depression, Cripps complains that "the old ones still survived in Southern programmers [*sic*] and Will Rogers films" (272). Since Paul Green wrote several screenplays for Will Rogers's movies, perhaps Cripps assumed he also wrote the screenplay for the film adaptation of his own play and did not notice that Green's name was listed in the film credits underneath "Screen Play Reginald Berkeley" with "From 'The House of Connelly' by Paul Green."[23] In any case, Cripps does not seem to realize how different *Carolina* is from Green's play or that the author of the screenplay, Berkeley, was from England (though it is true that the director, Henry King, was a native Virginian). Cripps does correctly describe the marriage plot of the *film* ("proud Rebel" meets "pragmatic Yankee"), which was a common trope in popular nineteenth-century plantation fiction romance novels, but in the *play*, Patsy is just as Southern as the Connellys.

The Civil War is long over by the time of *The House of Connelly*, but the film *Carolina* opens with the year 1861 superimposed over a Southern plantation house. The date is then replaced by a few lines about the great House of Connelly prior to this time; then the sound of "Dixie" plays as a marching band parades before the house. Men on horseback, presumably Will's father and Uncle Bob, ride from the house off screen, and then, after the foot soldiers pass in the procession, a man on horseback appears, General Connelly perhaps, waving back at the people in front of the house. That scene fades and then erupts with cannon fire, followed by "40 Years After the Civil War" and a statement on the current state of affairs: "The House of Connelly, a crumbling shell enclosing the family pride, but little more. Their cause lost, their wealth gone, the Connellys live in the past, resent the present and fear the future." Uncle Bob (played by Lionel Barrymore) crosses the lawn toward the house, calling out to two black women walking past. There is no flirtation between Uncle Bob and these women, no bawdiness, and certainly no air of threat and foreboding surrounding the two women.[24] Not even listed in the film's credits, these women merely seem to serve as pawns for establishing the setting of the film, which suggests that the way of life on this Southern plantation has changed little since the war, in spite of the tough economic times. Rather than the two black sisters in the play, it is Uncle Bob who serves the "chorus" role in the movie: his first conversation with Will (played by Robert Young) provides the kind of background information that the black sisters' dialogue in the opening scene gives to the play's audience.

In the next scene, following a brief exchange with Uncle Bob as he passes through the dining room on his way to see Will, Mrs. Connelly (played by Henrietta Crosman) complains to her daughter (there is just one daughter in the film) about her brother-in-law's "military nonsense." Both women are dressed in mourning, as Mrs. Connelly does in the play (there is no indication in either play or film as to how long ago Mr. Connelly died). In contrast to the dignified stoicism and weak invalidism of the play's matriarch, the Mrs. Connelly on screen is no invalid, regardless of the cane she uses. As the film progresses, the audience watches her family comply with her wishes out of intimidation, not concern for her fragility. Mrs. Connelly's villainy is much more overt on screen than it is in the play.

And Uncle Bob is much more bitter in the opening scenes of the film, as evidenced in the aforementioned conversation with his nephew, who seems to be rousing himself after a late night. This Will Connelly is already drinking in town at the start of the movie, rather than, as in the course of the play, driven to alcohol and late nights by his confused feelings for an inappropriate love interest and his own self-doubts. With this difference from the play, the viewer is again given the impression that the way of life in Connelly Hall has not changed much since before the war: the men of the Southern aristocracy would have had much more leisure time, as there would have been overseers handling the hard work of running the plantation. Apparently, it is taking Will and the rest of his family some time to adjust to their current poverty, particularly since, we learn, they have been allowed credit by the local merchant. But that credit—or rather, the merchant's willingness to "credit" caste when there is no evidence of *cash* to follow—is running out, and Bob is seeking some spending money from his nephew so that he can replenish his cigars. When Will admits he has none to spare, Bob brings up the Tates, who, to Bob's dismay, have arranged with Will to pay their lease with shares on their crop profits rather than rent money.

As noted previously, Uncle Bob is suspicious of the Tates because they are Yankees (not so in the play). He accuses the father of being shiftless, leaving the work to his children and a single "nigger" (the only time in the film that this term is used). Ignoring or not perceiving the hypocrisy in Uncle Bob criticizing someone else for not working, Will defends the new tenant, saying that Tate's daughter told him her father has been ill. With Uncle Bob's suspicions and criticism, the film begin to replace the discomforting, unseemly miscegenation issue of the play with the same old North/South conflict of traditional post-bellum plantation fiction that often brought North and South together by way of a marriage between young people, and rarely explored the more sordid issues surrounding interracial relations on plantations. The film viewer may be surprised and disconcerted, then, when Uncle Bob uses (gratuitously) the term "nigger,"[25] for other than this denigrating term, race is of little significance in this movie, beyond setting the Southern stage and, awkwardly, for comic relief.

When Uncle Bob and Will join Mrs. Connelly and Geraldine in the dining room, the conversation turns to the impending visit of Virginia Buchanan. Bob is critical of the Buchanans too, noting that their money comes from "human flesh sold to the planters of this state." Again his critical tone is hypocritical, given his own plantation background. The hypocrisy in this case is typical of members of Old Southern aristocracy who viewed themselves as superior to the often less socially polished businessmen involved in the slave trade. In response to Mrs. Connelly's defense of Virginia's family as "one of the first families of Carolina," he reminds her that they were slave and liquor dealers, now called "gentry," he implies, only because of their money. So his snobbery extends to people from both above and below the Mason-Dixon line, people with more as well as less money than he has. This man without enough money to buy cigars holds onto his pride in his family name, which is the only collateral he has, as indicated later by a scene in the local mercantile, added to the movie, presumably to reveal the poverty of the Connellys: the store manager admonishes his clerk not to sell anything to a Connelly without cash and then insists to Uncle Bob that he is out of cigars until Bob produces a coin to pay for one.

At the dining room table, Uncle Bob does concede that Virginia is "a nice girl," and when Geraldine adds, "She's a very rich girl," he responds cynically, "same thing." With the talk of Virginia and also Will's reference to Tate's daughter as his source of information about Mr. Tate being ill, as opposed to a slacker, the film is clearly setting up the common—and comfortable—movie trope of a love triangle. The movie also adds a young store clerk, who appears to be enamored of Joanna Tate (Patsy is inexplicably renamed in the film), and a rival suitor among Will's contemporaries, who shows interest in Virginia at the Connelly's ball—thus, a triple triangle for the unimaginative audience that, as Green suggested in "The Theatre and the Screen," movies cater to with such trite, predictable, uncomplicated complications.

Interesting, though, recalling how Green contrasted Patsy in his play (comfortable in the outdoor scenes, not so comfortable whenever she is indoors) with the Connelly sisters (always shown inside the decaying house), Virginia is mentioned around the Connelly table in the early *interior* scene of the movie. Then Joanna Tate (played by Janet Gaynor) is introduced in the next scene, outside, when Will calls to her from his carriage, asking her to send her father out to speak to him. Joanna tells Will that her father has died, and thus the movie transforms the play's strong female lead into a more traditional damsel in distress. The movie also gives this female lead two much younger (and of course endearingly cute) brothers, whom she is responsible for now that they are all orphans. (Patsy's brothers are only mentioned once in the play, with no indication of their age, and her father is very much alive through the play's last scene.)

As Green suggests in his criticism of the industry, the film's characterizations are simplified for a non-critical-thinking audience. Joanna Tate is not complicatedly ambitious. She shares Patsy Tate's work ethic and wants to try growing tobacco, which she believes will be more successful than whatever they have been growing here (in this ambiguous "Carolina"), but Joanna is not manipulating Will in order to get control of his land, nor is *she* the assertive one of the two. It is Will who pushes their relationship's development, beginning by inviting Joanna to the ball for Virginia when he comes upon her in dismay after the two black women from the opening of the film have picked flowers from her yard without her permission. And speaking of uncomplicated characters, this scene, added to the movie, is the closest these black women come to reminding the audience of their threatening role in the play. They argue with Joanna that the flowers growing in her yard belong to the Connellys since she is a tenant on their land, and Joanna succumbs when they mention that Mrs. Connelly wants the flowers to decorate for a party. Joanna's anger and outrage are replaced with (one might say more girlish) hurt feelings over not having been invited. Her knight to the rescue, Will quickly comforts Joanna by lying about the late invitation he then extends.

Janet Gaynor as Joanna Tate and Robert Young as Will Connelly in the Fox Film Corporation's 1934 movie *Carolina* (courtesy British Film Institute).

Carolina's Will Connelly may be introduced into the movie with a hint of a hangover, but in the movie, he is not the Quentin Compson–like conflicted character he is in the play. The movie's depiction suggests that he is merely a bit spoiled and that he lacks direction for his life—a true son of the aristocracy—at the start. He is not troubled by having to live up to, live with, or live down his father's reputation. In the movie, when Will talks about his father, a great leader and the youngest general in the Civil War, he is clearly proud, and there is no reference to anything about his father of which he might be ashamed. When early in the movie Joanna comes to the Connelly house and stops at the family cemetery plot to read the grave markers—aloud, so that the audience hears that there was a Connelly among the signers of the Declaration of Independence—Will enters and tells her, proudly, about an ancestor who started with nothing and built up the family fortune. Such details suggest the filmmaker's intent to remind the national audience that this Southern family is also a very "American" family. Joanna encourages Will with assurances that he could do the same, but she is not too aggressive, nor is she being manipulative—just a typically supportive potential helpmate.

Joanna tells Will a story too, of her Southern grandmother who had continued, throughout her marriage and life in the North, to love her Confederate beau, a casualty of the war.

Joanna's family story (fabricated for the movie's later revelation scene) contributes to her own romantic appeal, again contrasting significantly with the hard-edged Patsy Tate of the play (who, though not of the same class, was definitely as Southern as Will). In the movie, the two young leads share a romantic vision of the past, which culminates in their shared fantasy vision during the ball in Virginia's honor. As they sit on the swing and Will tells Joanna about past balls held at the Connelly house, the scene fades into a fantasy sequence of the two dancing together, Joanna wearing an Old South ball gown (over a hoop skirt, of course) and Will a Confederate uniform, while people like Jefferson Davis and Robert E. Lee arrive in the background. This dream sequence, another complete fabrication by the screenwriter, provides an illustration of what Edward D.C. Campbell, Jr. suggests (talking more about the movie *Gone with the Wind*) is a problematic message of popular romantic films that reflected "the persistence of a legend which decreed that an opulent South and its beliefs were being enjoyed at the expense of progress nationally in race relations and in a more accurate perception of the South's past and present problems" (140).[26] We are reminded by Campbell's observation that this movie was made during the Depression, which might explain its escapist tone, its resistance of the serious issues of the play that were more thought-provoking than "entertaining." Moviegoers enjoyed the hopefulness rather than resented the false romanticism of movies like this one and *Gone with the Wind*, in which people pulled themselves up out of poverty.

Carolina's dream sequence is interrupted abruptly when Mrs. Connelly approaches, finds Joanna dozing on Will's shoulder, and, after appearing nightmarishly witchlike in Joanna's dream, harshly snaps them both back to the present, sending Will inside to be a better host to their visitor, Virginia, while she speaks to Joanna. She offers Joanna her support of the Tates' tobacco crop if the young woman will stay away from Will. Maintaining her deference and respect toward the older woman, but also her faithfulness to Will, Joanna politely refuses to make any promise to Mrs. Connelly. Her behavior is "ladylike," certainly not "trashy," thus foreshadowing the movie's ending, in which she also very much looks the part of *lady* of the manor.

Uncle Bob enters when Mrs. Connelly leaves. He is troubled by what his sister-in-law might have been telling the young woman, whom he mistakes for a long ago love interest of his. Addled with drink and perhaps symptoms of dementia, he promises this "Barbara" that he will come back to her after the war. Will once again comes to the rescue, less violently than in the play's corresponding scene, since Uncle Bob is just a harmless old drunk in this movie. Will then walks Joanna home, pressuring her as they say goodnight to tell him she loves him. A good girl, much more traditionally proper than the play's Patsy, she responds, "Don't make me say it 'til I'm ready." The scene does continue with Will declaring his love for Joanna, telling her he will love her forever, and Joanna finally admitting she loves him too. Gone is the play's ambiguity of the two young people's feelings for each other, their confusion as to whether they are in love with each other or just attracted to what they can each do for the other. And certainly gone is any hint of the relationship involving sex; theirs is the innocent, romantic love of the era's movies.

If there is any premarital sexual activity in the movie, it is between Will and Virginia (played by Mona Barrie), though it is only vaguely hinted at. A scene from the screenplay that did not make it into the film shows Will in Virginia's home where, just as when she visited the Connellys, her family hosts a party during Will's visit. The stage directions indicate that Will has had a lot to drink. He comments on the scent of Virginia's hair, says he "feel[s] rather wicked" and notes how "dreadfully attractive" she is. Virginia is plying him with drinks—thus *she* is the one who is the more aggressive seducer (less traditionally feminine) in the movie, as Patsy is in the play. The scene cuts as Will leans "swiftly forward," presumably to kiss Virginia (Berkeley 82–83). Reading this scene in the screenplay makes more sense of their dialogue in the next scene, which *is* in the film. Will and Virginia are heading to the bank for a loan from Virginia's family's money for the Connelly plantation. The screenplay notes that when Will finally summons the nerve to speak, "Virginia smiles *provocatively*" (Berkeley 88; emphasis added). In the scene as it was filmed, there is no close-up on Virginia, and she seems merely naturally smiling at her presumed suitor, whom she refers to as "darling" as she encourages him to go ahead with whatever he has to say. Interestingly, when Will then says he can't borrow money from Virginia's family because he is "in love with someone else" and "can't marry you," Virginia laughs at him (in both the screenplay and the film): "Did anybody ever say a word about my marrying you?" she asks. Will's response in the screenplay indicates that they may have been intimate: "But after last night—I mean—I—When two people—" (Berkeley 89); however, in the actual film the line is changed to "I thought that after *what I said* last night.... I guess I had too much champagne" (emphasis added). The change in the dialogue removes the suggestion that Will may have been unfaithful to Joanna, his true love—even if the implication is that he led Virginia on while inebriated. A viewing audience can't know whether Virginia's response to Will's rejection is false bravado to cover up hurt feelings or genuine amusement at Will's expense, but in any case, the screenplay writer implies that Virginia is not a "nice girl"—as Joanna clearly is: "You thought because I chose to amuse myself with a country lout—" (which line *is* spoken in the film) and (only in the screenplay): "Do you suppose you're the first? Or that you're going to be the last?" (Berkeley 89). Thus, one might suggest that the screenplay writer conflated Virginia with Essie in his adaptation. But the film itself resorts to more clean-cut heroes: Will does not have a drunken affair—merely a drunken flirtation, which is apparently forgivable to the movie audience, as long as he remembers in the sober light of day that he loves the movie's heroine, as long as Virginia is femme fatale–like (and not as likeable as Joanna), and of course, as long as the woman he flirts with is white.

Two points of consistency between the play and the film are Mrs. Connelly's desire for Will to marry Virginia and her disapproval of his interest in the tenant farmer's daughter. Will's mother's failure to recognize her own hypocrisy is also repeated in the film, when she remarks upon "penniless Jack Hampton flirting with Virginia," since it has been clearly established that Will, too, is penniless. But in contrast to the physically weak but subtly manipulative Mrs. Connelly of the play, the movie's Mrs. Connelly is much more overtly villainous in the film (and Joanna a much more traditional victim). Poisoning Will's mind against Joanna doesn't work in this version of the story, in which her son is not so emotionally troubled and thus not so easily manipulated into doubting himself. So after sending Will away with Virginia on this loan business, Mrs. Connelly sets herself to getting rid of Joanna, informing the local merchant that she will not be financing Joanna's tobacco crop after all and that she is terminating the Tate lease.

Joanna is forced to pack up to leave, and when she goes to the Connelly house to say goodbye, a revelation scene takes place—quite different from the play's parallel scene. Rather than Will exposing the (sexual) sins of the father (and uncle), it is *Mrs.* Connelly's past duplicity that is exposed in the movie's climactic scene. It turns out that she was the cause of Uncle Bob's lost love, Barbara, predictably none other than the grandmother of Will's new love. Joanna's grandmother was Geraldine's governess. So the great threat then, in the movie storyline's past (as in its present with Will and Joanna), was the idea of a Connelly marrying out of his class. To thwart her brother-in-law's breach of decorum, Mrs. Connelly told the governess that Robert had been killed in the war. Distressed by the discovery of his sister-in-law's long ago betrayal and the resulting senseless loss of the great romantic love of his life, Uncle Bob snaps, exiting the scene with words suggesting he is once again addled and thinks he is going off to battle. But, as in the play, he commits suicide offstage.

There is no point to Uncle Bob's suicide in this film (especially since the movie was marketed as a comedy). Taking his own life is neither a sacrifice to motivate Will to move on with his life nor self-punishment for sinful and shameful behavior with the black women who worked on the plantation. Uncle Bob's death results in no catharsis, as in the play. Rather, his suicide merely emphasizes *Mrs.* Connelly's villainy; her past meddling has ultimately resulted in tragic violence: Robert Connelly commits suicide out of despair over the realization that he might have had a loving wife, if not for his sister-in-law's interference.

Following Scipio's off-stage cry that "Marse Bob done shot hisself" and Will's hasty exit to investigate, the camera zooms in on the horror-stricken faces of Mrs. Connelly and Joanna. But then the scene cuts abruptly to Joanna's brothers chasing a chicken that has gotten inside their tenant house—the tone instantly switching from tragic to comic (the film is not only promoted as but also referred to as a comedy by reviewers). Will soon arrives to talk Joanna out of leaving, with Mrs. Connelly not far behind to make sure he doesn't. So the shock of her brother-in-law's death does not hasten her own demise (as in the play), nor does a guilty conscience over her part in his motivation for suicide prompt her to stop interfering in other people's lives. Rather, Joanna eventually convinces Mrs. Connelly of the prosperous potential of a marriage between this young woman with big dreams for the House of Connelly and Mrs. Connelly's less motivated son and heir.

In this penultimate scene of the movie, which takes place in Joanna's now empty tenant house (she has packed up to leave), Will asserts to his mother that he and Joanna had plans for how they would bring the Connelly plantation back to life, and Joanna responds to Mrs. Connelly's skepticism by asking, "Why should it be nonsense for Will to want to carry on what his great-grandfather began and for me to have wanted to help him?" She begins describing her plans, and the scene fades into a montage of images showing her dreams coming true. Her speech then also fades and is replaced by the rising music of Negro spirituals. Within the montage is a sign referring to the "Connelly-Tate Mixture," as well as "Joanna Tobacco" and Tate cigarettes. It is interesting how this much less assertive leading lady eventually gets her name and her family name into their apparently successful business venture while the aggressive Mrs. Connelly is transformed into a doting, humbled grandmother in the final scene of the play.

The film transitions from the visions in Joanna's fantasy to the front porch of the House of Connelly where Mrs. Connelly is lighting a cigarette and fussing with Scipio as more "comedy" is inserted in this final scene when Scipio spills the lemonade he serves, trying Mrs. Connelly's patience yet again—some things may have changed, but he is still ridiculously inept, and she still resignedly tolerates him. Joanna enters to ask Mrs. Connelly if she needs anything at the store. The younger Mrs. Connelly commiserates amicably with her mother-in-law about the mess Scipio has made. Then, as Joanna and Will stand together in each other's arms on the Connelly front steps, Mrs. Connelly, transformed into a more familiar grandmother figure, gathers two grandchildren onto her lap on the porch to tell them a fairytale:

> Once upon a time, there was a young girl who lived in a cottage. And she loved the sunshine and the rain and the rich, dark earth. And in a great, lonely house, there was a tall, handsome prince who had nothing at all to do but shoot crows and twiddle his thumbs. And the young girl fell in love with the tall, handsome prince, and she wanted to give him her gayety and her faith and her courage, and she wanted to inspire him to do big things with his life. And the prince told the young girl that he'd follow her to the ends of the earth. But the prince's mother didn't understand and did everything she could to keep them apart.... Oh, of course, it all ended happily because the prince's mother found out that the young girl was the most wonderful person in the whole world and just the right wife for the prince and just the right mother for children.

Order is restored with a woman from the tenant farms firmly established and looking quite at home in her role as the mistress of the House of Connelly. The New South looks exactly like the Old to anyone unfamiliar with Joanna's humble beginnings. Against the familiar, romanticized backdrop of the plantation house, one certainly cannot imagine that this is what the Group Theatre had in mind when they asked Green to change his tragic ending. But this sentimentalized ending and the other cheap changes that take out the dark past of *The House of Connelly* remind us of the slippery slope between realism and romanticism when a work of art is altered to suit an agenda—in this case, the film industry's agenda of making money; in the case of the Group Theatre, their wish to reward the tenant farmer for her work ethic.

In September 1933, as Green was deciding whether to go to Hollywood to help with the adaptation of *The House of Connelly*, he wrote a letter to his friend and publisher Barrett H. Clark in which he responded to Clark's concern that so many playwrights "were working in Hollywood instead of writing plays" (Avery 220n). In this letter, Green says he'd rather stay home to put the finishing touches on some plays he has nearly ready for production, but will probably go to Hollywood, even though his experience with the movie *business* being what it has been, he would prefer not to. And yet, Green still held out hope for movies: "I maintain that the movies will also some of these days provide the writer with one of his most historical and glorious opportunities" (Avery 221). Between the writing of this letter and the publication of an essay on his Hollywood writing experience, Green consulted on the production and then saw the premiere of *Carolina*. And still he maintains in his essay his belief in the *potential* for film, and he predicts the rise of independent filmmakers from the "hundreds of dissatisfied creative minds, whose sole job day after day is the making of money for bankers, millionaires, and stockholders.... Already a few independent producers, writers, and artists are trying a few forlorn experiments in creating pure forms of cinematic art" (*Drama* 93). One must admire how he maintains his optimism after seeing what Hollywood did to his play in the film *Carolina*. He still believed that

> when this new art has broken itself loose from the industry and professionalism of Hollywood and started on its own path, we shall see moving picture dramas worthy of the name. Writers, actors, directors, and musicians will then take joy and pride in their work and will strive to the best of their minds and souls to deal with the camera as its essential nature provides. And what they create will be of their own making, and the writers will be free to write scenarios as full of imagination and poetry as their gifts will allow [*Drama* 93].

Paul Green Revisited

In a 2010 essay, "From the Newspaper Page to the Broadway Stage: Paul Green in the Poet/Priest Tradition," I argue for bringing the plays of Paul Green back into the canon of

Southern literature. It is far past time for *In Abraham's Bosom* to be performed on a Southern stage. The regularly anthologized and performed Tennessee Williams is not the only Southern playwright, and Paul Green deals much more directly and often with race issues than Williams does in his works. These Green plays are very complicated and quite troubling. Let us not make the same mistake that the film industry made when they created an almost unrecognizable, completely romanticized adaptation of *The House of Connelly*, one of Green's strongest plays by avoiding the difficult discussions that Green's provocative plays might elicit. The ambiguity of both endings of the play *The House of Connelly* leaves us pondering anew the old issues of a changing and unchanging South.

Afterword

by Jim Grimsley

Paul Green's *The House of Connelly* was a work unknown to me until I was introduced to the script and movie adaptation by Margaret D. Bauer. Being a North Carolina native, I was familiar with Green's outdoor dramas, the spectacles of history that have made his name something of a household word in my home state. These are strong, solid works of theater, rooted in regional history, adequate to their purpose but hardly daring. Because of them, I thought of Green as a mildly interesting historian, not as a dramatist who made much of an impact, and I certainly would not have associated him with the Group Theatre and its legendary, even transformative work.

I am admitting my ignorance of Paul Green's true body of work, the plays of harder, edgier construction, that brought him to the attention of New York, which is, for good or ill, the capital of American theater.

When Bauer told me about this play, comparing it favorably with the works of Tennessee Williams, the essential Southern playwright, I confess that I was skeptical of her assessment. Williams is a towering figure, probably the most significant American playwright before August Wilson, at least in my estimation. How could Green be spoken of as his peer?

A reading of the play quickly convinced me that I needed to reassess Green altogether, and I understood Bauer's enthusiasm.

While I doubt I will ever have much to complain about in discussing Williams, I found *The House of Connelly* to be honest, direct, and powerful in confronting aspects of the South and its heritage, in areas of subject in which Williams, for one reason or another, is more timid. I admire Williams for his hothouse language, his dialog as floridly scented as any magnolia; but I cannot recall a Williams play in which he wrote about the doom at the heart of the South. Issues of race are coded in Williams; in Green's play, the fact of slavery and the inheritance of white supremacy are exposed like the rawest nerves. In the work of Williams, the plantation is a fading memory. In *The House of Connelly*, it is the star of the play, and its pivotal place in the drama of Southern history is starkly and bleakly represented.

The play is only a little less concerned with history, and even pageantry, than Green's better known works, but in Connelly the presentation is more personal, focused as it is on the decay of a family and the people around them. What we witness is a plantation falling to ruins, an agrarian way of life that is dying, and a people who are gripped by the talons of a deadly past. History has turned malevolent in this play, and the shadow it casts on the present is poisonous.

That shadow is drawn quite directly, in explicit terms. As Bauer points out so well in her analysis of the play, the crossing of the forbidden zone between black and white, the presence of miscegenation, lies at the heart of the work. The word itself, miscegenation, is an ugly term for the fact that blacks and whites shared intimacy and produced children throughout the long, cruel night of slavery and its aftermath. The fact of this congress made a lie of the slave owner's laws against such pairings and offered a human rebuttal to the fiction of difference between what we call the two races, ignoring the science that tells us black and white people are no more different than black or white dogs.

The fact that the elder living Connelly has dallied with black women, the descendants of former family slaves, lies at the heart of the play, and this revelation is the point at which the drama tips into tragedy. In the face of this knowledge, the family crumbles, the elder Connelly kills himself, and the family legacy, that ruined house, sighs and sinks further toward oblivion.

One cannot credit Green's vision with real enlightenment; he struggles with his vision and, perhaps, yearns for that past world of Connelly wealth and glory in ways that we will question today. As in Faulkner, his African Americans are troubling portraits, presented as wily by nature, unreliable, often malicious. There are moments of astonishing reality in the presentation of these characters; the play's opening with Big Sis and Big Sue is a study in superb character-driven dialog, a moody preamble to a calamitous narrative. Green's former slaves are all presented in the manner one would expect from the era in which he writes: servile, cunning, prone to steal, the women eager to seduce white men, the men shiftless, shirking what we are led to think of as their duties to the family they serve. Green has not resolved the ideas of white supremacy with which he was surely raised, and his consciousness is not pioneering toward a prediction of the civil rights era.

But with his storyteller's instinct he has reached the core of the Southern dilemma. White people and black people never could keep their hands off one another. There is no more tacit admission of equality than desire. The great dynasty of Connelly was built on a corrupt falsehood, a notion of property that reduced human beings to exploitable chattel, a lie maintained by a separation of the races that could never be sustained. (In making this assertion, I am presuming that there were regular instances of consensual relations between blacks and whites; I am fully aware that much of the sex forced by whites on blacks is better described as an expression of power than of desire.)

This is an honesty that, even if partly accidental, buttresses the play with the certainty that it has touched something essential. Green's drama helps us to see that the story of the South cannot be staged with slavery and its repercussions politely concealed behind a backdrop of charm and oddity. Relations between black and white are not the subtext of Southern art; they are its core. Tapping into this furnace of dramatic energy, Green created a play so disturbing that the Group Theatre forced him to write a more palatable ending. Before Bauer told me the tale, I would not have believed this legendary theatre collective could be so cowed by the drama it craved to produce.

I am grateful to have encountered this play, and believe, as does Bauer, that it should take a place among much better known works in the Southern canon. Green was a seminal force in early twentieth-century American theater and deserves to be understood as the forebear of later Southern writers. *The House of Connelly* comes down to us as a raw, powerful example of what a playwright can do when tracing the course of tragedy through our complacent ideas of the past. The Connelly family stands as a fierce depiction of the power of the past, and a true portrait of the landscape of white supremacy and its hypocrisy.

Appendix: Reviews of the 1931 Broadway Performance

Atkinson, Brooks. "October Nights in the Playhouses of Manhattan: Acting the Drama." *New York Times* 4 Oct. 1931: sec. 8:1.

———. "The Play: Epic of the South." *New York Times* 29 Sept. 1931: 22.

Benchley, Robert. "The Theatre: More Like It." *New Yorker* 10 Oct. 1931: 32+.

Brown, John Mason. "Paul Green's *The House of Connelly*: The Play." *New York Evening Post* 29 Sept. 1931: 14.

Carb, David. "Seen on the Stage: *The House of Connelly*." *Vogue* 1 Dec. 1931: 100+.

"Coming Stage Attractions." *Washington Post* 17 Jan. 1932: A2.

"Critics Acclaim Opening of New Play." *Daily Tar Heel* [Chapel Hill, NC] 3 Oct. 1931: 1–2.

DeCasseres, Benjamin. "Broadway to Date." *Arts and Decorations* 36.2 (Dec. 1931): 68.

Fergusson, Francis. "The New Group and Others." *Bookman* 74.3 (Nov. 1931): 298–99.

———. "A Month of the Theatre: Recalling the High Lights." *Bookman* 75.3 (Jun/Jul 1932): 288–91.

"First Week's Earning—Second only to Grand Hotel—$13,000." *News & Observer* 17 Oct. 1931.

Hammond, Percy. "The Theaters: A Good Show, though Presented by a Group of Eager Idealists." *New York Herald Tribune* 29 Sept. 1931: 18.

"'House of Connelly,' Stage Hit, Pleases New York Fans." *Chicago Defender*, nat'l. ed. 10 Oct. 1931: 5.

"Justice to the South in a Play." *Literary Digest* 3.14 (24 Sept. 1931): 17.

Krutch, Joseph Wood. "Drama: A Promise Fulfilled." *Nation* 133.3458 (14 Oct. 1931): 408.

Lockridge, Richard. "*The House of Connelly*." *New York Sun* 29 Sept. 1931: 32.

"New Plays and Old Plots." *Saturday Review of Literature* 8.13 (17 Oct. 1931): 199, 202.

"Paul Green's Great Night." *News & Observer* 4 Oct. 1931: 4.

Skinner, Richard Dana. "The House of Connelly." *Commonweal* 14.24 (Oct. 1931): 583–84.

Wyatt, Euphemia Van Rensselear. "Plays of Importance." *Catholic World* Nov. 1931: 206–11.

Young, Stark, "The Shadow of Wings." *New Republic* 14 Oct. 1931: 234–36; rpt. in *Immortal Shadows: A Book of Dramatic Criticism*. New York: Scribner's, 1948. 127–32.

"Young Group Offers Play about South." *Washington Post* 24 Jan. 1932: A2.

Notes

THE PLAY

1. A mask made of dough.
2. Adapted from the translated phrase "While Rome debates, Saguntum perishes," suggesting doing something unnecessarily slowly as a result of people just talking, without any productive action.
3. Arguably, a slight corruption of "We who are about to die salute you," a saying attributed to those engaged in gladiatorial combat.
4. Hebrew for "God has spoken," an idiomatic call to "Listen."
5. Perhaps a fragment of "*de mortuis aut bene aut nihil*": "of the dead, if not good, [say] nothing," cut off when he realizes the inappropriateness of the dictum.
6. *Desiccare* is the infinitive of "to dessicate."
7. From Horace's *Odes*, "the honorable man has no need of a javelin" (for self defense).
8. This is a corruption of the Greek opening of *The Iliad*, roughly translated, "Achilles's anger now be your song, o goddess of wrath."
9. This is the first line of *The Aeneid*, usually translated, "I sing of arms and of a man."
10. Set in seventeenth-century England and written in the historical romance tradition of Sir Walter Scott, *Lorna Doone: A Romance of Exoor* (1869) by Richard Doddridge Blackmore was a popular novel in its day and continued to be so in the early years of the twentieth century (during which time Green's play is set). *Lorna Doone*, similar to *The House of Connelly*, is the story of star-crossed lovers: the title character is a member of a once noble, now outlaw family who falls in love with the son of one of this family's victims, who, like Will Connelly, takes care of a mother and two sisters.
11. Henry Wadsworth Longfellow's "Excelsior" was written and published in 1841. The Latin title is translated "ever higher" or, more popularly, "onward and upward." The narrative of the poem continues "onward and upward" with a banner that bears the motto "Excelsior," not heeding others warnings or temptations to stay, and he is eventually found dead, half-buried in snow.
12. Uncle Bob is here adapting lines from a poem by Thomas Hood, "Fair Ines": "O saw ye not fair Ines? / She's gone into the West."
13. Uncle Bob seems to be misquoting Catullus here: the last words of the elegy to his deceased brother are "*ave atque vale*," "hail and farewell."
14. Arbutus is a flowering plant of the Ericaceae family, native to areas of warm climates in the Mediterranean, western Europe, and North America. Sometimes called a strawberry tree because of its edible red berry, some species are cultivated for ornamental purposes.
15. This phrase should begin with *Abusus*, not *Abusum*; it translates "abuse does not take away use," meaning that abuse is not an argument against improper use.
16. "The palace of the sun stood on sublime tall columns that shone with bronze [brightness] that was as if flames, bright [shining white] ivory covering its posts and each door [of a pair] radiating silver": from Ovid's *Metamorphoses*, Book 2 first lines. This introduces the encounter between the son Phaeton and his father Phoebus, as the son queries his father about his own birth origins; see below.
17. From Ovid's *The Metamorphoses* (an apostrophe to Phoebus, lines 35–38): "O universal Light of the world, Father Sun, if Clymene has not been false with me, give me a sign of your blessing."
18. It is certain by the fact itself.
19. In the name of the church, a trifle mocking and irreligious, perhaps a play on "*in nomine Christi*").
20. Traditionally translated (from the Greek), "Why wasn't Sophocles more cosmopolitan? Why was he out of touch?"; a rough rendering of the spelling in Greek might be "*ekhei* [or *exei*] *o anthropos ten physin* [or *phusin*] *apotetelesmenen*."
21. Shortening of "Hail Caesar, we [who are about to die] salute you"; also probably from the Greek originally: "*Khaire autokrator*"; supposedly said by those engaging in gladiatorial combat (see also "*te morituri*" above).
22. "It's easy to descend to hell," with an allusion to the Italian volcanic lake Averno; then Uncle Bob's memory seems to falter, and he says something like

"who/what/although my memory is not what it used to be."

23. Mrs. Connelly's line "I failed you" is not in the original publication of this play in *The House of Connelly and Other Plays* (New York: Samuel French, 1931).

24. There is no "Jerry" in the cast list and no explanation as to why Green changed the name here from "Duffy" to "Jerry" in the revision for the Group Theatre.

The Analysis

1. In addition to *In Abraham's Bosom* and *The House of Connelly*, miscegenation is also the source of the central conflict in Green's early play *White Dresses: A Tragedy in White and Black in One Act* (1920). For more information about this play, see my introduction to its reprint publication in the 2009 issue of the *North Carolina Literary Review* (Green, *White Dresses* 23–24). Pending miscegenation is also implicit in the ending of the 1923 Green play *End of the Row*.

2. According to Harold Clurman, the Guild also demanded a couple of casting changes, which the Group Theatre objected to as well (55).

3. See, for example, the *New York Sun* review by Richard Lockridge.

4. Green felt strongly enough about this issue that he researched the statistics on state executions in North Carolina, and in an essay he published in the Raleigh *News & Observer* in 1962, he quoted the information he'd found, which showed that more than three times as many black men were executed than white and that everyone who had been executed by the state of North Carolina had been poor (Green, "Let Us" 2).

5. See my article on the Wright-Green collaboration (Bauer, "Call me Paul").

6. In the first production of this play, Duffy is played by Hungarian born J. Edward Bromberg, a member of The Group Theatre. The Group Theatre acting troupe did not include any African American members. They seem to have hired only two black actresses for the roles of Big Sis and Big Sue.

7. In the Group Theatre production, Essie was played by Ruth Nelson, a white actress. Nelson reports that she was only to rehearse the part during the Group Theatre's summer retreat in Brookfield Center, Connecticut. A black actress was to play the role "when they opened in New York," but whoever it was "wouldn't join them for the summer." When they returned to the city, however, Nelson continues, "there was no talk of getting this Negro girl. She disappeared, and I played the role. ... I did my hair up in leather curlers, in little tiny sections, all over my head, and then combed it out with grease, so that I got an authentic kink, and it looked much darker. I put brown all over" (Clurman et al. 58). One wonders what Paul Green thought of this, which sounds like something akin to blackface, but no mention could be found of it in his letters or diaries.

8. I thank Marsha Ironsmith for informing me of the lavaliere engaged to be engaged tradition, comparing it to "promise rings" in high school and being pinned in sororities and fraternities.

9. In the revised ending, the carriage driver who comes for the sisters is called Jerry, though no Jerry appears in the cast list. While the name Jerry by itself would not be noteworthy, the change from one version of the play to another calls ominous attention to an absent Duffy in this scene following just after the death of Uncle Bob, and one remembers that Duffy called the dead Uncle Bob "Pappy" in the previous scene. As Big Sis and Big Sue noted of Purvis in the play's opening scene, a black man was not supposed to acknowledge his white father. Has Duffy, then, like Essie, been fired?

10. In the revised ending, the sisters also behave threateningly and disrespectfully toward Patsy when Will leaves the room in search of his sisters in the house.

11. Green's diaries are available in the Paul Green Papers in the Southern Historical Collection of Wilson Library, at the University of North Carolina at Chapel Hill.

12. Recall that, as indicated previously, Dusenbury makes no mention of (and likely had no awareness of) the original tragic ending of the play in her analysis, which was based on the "comic" marriage plot ending performed on Broadway and in the original publication of the play.

13. Green also collected *The House of Connelly* with only the Broadway ending in his 1939 volume *Out of the South: The Life of a People in Dramatic Form*. This volume added a subtitle to the play that does not appear in the earlier publication: *A Drama of the Old South and the New*.

14. Green is referring here to the mill strikes of the 1930s, in protest of poor working conditions. In Burlington, North Carolina, six workers were convicted of plotting to bomb one of the mills. Green was among several Chapel Hill liberals who set up the League for Southern Labor, which they hoped would be more effective in protecting the accused than the Communists, who were using them as martyrs for the cause.

15. Cox does not mention *Carolina* in her chapter—probably because, until recently, the movie had all but disappeared. The film is mentioned in Anna Everett's *Returning the Gaze: A Genealogy of Black Film Criticism, 1909–1949* (287), in addition to the sources referenced in the discussion to follow here.

16. After much searching, I finally found a copy

of the film at the George Eastman House, International Museum of Photography and Film, in Rochester, New York.

17. Green complains that this ending sequences damages "an otherwise beautiful ending" (Avery 223), and since this ending does not kill off the leading lady, one might see in this praise further evidence that Green was fine with the revised, happy ending of his play that he wrote for the Group Theatre. Still, one may be surprised to hear him praise anything about this movie.

18. Originally published as "A Playwright's Notes on Drama and the Screen" in the *New York Times* (4 Feb. 1934, sec. 10, p. 1–2), an excerpt of this essay (skipping the first half that discusses *The Birth of a Nation*, as well as Charlie Chaplin, and getting straight to Green's own screenwriting experience) was published as "Dimes vs. Art" in the Raleigh (NC) *News & Observer* (7 Feb. 1934, p. 4). Under the title "The Theatre and the Screen," Green included it in his *Drama and the Weather* (from which it is here quoted). It is also included in Green's *The Hawthorn Tree*. Most recently, it has been reprinted in *NCLR Online* 2012.

19. In his interviews with James R. Spence, Green discussed *The Birth of a Nation* more extensively, explaining his view that much of the power of the film came from the music, but also, "The effect of *The Birth of a Nation* was doubly strong in that it was a darned good dramatic story. It was well done. It had pathos, heartache, fervor, antagonism, even hate in it. The power of the drama was such that the spillover effect was not spiritually healthy" (qtd. in Spence 158).

20. Green explains the "unfortunately" in this passage from his interview with Spence: "After you had gone through the experience of seeing this thing and appreciating it, there was this hangover of antagonism. There's no question about it that … when you came out from it and [saw] a black man, you didn't feel more like embracing him … you felt more like pushing him away" (qtd. in Spence 158).

21. The *Los Angeles Times* reviewer noted the film's tendency toward anachronism, but the examples he calls attention to do not include the scene of black field hands singing for the white folks on the porch forty years after Emancipation. Rather, he focuses on the inaccurate references to the tobacco industry in the film and the oddity of Virginia, a Southern lady, smoking a cigarette so casually in front of Will. The reviewer remarks, "The manufacturers, at any rate, will be delighted" (Scheuer 12). Research has produced evidence of very few reviews of this film, but among the few found, this is the only one that is negative.

22. See the Motion Picture Production Code appendix in *The Dame in the Kimono* by Leonard J. Leff and Jerold Simmons.

23. A copy of the screenplay, written by Reginald Cheyne Berkeley, is in the Paul Eliot Green Papers (#3693) in the Southern Historical Collection at UNC-Chapel Hill.

24. Interesting, though, the film version of the play includes a flirtatious, innuendo-filled conversation between Uncle Bob and Essie similar to the one in the play between Will and Essie about engagement rings and lavalieres. With this change, the filmmakers maintain Will's one-dimensional characterization (to be discussed): movie *heroes* do not flirt with black servants.

25. According to Leonard J. Leff and Jerold Simmons, "when Lionel Barrymore uttered 'nigger' in *Carolina*, blacks in Chicago, Washington, Baltimore, New York, and Los Angeles had thrown bricks at the screen" (98).

26. Campbell points out an error in this dream sequence, noting that the ball apparently took place "after the victory at First Bull Run," but Lee is "mistakenly identified as the commander responsible for the glorious victory" (77).

References

WORKS CITED

Atkinson, Brooks. "October Nights in the Playhouses of Manhattan: Acting the Drama." *New York Times* 4 Oct. 1931: sec. 8:1.

———. "The Play: Epic of the South." Rev. of *The House of Connelly* by Paul Green. *New York Times* 29 Sept. 1931: 22.

Avery, Laurence. *A Southern Life: Letters of Paul Green, 1916–1981*. Chapel Hill: University of North Carolina Press, 1994.

Barnes, Billy E. Interview with Paul Green, May 7, 1975. Interview B-0005-2. Southern Oral History Program Collection (#4007). Southern Historical Collection. University of North Carolina Library. Chapel Hill.

Bauer, Margaret D. "'Call me Paul': The Long, Hot Summer of Paul Green and Richard Wright." *Mississippi Quarterly* 61 (2008): 517–38.

———. "From the Newspaper Page to the Broadway Stage: Paul Green in the Poet/Priest Tradition." *South Atlantic Review* 75.2 (2010): 45–53.

Berkeley, Reginald. "House of Connelly" Screen Play. 1933. Typescript. Paul Green Papers (#3693). Southern Historical Collection. University of North Carolina Library. Chapel Hill.

Bogle, Donald. *Toms, Coons, Mulattoes, Mammies, & Bucks: An Interpretive History of Blacks in American Films*. 4th ed. New York: Continuum, 2001.

Campbell, Edward D.C., Jr. *The Celluloid South: Hollywood and the Southern Myth*. Knoxville: University of Tennessee Press, 1981.

Carolina. Adapt. of play *The House of Connelly* by Paul Green. Dir. Henry King. Fox, 1934. Film.

Chinoy, Helen Krich. *The Group Theatre: Passion, Politics, and Performance in the Depression Era*. Ed. Don B. Wilmeth and Milly S. Barranger. New York: Palgrave Macmillan, 2013.

Clurman, Harold. *The Fervent Years: The Story of the Group Theatre and the Thirties*. New York: Knopf, 1950.

———, et al. "Reunion: Self-Portrait of the Group Theatre." *Educational Theatre Journal* 28.4 (1976): 471–552.

Cox, Karen L. *Dreaming of Dixie: How the South Was Created in American Popular Culture*. Chapel Hill: University of North Carolina Press, 2011.

Crawford, Cheryl. *One Naked Individual: My Fifty Years in the Theatre*. Indianapolis: Bobbs-Merrill, 1977.

Cripps, Thomas. *Slow Fade to Black: The Negro in American Film, 1900–1942*. New York: Oxford University Press, 1977.

Dusenbury, Winifred L. *The Theme of Loneliness in American Drama*. Gainesville: University of Florida Press, 1960.

Green, Paul. Diary. Paul Green Papers (#3693). Southern Historical Collection, Southern Historical Collection, University of North Carolina Library, Chapel Hill.

———. *Drama and the Weather: Some Notes and Papers on Life and the Theatre*. New York: French, 1958.

———. *The Field God and In Abraham's Bosom*. New York: Robert M. McBride, 1927.

———. *Five Plays of the South*. New York: Hill and Wang, 1963.

———. *The Hawthorn Tree: Some Papers and Letters on Life and the Theatre*. Chapel Hill: University of North Carolina Press, 1943.

———. *The House of Connelly*. *Best American Plays: Supplementary Volume, 1918–1958*. Ed. John Gassner. New York: Crown, 1961. 169–215.

———. *The House of Connelly and Other Plays*. New York: New York: Samuel French, 1931.

———. "'Let Us Outlaw the Gas Chamber,' Urges a Pulitzer Prize Winner." *News & Observer* [Raleigh] 2 Dec. 1962: sec. 3:2.

———. *The Lord's Will and Other Carolina Plays*. New York: Henry Holt, 1925.

———. *The No 'Count Boy: A One-Act Comedy of American Country Life*. New York: Samuel French, 1953.

———. *Out of the South: The Life of a People in Dramatic Form*. New York: Harper, 1939.

———. *Plough and Furrow: Some Essays and Papers on Life and the Theatre*. New York: French, 1963.

———. *A Southern Life: Letters of Paul Green, 1916–1981*. Ed. Laurence G. Avery. Chapel Hill: University of North Carolina Press, 1994.

———. *White Dresses: A Tragedy in White and Black in One Act*. 1920. *North Carolina Literary Review* 18 (2009): 22–33.

Hall, Jacquelyn. Interview with Paul Green, May 30, 1975. Interview B-0005-3. Southern Oral History Program Collection (#4007), Southern Historical Collection, University of North Carolina Library, Chapel Hill. Web.

Hall, Mordaunt. "The Screen: Janet Gaynor, Lionel Barrymore and Others in a Film Version of 'The House of Connelly.'" Rev. of *Carolina*. *New York Times* 16 Feb. 1934: 17.

"'House of Connelly,' Stage Hit, Pleases New York Fans." Rev. of *The House of Connelly*. Chicago *Defender*, nat'l. ed. 10 Oct. 1931: 5.

Ilacqua, Alma A. "Paul Green—In Memoriam: A Bibliography and Profile." *Southern Quarterly* 20 (1982): 76–87.

Leff, Leonard J. and Jerold Simmons. *The Dame in the Kimono*. Lexington: University Press of Kentucky, 2001.

Lockridge, Richard. "*The House of Connelly*." *New York Sun* 29 Sept. 1931: 32.

"New Plays on Old Plots." Rev. of *The House of Connelly* by Paul Green. *Saturday Review of Literature* 17 Oct. 1931: PG #?.

Noble, Peter. "The Coming of the Sound Film." *The Negro in Films* by Peter Noble. London: Knapp, Drewett, 1948. Rpt. in *Anthology of the American Negro in the Theatre: A Critical Approach*. Ed. Lindsay Patterson. Inernational Library of Negro Life and History. New York: Publishers, 1967. 247–66.

"Paul Green's Play, 'Carolina,' At State All This Week: Barrymore, Janet Gaynor Head Cast in Story of Southland." Rev. of *Carolina*. Raleigh [NC] *News & Observer* 4 Feb. 1934: 7.

Rabkin, Gerald. *Drama and Commitment: Politics in the American Theatre of the Thirties*. Bloomington: Indiana University Press, 1964.

Reddick, Lawrence. "Of Motion Pictures [1944]." *Black Films and Film-makers: A Comprehensive Anthology from Stereotype to Superhero*. Ed. Lindsay Patterson. New York: Dodd, Mead, 1975. 3–24.

Scheuer, Philip K. "Janet Gaynor Invades South." Rev. of *Carolina*. *Los Angeles Times* 9 Feb. 1934: 12.

Spence, James R. *Watering the Sahara: Recollections of Paul Green from 1894 to 1937*. Ed. Margaret D. Bauer. Raleigh: North Carolina Department of Cultural Resources, 2008.

Watson, Charles S. *The History of Southern Drama*. Lexington: University Press of Kentucky, 1997.

Wynn, Rhoda. Interview with Paul Green, Feb. 1974. Southern Oral History Program Collection (#4007). Southern Historical Collection. University of North Carolina Library. Chapel Hill.

Works Consulted

Cripps, Thomas R. "The Myth of the Southern Box Office: A Factor in Racial Stereotyping in American Movies, 1920–1940." *The Black Experience in America: Selected Essays*. Ed. James C. Curtis and Lewis L. Gould. Austin: University of Texas Press, 1970. 116–44.

Gassner, John. "Introduction." *The House of Connelly* by Paul Green. *Best American Plays: Supplementary Volume, 1918–1958*. Ed. John Gassner. New York: Crown, 1961. 170–72.

Lupack, Barbara Tepa. *Literary Adaptations in Black American Cinema: From Micheaux to Morrison*. Rochester, NY: University of Rochester Press, 2002. [no mention of *Carolina*]

Smyth, J.E. "Classical Hollywood and the Filmic Writing of Interracial History, 1931–39." *Mixed Race Hollywood*. Ed. Mary Beltrán and Camilla Fojas. New York: New York University Press, 2008. 23–41.

About the Contributors

Laurence G. **Avery** is a professor emeritus at the University of North Carolina Chapel Hill. The editor of three Paul Green books: *A Southern Life: Letters of Paul Green, 1916–1981* (1994), *The Paul Green Reader* (1998), and *The Lost Colony* (2001), in 2006 he received the R. Hunt Parker Award for his contribution to North Carolina literary studies. His first collection of poetry, *Mountain Gravity*, was published in 2014.

Margaret D. **Bauer** is the Ralph Hardee Rives Chair of Southern Literature at East Carolina University in Greenville, and editor of the *North Carolina Literary Review*. She edited and prepared for publication a draft of a Paul Green biography, *Watering the Sahara: Recollections of Paul Green from 1894 to 1937*, by the late James R. Spence (2008), and is the author of *The Fiction of Ellen Gilchrist* (1999), *William Faulkner's Legacy* (2005), *Understanding Tim Gautreaux* (2010) and *A Study of Scarletts: Scarlett O'Hara's Literary Daughters* (2014).

Jim **Grimsley**, a fiction writer and playwright from Rocky Mount, North Carolina, teaches at Emory University. His first novel, *Winter Birds* (1994), won the 1995 Sue Kaufman Prize for First Fiction and the Prix Charles Brisset. His second novel, *Dream Boy* (1995), won the 1996 Award for Gay, Lesbian and Bisexual Literature from the American Library Association.

Index

*Numbers in **bold italics** indicate pages with photographs.*

Absalom, Absalom! 107; character in 115
Adam and Eve (role models for "false Eden of the Old South") 132
Adler, Stella ***84***
African Americans 138, 139, 140
Alec (character in *The House of Connelly*) 123
Atkinson, J. Brooks 109
Avery, Laurence 107, 129, 130, 131, 132, 135, 136, 146

Barker, Margaret ***104***
Barrie, Mona 143
Barrymore, Lionel 139, 154n25
Bauer, Margaret D. 146
Berkeley, Reginald 134, 139; screenplay by 143, 144
Best American Plays: Supplementary Volume, 1918–1953 132
Big Sis (character in *The House of Connelly*) 109, 113, 115, 118, 122; actress portraying ***108***, ***120***; adopts threatening tone toward Patsy Tate 119, 127; murders Patsy 128, 129; possible motives for murdering Patsy 111, 129–30; spoken lines affected by alternate ending to play 131; spreads rumors about Patsy 119, 122, 124; threatened by Patsy's plans for Connelly land 114, 122, 126
Big Sue (character in *The House of Connelly*) 109, 113, 115, 118, 122; actress portraying ***108***, ***120***; adopts threatening tone toward Patsy Tate 119, 127; murders Patsy 128, 129; possible motives for murdering Patsy 111, 129–30; spoken lines affected by alternate ending to play 131; spreads rumors about Patsy 119, 122, 124; threatened by Patsy's plans for Connelly land 114, 122, 126
The Birth of a Nation (film) 136
Bogle, David 138
Breen, Joseph 137
Bromberg, J. Edward 153n6
Buchanan, Mr. [father of Virginia Buchanan] (character in *The House of Connelly*) 119
Buchanan, Mrs. [mother of Virginia Buchanan] (character in *The House of Connelly*) 119
Buchanan, Virginia (character in *The House of Connelly*) 137; chastises Will Connelly 119; as represented in film *Carolina* 140, 141, 143, 144; seen by Connelly family as object of courtship by Will 117, 118, 122
Buckingham, Claire ***73***

Cabin in the Cotton (film) 136
Campbell, Edward D.C., Jr. 135, 143
Carolina (film) 134, 135, 136, 137; characters in 137–139, 141–145; contrasted with *The House of Connelly* 138, 139, 140, 141, 143, 144, 145, 146; reviews of 137, 138, 139; scene from ***142***; and theme of miscegenation 137
Carolina Playmakers 3
The Celluloid South: Hollywood and the Southern Myth 135, 143
Chaplin, Charlie 136
Chicago Defender 109
Chinoy, Helen Krich 130
Clark, Barrett 109, 146
class conflict 111, 114, 117
Clurman, Harold 130, 131, 153n2
"The Coming of the Sound Film" (essay by Peter Noble) 138
Connelly, Evelyn (character in *The House of Connelly*) 112, 118, 128, 132; physical appearance 116, 127; rejects suitor 117
Connelly, General [William Hampton] (character in *The House of Connelly*) 113, 114, 115, 116; as portrayed in film *Carolina* 139
Connelly, Geraldine (character in *The House of Connelly*) 112, 118, 128, 132; departs Connelly Hall 127; physical appearance 116, 127; as portrayed in film *Carolina* 140, 141
Connelly, Mrs. (character in *The House of Connelly*) 112, 116, 117, 132, 138–39; condemns Patsy Tate 122; defends late husband and Uncle Bob 125; as portrayed in film *Carolina* 140, 141, 143, 144, 145
Connelly, Robert [Uncle Bob] (character in *The House of Connelly*) 132; commits suicide 125; encourages Will Connelly to marry Patsy Tate 124; engages in bawdy dance scene 120; expresses animosity toward Will 121; interacts with mulatto tenant farmers 121; makes advances toward Patsy 119; portrayed as dissipated 116; as portrayed in film *Carolina* 139–140, 141, 143–145; praises his brother 113, 117; resents request for meat by mulatto Duffy 112; sacrificing himself for nephew 126, 130
Connelly, Will (character in *The House of Connelly*) 111, 112, 114, 116; addresses tenant farmers on future plans 121–22; affected by misdeeds of late

158

father 113; appears disinterested in Virginia Buchanan 117, 118; attacks uncle Bob in long rant 125; attracted to Patsy Tate 117; behaving like father and uncle 124; confronts Patsy 124; departs Connelly Hall to retrieve absent sisters 128; expresses doubts concerning Patsy's affections 123; lashes out at Virginia 119; as portrayed in film *Carolina* 140–145; spoken lines affected by alternate ending to play 131; suffers from white male guilt 115; teases black servant girl 123
Cox, Karen L. 135, 136, 137
Crawford, Cheryl 109, 130
Cripps, Thomas 139
Crosman, Henrietta 140

Davis, Bette 136
death penalty 111
deKnight, Fanny **84, *104*,** 109
dialect (spoken by characters in Green's plays) 3, 4
"Dixie on Film" (book chapter) 135
Drama and Commitment: Politics in the American Theatre of the Thirties 132, 133
Drama and the Weather: Some Notes and Papers on Life and the Theatre 136, 137, 146
Duffy (character in *The House of Connelly*) 125, 137, 138, 139, 153*n*9; physical appearance 121; requests meat for family 114, 116; revealed as cousin to Connelly children 112
Dukes, Selena C. **50, 108, *120***
Dusenberry, Winifred L. 126, 130, 131

End of the Row 153*n*1
Essie (character in *The House of Connelly*) 120, 123, 124
Everett, Anna 154*n*15

Faulkner, William 107
The Fervent Years: The Story of the Group Theatre and the Thirties 130, 131, 153*n*2
Fetchit, Stepin 138, 139
The Field God: characters in 5–7; revisions to 7, 8
film industry: and depictions of South 135, 136, 137, 140; and treatment of African Americans 138, 139, 140
Five Plays of the South 132
freed slaves 112, 118, 130
French, Samuel 109
"From the Newspaper Page to the Broadway Stage: Paul Green in the Poet/Priest Tradition" 146

Gaines, Ernest J. 111
Gassner, John 132
Gaynor, Janet 141, ***142***
Gone with the Wind: character in 113
Green, Paul **6, *110***; complains about script changes 136; diary 132; essay by 136; and film industry 134, 136, 139, 141, 146; and folk plays 3; interview 136; letters from 107, 135, 146; and miscegenation 107, 111, 121, 150; opposes death penalty 111; quoted 109, 116, 129, 130, 131, 133, 134, 147; and revision process 3–5, 7, 8; works of, contrasted with those of Tennessee Williams 107, 133; writes alternate ending to *The House of Connelly* 130
Griffith, D.W. 136

Group Theatre (New York) 107, 109, 130, 150; performs *The House of Connelly* 27, **66, *84, 104***
The Group Theatre: Passion, Politics, and Performance in the Depression Era 130

Hall, Jacquelyn 133, 134
Hall, Logan James *73*
Hall, Mordaunt 137
The History of Southern Drama 107

Ilacqua, Alma A. 109
In Abraham's Bosom 107, 147; characters in 3, 4; dialect written for characters in 3, 4

"Janet Gaynor Invades South" (review of film *Carolina*) 154*n*21

King, Henry 139
Koch, Frederick 3

Laciura, Anthony **50, *120***
League of Southern Labor 153*n*14
Leff, Leonard J. 154*n*25
Light in August 115
Lockridge, Richard 109
The Lost Colony (outdoor symphonic drama) 107; characters in 5; Green's revisions to 5

McClendon, Rose 84, 104, 109
miscegenation: absent from film *Carolina* 137, 140; prohibited in film industry 137; as theme of Green's plays 107, 111, 121, 150
Motion Picture Production Code 137
"mulattoes" (term employed by Green) 121

Native Son 111, 138
Negroes *see* African Americans
Nelson, Ruth **66**, 153*n*7
The No 'Count Boy: A One-Act Comedy of American Country Life: characters in 4, 7; dialect written for characters in 4
Noble, Peter 138

"Of Motion Pictures [1944]" (article by Lawrence Reddick) 138
Old South: decline of, represented in characters in *The House of Connelly* 116; persistence of ethos of, in films 135, 137, 139, 140
One Naked Individual: My Fifty Years in the Theatre 109, 130
O'Neill, Eugene 109
Out of the South: The Life of a People in Dramatic Form 4, 7, 153*n*13

Plough and Furrow: Some Essays and Papers on Life and the Theatre 109, 116, 131
Purvis (character in *The House of Connelly*) 113, 125, 138

Rabkin, Gerald 133
racial conflict 111, 114
Reddick, Lawrence 138
ReGroup Theatre Company (New York) 107; performs *The House of Connelly* **50, *73, 108, 120***; poster advertising ***108***

Returning the Gaze: A Genealogy of Black Film Criticism, 1909–1941 154n15
revision process (as practiced by Green) 3, 4, 5, 7, 8

Saturday Review of Literature 109, 131
Scheuer, Philip K. 154n21
"The Screen: Janet Gaynor, Lionel Barrymore and Others in a Film Version of 'The House of Connelly'" 137
Shepherd, Sid (character in *The House of Connelly*) 116, 117
Simmons, Jerold 154n25
Simmons, Sheila **50**, *108*, **120**
slaves 112, 115, 119
Slow Fade to Black: The Negro in American Film, 1900–1942 139
The Sound and the Fury 115
A Southern Life: Letters of Paul Green, 1916–1981 107, 129, 130, 131, 132, 135, 136, 146
Southern literary themes 107, 112, 116
Spence, James R. 136, 154n19
Stockard, Eunice **84**
Strasberg, Lee 130
A Streetcar Named Desire 133
Sweet Bird of Youth 133

Tate, Jesse (character in *The House of Connelly*) 115, 116, 121, 122, 128
Tate, Joanna (character in film *Carolina*): contrasted with Patsy Tate in *The House of Connelly* 141, 142, 144; resists attempt to discourage relationship with Will 143; reveals plans to revive Connelly plantation 145
Tate, Patsy (character in *The House of Connelly*) 115, 116; attracts romantic interest of Will Connelly 117; confesses love for Will's land 124; contrasted with Joanna Tate of film *Carolina* 141, 143, 144; declares love for Will 119; fate of, compared with that of Chance Wayne in *Sweet Bird of Youth* 133; joins in working Connelly land 123; as portrayed (and renamed) in film *Carolina* 141; resents Will's doubts concerning sincerity 123; returns to Connelly Hall as Will's wife 127; role affected by alternate ending to play 134; seen as mastermind of plans for Connelly land 112, 122; spoken lines affected by alternate ending to play 131, 134; threatens security of Big Sis and Big Sue 111, 113, 114, 118; urges Will not to retrieve absent sisters 128
"The Theatre and the Screen" 136
Theatre Guild (New York) 109
The Theme of Loneliness in American Drama 126
tobacco 136
Toms, Coons, Mulattoes, Mammies, & Bucks: An Interpretive History of Blacks in American Films 138
Tone, Franchot **66**, *104*, 109

Watson, Charles S. 107
White Dresses: A Tragedy in White and Black in One Act 153n1
white guilt 111, 122
white male guilt 115
Williams, Tennessee: works of, contrasted with Green's *House of Connelly* and other plays 107, 133, 147, 149
Wright, Richard *110*, 111, 138

Yeats, William Butler 3
Young, Robert 140, **142**

www.ingramcontent.com/pod-product-compliance
Lightning Source LLC
Chambersburg PA
CBHW081600300426
44116CB00015B/2947